Unity Initiative

Unity Initiative

UnityInitiative.org

"Healing and enriching our lives; uniting our communities"

~

"Living united and absolutely free"

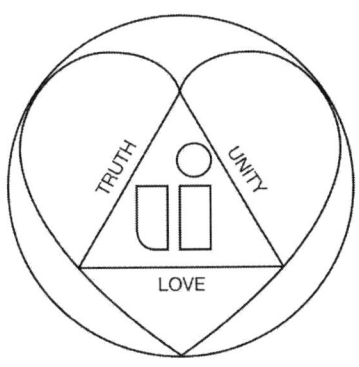

Our Vision

Unity Initiative wants to unite people of *all* diversities into a harmonious community to foster an environment for overcoming prejudice.

Name:	
Membership Date:	

Unity Initiative

Published by
Unity Initiative Book Publishing
E-mail: info@unityinitiative.org
Website: UnityInitiative.org

Copyright © 2013 Unity Initiative Book Publishing

Table of Contents

Preface VIII

SECTION I: Roots of UI Philosophy 1

Chapter 1: Introduction
    The Continuing Need for a Solution to Racism 2
    The Courage to Face Racism 4
    A Path towards Healing through Unity 6
    Our Primary Purpose 8

Chapter 2: Origins of the UI Concept: Founder's Experience 10
    The Impact of Childhood Lessons 10
    Introduction to the 12 Traditions 13
    Role Models of Service 15
    Discovering the Roots of Personal Bigotry 16
    Forced Into Action 18

Chapter 3: Introduction to Pioneers Addressing Racism 20
    Literature on the Pioneers 20
    Mohandas K. Gandhi 21
    Jo Ann Robinson, Rosa Parks & Dr. Martin Luther King Jr... 23
    Malcolm X 28
    Contradicting Messages 30
    Re-converging Philosophies 31

Chapter 4: Origins of UI Principles 32
    The Sources 32
    Principles emphasized in the Civil Rights Movements 32
    Principles emphasized through the 12-Steps 36
    Commonality of Principles 37
    The Three Legacies 38

Chapter 5: Establishing Concepts for the Principles 39
    Unity 39
    Truth 41
    Love 44
    Spirituality 47
    Humility 48
    Discipline 55
    Self-Cleansing 57
    Surrender 61
    Service 68
    Self-Sacrifice 69

    Nonviolence 71
    Direct Action 73
    Principles Conclusion 74

SECTION II: Observing Racism in Our Society 77

Chapter 6: Historical Review 78
    Historical Racial Events: Snapshots in Time 78
    Historical Events Summary 90
Chapter 7: Assessing Our Past 94
    Difficult Hurdles for a Split Society 94
    Racism and Past Politics and Economics 99
    Our Dysfunctional Society 101
    The Missing Acknowledgement 108
    Black Nationalist Ideals for Resolving Racial Inequality 111
    Civil Rights Movement Efforts for Ending Discrimination 115
    Overwhelmed by Racism 118
Chapter 8: Institutional Racism 120
    Racism in the United States 120
    Evolution of Systemic Racism in our Institutions 123
    Community Segregation and Social Oppression 126
    Blaming the Victim 127
    White Privilege: Racism by Proxy 133
    Privilege of Class and Proximity 139
    Healthcare 143

SECTION III: Principles in Action 145

Chapter 9: Getting Started 146
    HOW 146
    Sponsorship 146
Chapter 10: Self-Assessment 149
    Examining Our Egotism 149
    Examining Our Prejudices 155
Chapter 11: The Twelve Steps 161
    Overview of the Steps 161
    Step One 167
    Step Two 169
    Step Three 172
    Step Four 174
    Step Five 180
    Step Six 183

Step Seven	184
Step Eight	185
Step Nine	189
Step Ten	196
Step Eleven	207
Step Twelve	211
Chapter 12: Taking Direct Action to Unite	222
Uniting of Diverse Groups	222
Our Fellowship	223
Community Outreach	227
Integration: The Final Frontier	228
Appendix A	232
Unity Initiative Preamble	232
Appendix B	234
The Twelve Steps of Unity Initiative	234
Appendix C	235
The Twelve Traditions of Unity Initiative	235
Appendix D	236
Alcoholics Anonymous Statement of Non-Affiliation	236
The Twelve Steps of Alcoholics Anonymous	236
The Twelve Traditions of Alcoholics Anonymous	236
Appendix E	239
Starting a New Unity Initiative Group	239
Appendix F	243
FAQ: Frequently Asked Questions	243
Appendix G	248
Why we are here	248

Preface

This is the first edition of the book "*Unity Initiative*". The main purpose for this text is to act as a guide for building a diverse, unified community. This fellowship will be modeled after other twelve-step organizations that have already made natural strides in providing a united fellowship.

Because this volume is being introduced prior to the establishment of the organization, the initial edition is covering uncharted territory with many unknowns. As such, this first printing will be in small numbers to provide the pioneers with the suggested framework for the organization. The personal experiences and stories described in this book are based on lessons learned from similar organizations. Once Unity Initiative has established a solid foundation, a new edition can be published to incorporate refinements along with the stories from the members of this emerging society.

SECTION I:
Roots of UI Philosophy

Chapter 1: Introduction

The Continuing Need for a Solution to Racism

We are living in an era of opportunity, as no past generation has ever known. We are the beneficiaries of our ancestors who have endured innumerable trials and tribulations to put freedom, security and prosperity within the reach of an ever-expanding portion of the population. We have much to celebrate in the challenges that have been overcome and the level of abundance that has been achieved. An enormous amount of our material gains have been attained through the labored efforts of past generations as well as advances in government, science and education.

Progress has also been the result of the increased value of compassion swelling up from the communities of nations around the world who desire to see an increase in the spread of peace and unity. An overall sense of understanding is gradually evolving. Although making strides in these areas is sometimes painfully slow, tyranny and oppression are becoming less tolerated, opening the door for expanding freedom and human rights. As technology makes our world smaller, we are seeing more respect gained for all nations as well as increased appreciation for varying cultures. Throughout history, we have seen turning points by various nations who have transformed their societies, radically changing their courses by freeing themselves of philosophies and practices that bring about destruction.

Of course, we still have a long way to go. Violence continues to persist as an option that is too quickly chosen as the answer for settling disputes. Human rights are still not universally practiced. Age-old maladies such as bigotry and racism continue to resist eradication, impeding our growth resulting in continued corrosion for our civilization as a whole. While the factors producing the current climate of a cross-cultural experience are bringing a sense of openness to some, they are exposing the fears and prejudices of others that would otherwise stay dormant with the status quo.

Introduction

Finding, then implementing solutions to these problems will make way for our progress, while not addressing these issues will guarantee stagnation with the obstruction of our growth. There will never be a better time than now to take up this challenge. As our transformation continues, we must become willing to look honestly at ourselves and stay open to new perspectives so that we may overcome these social ills.

To accomplish this, we will first need to ask ourselves why our world is still plagued by racism. In the United States, so many decades have passed since the issuing of the Emancipation Proclamation, the adoption of the thirteenth, fourteenth and fifteenth amendments and the many Civil Rights Acts, as well as innumerable struggles throughout the world for similar causes. Although we are surely making progress as a society, our world is still suffering from fear, resentment and bigotry between various racial and ethnic groups. Why have we barely matured beyond the passing of legislation in an attempt to force an end to overt racism?

While the observation may be accurate that the relationships between Blacks and Whites in the United States and other parts of the world have exposed some of the most extreme cases of these issues, bigotry has eroded the relationships of every racial group across the spectrum. Regardless of the color of our skin, our belief system or our cultural heritage, we are all adversely affected. Today, factions around the world continue to fall prey to fear and violence. In spite of the fact that this mayhem has only brought heartbreak and sorrow in these conflicts, diverse groups continue to become hopelessly entangled in bigotry-fueled destruction.

For those of us who want to see a true and lasting healing take place in our lives, what can we do? Numerous organizations have been established for carrying out the essential needs of combating the effects of racism, but there seem to be sorely few organizations with the mission of actively facilitating in the uniting of diverse individual and community relationships; efforts that ultimately address the root causes. Unfortunately, the few organizations that have followed this path usually get less attention by our society than do divisive groups. Although it would be tempting to simply cast the blame on those who wish to maintain division through the status quo, we must take a look at ourselves and recognize that a number of us have been stymied by our own denial that significant problems still exist.

The gains made during the Civil Rights Movement of the fifties and sixties have lulled us into a false sense of hope. We declared victory, and then ended our efforts assuming the momentum of those successes would carry us forward through self-propulsion. The end of racism, we thought, was inevitable. But the materialization of that dream is still nowhere in sight. The root of the problem is far from being resolved. Consequently, our complacency has given the ideologies of divisive groups the opportunity to spread, regaining their foothold. We have stopped moving forward in many critical areas of our progress towards equality, and advances gained so far are slowly eroding. What can we do to reverse this backslide so that we can move forward again? Can we stop the cycle of continually handing off this problem from generation to generation? How can we transform our world so that our children and grandchildren will have a better future?

The Courage to Face Racism

Overcoming bigotry is a lifelong, soul-searching endeavor that takes patience and courage. Part of the difficulty lies in the inherently sensitive nature of the controversy in the topic of racism, which often exposes the deep-seated feelings of our passionate opinions. The complexity is multiplied by the 360 degrees of angles in which we perceive this problem. Coming to a consensus on solutions is improbable.

As of the writing of this book, a large portion of our population had grown up during the era of legislated segregation. The negative feelings associated with that bitter past have mostly become dormant, but they are nonetheless quite prevalent throughout our society. Those reviewing or participating in open forums discussing racism or other problems facing diverse groups will inevitably hear responses of frustration, disappointment, anger, animosity and disillusionment. For this reason, prejudice, bigotry and racism are topics we simply try to avoid altogether. The observations, experiences and ideas expressed in this book will hopefully be well received, but in spite of our goal of unity, they will undoubtedly evoke strong dissent in some.

Facing such controversial issues takes courage. Those who dare to come together to discuss them do so with a measure of risk.

Introduction

Not only might others criticize one for "stirring the pot" but we also inevitably take a deep look into ourselves, exposing our own bias. We sometimes endure great discomfort when discovering how we contribute to, or collude with racism. Maintaining our innocence is not guaranteed. On the contrary, this discovery is necessary, but exposing our prejudices in front of others can be very difficult. This is true despite the reality that practically no one can claim absolute freedom from bias, regardless of color.

However, although racial-prejudice is a problem that individuals of every race must resolve within themselves, oppression in the United States has historically been overwhelmingly carried out by Caucasians upon people of color. Spotlighting the historical events that reflect this and examining current institutional racism may be uncomfortable for many nonwhites as well as Whites.

These critical reviews are not meant as attacks, but as necessary measures for acknowledging the facts of our history. The society we inherited from generations of unresolved racism is still dysfunctional as the result of our inability to find answers to our social problems. Just as a therapist must guide individuals to dig deep into their past to help them discover personal issues before finding a resolution, we must dig into our own country's history in order to understand and resolve our nation's difficulties. If we are going to work together, we must prepare ourselves for this inevitable discomfort. This is a necessary part of the healing process.

Equal to the importance of not demonizing Whites, is to not erroneously portray people of color as helpless. Although minorities continue to be victimized by institutional racism, exposing such problems is not to be misconstrued as weakness. On the contrary, the disciplined courage, exercised in the effective measures of minority communities, continues to shape and strengthen our society as a whole.

People of *all* races will be needed for joining in the participation of contributions towards unity in order to continue our growth. Hopefully, as you read these pages, you will keep an open mind as well as an understanding heart and courageously face the uncomfortable emotions that may surface. Please do not allow that discomfort to deter you. Know that you are not alone. Your courage will pay handsomely. In the end, we hope you will be moved to participate in following the suggested action laid out for *all* individuals to reduce personal bias and to help build a united community.

A Path towards Healing through Unity

Our world is filled with such wonderful diversity. Our combined contributions in musical, visual, culinary and performing arts, as well as those in math and science, philosophy and spirituality make up the rich tapestry of our existence. Although this diversity is widely appreciated as a beautiful part of nature that adds spice and texture to our lives, we only need to look back at century upon century of overall racial and ethnic strife, marked by exploitation, violence and oppression to see that we are a long way from this becoming a universal view. Can we unite a world where division sometimes seems to stretch like an unbridgeable chasm? What would a united world look like? What would it be like to travel to any country and experience brotherly love instead of tension, fear and hostility? A world where you can go to any community in your own country, state or city and experience this same oneness?

To some, efforts towards widespread unity probably sound like a fool-hearted undertaking only to be attempted by individuals with Pollyanna-like optimism; a hopelessly impossible endeavor. But then when you witness, year after year, the miraculous transformation of people's lives when fully embracing principles, such as those practiced in the Civil Rights Movement and in 12-step programs[*], the vision of our whole world benefiting seems quite plausible. And unless we are resigned to having all future generations continue to have their lives eroded by the same problems of our past, we must make an effort by taking further action.

There will still be others who will feel anxiety, simply at the thought of such an undertaking, viewing this as an overwhelming and unthinkable burden. Thankfully, experience has revealed that such efforts are actually very exhilarating, fulfilling and joyful. This is not a burden to be endured, but a pleasure that makes life worth living.

---

* The first 12-step program was introduced by Alcoholics Anonymous® June tenth, 1935. Since its foundation, many 12-step programs have been established to resolve various problems and promote personal healing and growth. Millions of lives have been significantly enhanced in practicing the common principles these groups all share.

Introduction

Change is certainly neither going to be simple, nor will it happen overnight. The perceptions underlying our problems have evolved over several millennia, so it will take time to heal. But if the successes of other organizations are of any indication, a difference can be made as long as we have the willingness and maintain our persistence in our efforts.

Keeping our scope in perspective for the individual, we need to look no further than changing our own personal lives. We will make a difference simply by participating in the unifying action of our local communities. Personal happiness and freedom from bigotry will come through the action we take to embrace the principles discussed later in this book. Uniting together will require widespread joy and happiness, as well as an abundance of compassion. With these elements in place, reducing bigotry for many will be a natural byproduct.

Conversely, brushing off widespread unity as "impossible", without trying, may seem negative and cowardly to some as if we are irresponsibly sticking our heads in the sand. But we can't expect much more from ourselves or from others without clear direction on how such an undertaking can be achieved. That is precisely the purpose of this book: to examine these problems through the lens of common values and to propose a path to community healing.

This book is a call to action; an initiative to unite.

We will take advantage of combined methods and philosophies that have been successfully practiced by others in past generations. Along the way, we will see how we can find a deep and sustained peace and happiness in our own personal lives by practicing the principles that are laid out in later chapters.

In this text, we will expose and discuss some of the problems of bigotry and racism in today's society. Because of the fractured relationship that has evolved from the roots of slavery to the divided communities of today, we will primarily be focusing on problems in the United States between Blacks and Whites.

However, the underlying issues that will be exposed, as well as the proposed solutions, apply to all diverse relations. Whether trying to advance human rights or improve race relations, whether looking for resolution to political strife or searching for common ground in conflicting religious and ideological beliefs, following the presented ideals will pave the way towards unity.

Next, we will examine ourselves as individuals and search for our own prejudices. We will then lay out the solution for cleansing ourselves of the root causes of our bias. Finally, we will discuss ideas on how we can bring this healing to our communities.

Our Primary Purpose

Unity Initiative seeks to foster unity amongst diverse communities by providing an environment where healthy relations can grow. *We want to bring people of all races, ethnicities and every other diversity together as a fellowship to grow individually and as a society while freely pursuing individual cultural identities.* This is what Dr. Martin Luther King, Jr. described when he envisioned the *Beloved Community;* where the brotherhood and sisterhood of humankind binds all people regardless of race or class.

While historical legislation towards desegregation has removed legal barriers for integration, these efforts have addressed neither the social structures nor psychological roadblocks that keep our communities separated. Only a deliberate effort towards these ends will allow us to achieve true integration and only then will we set up an environment where animosity of our past can be healed, prejudices removed, and sharing of opportunity balanced.

Dr. King also repeatedly emphasized the need for *Direct Action*. For this, we have adopted the principles of 12-step programs for our personal healing and growth. Just as the only way to overcome fears is to face them, the only way we will be able to overcome prejudice is by getting in the same rooms together and building relationships. But even this will not be enough if we have fears, resentments or other mental or psychological blocks that prevent healthy relations from taking root. We will thus need to take measures to rid ourselves of these obstacles by following the suggested 12 steps. We couple this with the philosophies emphasized by King and Gandhi, plus meetings, anti-racism education and group discussions as well as dialogs with like-minded individuals from diverse races and cultures.

UI has no other purpose.'This is a nonprofit organization with no political, financial, religious or any other ambition. Furthermore, although UI wishes to express hopes for success in the endeavors of other institutions pursuing similar goals, we have no direct affiliation

Introduction

with any other organization. We are simply a fellowship* with the common desire to live in harmony with people of *all* diversities. If you share this aspiration, we hope you will join us.

If you are plagued with bigotry and want to replace bitterness and prejudice with love and compassion, we welcome you. Regardless of the level of animosity you may have, we can help if you are ready. If on the other hand, you carry such bias, yet desire neither to join us in these efforts nor change your perceptions, you are no less our brother or sister. We respect your right to choose and wish you well. If at some point you wish to experience life with less fear and judgment of others, our doors will always be open to show you the peace that can be found.

* *2013; UI is a newly forming program whose fellowship is just beginning. This book is meant to be the basis for the organization's foundation. By the time this book becomes public a fellowship will have been started.*

Chapter 2: Origins of the UI Concept: Founder's Experience

To explain the origins of this organization and the purpose for its establishment, the founder's personal experiences that led to this fellowship are presented here...

The Impact of Childhood Lessons

I was born in southern California in 1961 to a mother captivated by the history being made during that era. She was strong, beautiful and filled with compassion. As a member of SCLC*, she was very active in the Civil Rights Movement and other honorable causes. Through these experiences, she acquired unconditional love along with other priceless values that enriched our whole family.

Occasionally she gave my brothers and me exposure to this Movement by bringing us to the SCLC offices to participate in various activities. We were very young so they would have us perform simple services such as printing bumper stickers, passing out flyers or painting picket signs. Our mother would sometimes let us take a day off from school to join others in protests, peace marches, rallies and voting campaigns. She would proclaim that the public school system could never offer a better education. I am forever grateful for her prophetic insight. These experiences have impacted every facet of my life.

In 1969 my father was given a career opportunity that brought our family to Texas. My mother immediately made contact with the SCLC chapter there to continue her part in the struggles against racial injustices and the expansion of Civil Rights.

* SCLC (Southern Christian Leadership Conference) is a multi-cultural organization of diverse races and religions that was created by Martin Luther King Junior together with several other Southern ministers, to organize efforts for the Civil Rights Movement

Origins of the UI Concept: Founder's Experience

In those days, the racial-tension in Dallas was very high. In the early seventies, my mother took me to march downtown to protest the shooting-death of a Hispanic boy. He had just been arrested and was handcuffed behind his back when he was shot. The day ended with the police chasing protesters down the streets with tear gas. Tension also penetrated the junior high I attended which on a few occasions culminated in race riots. Although I avoided this violence, I remember the fear, sadness, anger and shame I felt. More than any other emotion though, was the confusion I felt due to the polarity of the teachings of unconditional love from my mother and the immense fearful divisiveness of my school friends.

Soon after we arrived in Texas, I had another life-changing experience. I became involved in drugs and alcohol. Some of the first children that my brothers and I met in our new neighborhood introduced us to marijuana. I was eight years old at the time and what started off as an innocent adventure of curiosity, evolved over the next seven years into suffering to the extent of thoughts of suicide. During that period, my ego ran out of control. It consumed me faster than I could find the relief needed to escape my self-imposed prison and ever-increasing fears.

Our family suffered terribly through this period, and in 1976 my parents finally intervened when my younger brother was arrested at his elementary school for possession of marijuana. Their intervention forever altered the course of my life. My brothers and I were pressured into joining a 12-step organization modeled after the program of Alcoholics Anonymous but geared towards young people with drug and alcohol problems. However, I was trapped in perpetual misery and drugs and alcohol were my "anti-depressants". They were my only solution for finding relief. I feared that if they were taken from me, I would surely perish. I was not about to trade them in for a life of tortuous boredom, without a fight. To my parents, it must have seemed like they were performing an exorcism as they put on the pressure for me to go to a meeting. But because of their persistence and not giving in to my incessant wailing, I finally tired and gave up the fight. I reluctantly agreed to attend for thirty days, although I had no intention of staying sober.

I will never forget that first meeting which seemed like some bizarre world. It was filled with people who had overcome their addictions. Although they were drug and alcohol free, they looked truly happy. They talked freely about themselves showing a great deal of compassion towards each other. This fellowship was so alive it was intimidating at first. Some very kind members reached out to me, helping me to feel welcome, but I remained aloof and unreceptive. Like my parents though, they gently persisted. If it wasn't for their kindness, I might not have stayed. If I hadn't stayed, I am convinced I would have eventually taken my own life, having been left unarmed to face the hopelessness of my bleak future. In that respect, these friends helped save my life.

Even though I was still filled with skepticism those first few days, I was experiencing a small glimmer of hope that I dared not acknowledge for fear of the agony of something bursting my bubble. Ironically, part of me still had many concerns about being sober and at some level I tried to sabotage this experience. In spite of those doubts, I continued to attend meetings and my worries began to fade as hope turned into reality.

I was agonized by depression before I came into the program and that didn't go away overnight. The hope I gained from the positive example I saw in others, however, led me to take the recommendation of getting a sponsor to mentor me as I walked through the twelve steps of the program. The steps were extremely difficult because of the level of honesty required, but the more rigorously I struggled with them, the freer I became.

Members of the group had told me that the twelve steps were the key to their happiness, which made no sense upon first review. I simply could not understand how they applied to my problems, but I soon experienced the benefits for myself. Thanks to the steps and the fellowship, except for a few slips in the first week, I have remained completely clean and sober. My life is now filled with joy and I have been blessed with wonderful relationships.

I never dreamed of the gratitude I would feel for my parents and their use of tough love in forcing me into recovery. I see now that this required courage when faced with the risk of alienating their children. The twelve steps and that fellowship literally saved my life. Decades later, I continue to work the steps on a daily basis in order to maintain my personal growth. The steps and the wisdom of my friends have provided effective solutions to fundamental life struggles that had previously seemed insurmountable.

Origins of the UI Concept: Founder's Experience

The friends, parents and other relatives of the members of that program also worked the steps. Their meetings were modeled after the Al-anon program, which is open to all friends and family members of the alcoholic or addict. Such family groups are technically separate organizations, but they follow the same twelve steps since it was found that they are as effective in the lives of the non-addicted person. Many without such obvious afflictions, but facing their own internal struggles have likewise given credit to the steps for saving their lives.

Introduction to the 12 Traditions

Along with the 12 steps, I found that AA developed the concept of the *12 traditions**. The traditions were born from the lessons learned from previous organizations and from the early growing pains of AA's pioneering days. The traditions of such programs have a similar function as the constitution does for the United States in that they set up a foundation on which our society can be built upon and thrive. They set guidelines for such organizations so that they may preserve their integrity and keep their focus on their fundamental vision. They also provide a set of critical boundaries to maintain respect for our rights as individual members as well as suggesting guidelines for ensuring the organization is not adversely affected by the actions of its members.

After becoming educated on the traditions, I was able to observe the fallout from incidents where these customs were disregarded in similar organizations. In some cases, the consequences were disastrous with multiple groups shutting down. Who knows the number of individuals whose lives could have been saved if those groups were able to continue to carry their message? In the aftermath of these tragedies, the vital need for the traditions became clear. I became even more appreciative of the wisdom of AA's founders in architecting this framework of humility.

---

* See the appendices for a complete listing of the traditions as well as the statement of non-affiliation to Alcoholics Anonymous. Further information can be found in the Alcoholics Anonymous publications *Twelve Steps and Twelve Traditions* and *Alcoholics Anonymous Comes of Age: A Brief History of AA*.

To inherit the stability enjoyed by the organizations that have followed these customs, UI has adapted the 12 traditions along with the steps. For example, UI's first tradition states, *"Our common welfare should come first; personal growth depends upon UI unity."* This emphasizes the critical role of our fellowship. Our third tradition states that *"The only requirement for membership is a desire to live in harmony with people of all diversities."* This provides a safeguard for the individual's rights for membership while expressing the spirit of the organization to welcome people of every race, culture and belief system.

The fifth tradition states, *"Each group has but one primary purpose - to foster an environment of unity and to carry its message to all who wish to be free from prejudice."* This ideal prevents us from getting sidetracked with other causes that might dilute our efforts towards unity and derail us from our primary objective.

The seventh tradition states, *"Every UI group ought to be fully self-supporting, declining outside contributions."* This means that we must pay our own way. We can neither accept funds from the government nor donations from corporations, institutions or individuals outside of our organization. This tradition not only helps us to avoid becoming distracted by motives of profit, but also prevents unhealthy dependencies that could lead to influences from outside enterprises potentially diverting us from our objective.

The eighth tradition states that as UI members, we remain nonprofessional. Although we can hire special workers to provide services for UI, we have no membership dues nor take fees for helping others work through the steps or any other service provided by our organization. The tenth tradition states, *"Unity Initiative has no opinion on outside issues; hence the UI name ought never be drawn into public controversy."* This keeps us from becoming embroiled in religious, political or controversial issues that might otherwise divide us. The eleventh and twelfth traditions address our anonymity. To further promote a spirit of humility for the organization as well as the individual, we avoid the public spotlight and strive to always place principles before personalities.

History has plenty of examples of the pitfalls that await well-meaning organizations when they fail to adopt such guidelines. The traditions keep us honest and humble. They help ensure the continuity of the organization by keeping the program and its members on track, allowing us to maintain our effectiveness in our primary purpose.

Origins of the UI Concept: Founder's Experience

Role Models of Service

In the '70s, a close friend of my mother's from the Civil Rights Movement, created a service-based organization, the *Bethlehem Foundation*, to provide basic living assistance to indigent citizens of Dallas County. Most of the recipients were minorities segregated from prosperous communities and struggling to make ends meet. My mother was very moved by her friend's vital community service and became involved on a volunteer basis. She eventually went to work for them part-time while teaching art for the Richardson Independent School District.

The Bethlehem Foundation one day found they were left with no IT personnel; and in the hopes I could help resolve their problem in retrieving their client information from their database, my mother approached me with an offer for a side job to take on this project. By this time, my life had completely turned around from my previous path of destruction. I had worked my way through school, earning a bachelor's degree in computer science while employed at a local electronics manufacturer. Service to others is an integral part of recovery and vital to lifelong growth, so I was honored to volunteer my time. This turned into a sizable service commitment that stretched out over a decade requiring periodic technology upgrades and continued training for new volunteers and employees.

Involvement in this service work provided me with enormous gratitude. This was also in alignment with the twelfth recommendation of 12-step programs to practice the principles of the steps and serve others in our daily lives in order to ward off a return to selfish deterioration. I continue to be very active in service work because it has proven to be an effective deterrent from self-pity and an essential ingredient for happiness and self-esteem.

I now see that my mother had this same experience although this was not my perception when I was younger. Back then, I could see that she enjoyed giving to others, but I thought her ability to do so was because she was so filled with life. I now understand I had it backwards. She was granted a life filled with joy because she accepted the privilege to do that service. It made her strong and provided her with love that she was then able to give to our family along with almost everyone else who came into her life.

I also came to realize that I had often trivialized her accomplishments by saying "she has a gift". Subconsciously I felt I could justify not following her example because I wasn't endowed with her abilities. To some extent, this is an irresponsible denial of the truth. When King and Gandhi encountered these same misperceptions in others, they worked to derail such rationalization by making it clear we are all capable of transformation; we merely need to take action.

These extraordinary people were simply human beings who accepted the challenge of carrying the torch of humility passed on by those who went before them. And like those who taught them, they hoped we would accept the torch and continue to advance it forward. Advancing these ideals through our actions is the highest form of honor we can show them. The knowledge they passed along carries a message of hope and we have a duty to keep it alive, but the rewards for this responsibility are invaluable.

Discovering the Roots of Personal Bigotry

My family owes a great debt of gratitude for the love and the lessons our friends from SCLC and the Bethlehem Foundation had given us. Those friends stuck by our side in our time of need as my mother was dying from cancer. They gave my family a tremendous amount of strength with their caring support.

After my mother passed away, my involvement with the Bethlehem Foundation continued. Watching their dedication, I couldn't help but to reflect on the issues that were fought for during the Civil Rights era, but I was now seeing them in the light of a new set of principles. I was granted a new pair of glasses giving me a clearer perspective. The seeds that were planted during the Civil Rights Movement had germinated and were starting to sprout in the nourishing soil of my 12-step recovery.

I started looking at the underlying causes of my own prejudices that were common with the fundamental issues fueling my addiction. I realized that a byproduct of working through the 12 steps was that it helped me overcome several misconceptions. The root cause of this discrimination now became crystal clear. *Like my addictions, my prejudice was based on fear, selfishness and disillusionment.* As my fears in life began to disappear, my ego began to diminish and the freeing of my heart had begun.

Origins of the UI Concept: Founder's Experience

I have heard this echoed by others confessing they were plagued by various forms of prejudice when they came into the program. Their bigotry, homophobia, sexism and other fears partially dissolved as an outgrowth of their step-work along with their exposure to the diversity of the fellowship. None of us specifically sought to have these biases reduced; it just happened naturally. It was simply an additional benefit to the freedom we found.

When we end destructive and abusive behavior, clean up our past through the steps, begin taking responsibility for our lives, and get involved in a fellowship striving for the same values, we spend less time blaming others for our problems. We were not all rendered completely free of our prejudices, but a significant improvement had been made. It was then a logical conclusion that further progress could be made with an organization that directly applies step-work on the destructive nature of racial discrimination.

Of course, the two maladies of prejudice and addiction have stark differences and implications for our society. Unlike addictions, racism, the product of prejudice plus power, permeates every institution of our country and will eventually affect every one of its citizens. None of us can escape it. When you consider the effects of phenomena such as white-privilege that afford one race advantages over another, we also see there are no innocent bystanders. We were all assimilated from birth into an unfair system, in which we must all take a stand, while not taking a stand allows the same unfair, unjust system to speak on our behalf.

Regardless of the differences though, experience has shown that like addiction, most prejudice today is based on fear. So although the likelihood of there being a common solution for such disparate maladies may seem far-fetched, that has turned out to be the case for many of us who have worked the steps. On the other hand, since both are founded on fear, it makes sense that a remedy, which addresses the anxiety at the root of one malady, will possibly produce positive results in any problem that is also based on fear. This is exactly the purpose of the 12 steps and the fellowship; to overcome the insecurities that are at the root of these maladies.

Further, when friends and family members of addicts and alcoholics started working the twelve steps, they too found relief even though much of their fear and suffering was brought on by the injurious behavior of their loved ones trapped in their disease. In many cases, abuse threatened to destroy the relationship, but family members still often reported finding a measure of healing, even in circumstances where the addict refused to seek recovery for themselves. .

But when both parties of each side of the malady rigorously took up the program of recovery, it often put them on the same page that helped establish a new foundation in which they could rebuild their relationship. The steps were thus found to be a common solution for the oppressed, as well as the oppressor.

Forced Into Action

Although I thought about these ideas for quite some time, I was continually side-tracked by college, career and other diversions that prevented me from making any progress in pursuing this potential solution for overcoming prejudice. Seeming like they could wait until post-retirement, these plans were eventually set aside and decreased their priority in my life. However, the crisis brought on by the attacks on 9/11/2001, the violence that has ensued over the years since and the racism exposed by these events has made clear the urgent need for immediate action.

I then experienced an incident in September of 2006 at an Asian market in Chandler Arizona, where a Caucasian man broke out in an enraged verbal attack, yelling profanities at two dark-skinned gentlemen as they were trying to back out of their parking space. Apparently they didn't get out of his way fast enough. I watched the event unfold as the men in the vehicle were cautiously avoiding several people who were walking behind them, preventing them from safely backing out.

These men did nothing wrong, but their attempts to calm down the angry man were to no avail. His screaming response was that "if they can't learn to drive, they should go back to where they came from" (sprinkled with colorful expletives). With my adrenaline rushing, I was afraid my intervention would trigger an escalation into violence, so I simply observed. I was prepared to intervene and assist in restraining the angry man if he attacked. But thankfully to everyone's relief, the men were finally able to back out and everyone went on their way without further incident.

Origins of the UI Concept: Founder's Experience

Nevertheless, I found this event to be deeply disturbing. I could not stop thinking about it for several weeks. I could suddenly identify with those witnessing similar overt expressions of hate in Nazi Germany and during the Civil Rights movement. They must have felt shock and helplessness to a far greater extent. I'm sure many must have also felt shame for passively allowing the abuses to occur without intervening. By not taking a stand, it felt like I was allowing the attacker to have the last word; that I gave him the proxy to speak on my behalf. I too felt a little shame.

I could only imagine the anguish felt by the victims of that vicious verbal attack. I regret not saying anything to those men who were left to drive away and process it on their own. I regret not taking a stand. Given another chance, I would have offered moral support to them at that crucial time.

These traumatic events were simply more examples confirming that the United States, and in fact, the whole world, is still in the grips of racism. I am further reminded with each new story I hear or read concerning groups or individuals publicly expressing hateful divisiveness. I can no longer sit on my hands paralyzed into non-action. The incident at the market made it impossible to delay any further. I felt a strong need for a fellowship where I could take refuge from such turmoil. *The malady of racism hurts everyone, including the racist who must face each day with his or her own fear-driven hatred.* It was clear that an organization like UI could offer some hope and provide the support I needed, so the next step was to start the process of becoming educated on bigotry, as well as the tools and principles to overcome such maladies.

Chapter 3: Introduction to Pioneers Addressing Racism

Literature on the Pioneers

Although innumerable women and men have dedicated their lives in the pursuit of raising the value of all life, sacrificing all to promote basic human rights over the period of a millennia, we will only take time here to spotlight a few.

The extraordinary application of Christian ideals in the life of a Hindu Indian to free his country can be found in the books of Mohandas K. Gandhi. His book *"Satyagraha in South Africa"* gives a moving account of the birth, development and expansion of Gandhi's *Satyagraha* philosophy, which reveals Martin Luther King, Jr.'s inspiration for his ideals adopted for the Civil Rights Movement. Their action based on love succeeded where hatred and violence could not.

Books such as *"Eyes on the Prize"* chronicle many important events and the role of several of the movement's unsung heroes. Other books such as *"Women in the Civil Rights Movement"* provide intimate insight into the courage of the women who were responsible for the early initiatives that led to the momentum for the pursuit of Civil Rights in the United States. The story of Dr. King is best told through his own words in his book *"The autobiography of Dr. Martin Luther King, Jr."* The influence of the Black Nationalists is well illustrated in *"The Autobiography of Malcolm X"*.

Yolanda King coauthored the book *"Open my eyes, open my soul"* exemplifying the passing of her father's loving legacy onto his children. This book contains samplings of letters from people of all races describing inspirational experiences of racial interactions and ideals. These stories make clear our society's shared desire to turn the dream of the Beloved Community into a reality.

The crisis of oppression drove these pioneers to initiate efforts that redefined the world's perceptions on human value and human rights. Because of the vital role they played in positively shaping our current racial climate, the lessons they learned and have to pass along are invaluable. These books are especially helpful to our education since they focus so heavily on issues stemming from racism.

Introduction to Pioneers Addressing Racism

Other insightful books on anti-racism education are available from contemporary writers offering a current outlook on these issues. The eye-opening book *"Teaching/Learning Anti-Racism: A Developmental Approach"* is based on the collaboration of a Black and a White professor who teamed up to teach college students about the effects of institutional racism. The patience and tolerance they practiced during these classes helped lead the students to a new understanding of prejudice and how they unintentionally collaborate with racism. Many students were then able to transform into "anti-racists" and actively worked to dismantle racist constructs.

Reading such books allows us to deepen our own understanding of our history of race relations while preserving their perspective and experiences. For now, here is a brief introduction to some of these pioneers.

Mohandas K. Gandhi

Starting with his arranged marriage at age 13, Gandhi's life was a nonstop series of events and experiences that were consistently rooted in love and the relentless search for truth. Personal encounters with racism in South Africa drove Gandhi to develop the philosophy behind *Satyagraha, love and truth force*.

In April of 1893 at the age of 23, two years after being called to the bar in England, he set sail from India to South Africa to contract as a barrister for a company in need of legal counsel. From the first day of his arrival, Gandhi witnessed verbal assaults and physical abuses that nonwhites had to endure by residents of European descent. The climax of abuses came a few weeks later while on a train en route to his destination in the Transvaal province. Nonwhites were restricted to coach seating, so despite having a legitimate first-class ticket, Gandhi was ordered to the coach section. He refused to forfeit his right to the seat and was forcibly thrown off the train. White-owned hotels denied him lodging. At every turn he encountered oppressive, racially-based restrictions on people of color by the minority white regime.

Later when Gandhi recounted these incidents with his colleagues, they agreed the treatment was wrong but explained that this was just the way things were. They each reported similar abuses but they had all chalked it up as part of doing business in that country.

Gandhi could not resign himself to this "reality", but the work of his contract consumed his time and diverted him from taking any action, so for the next year he simply endured the abuse.

At the end of his contract, he attended a farewell party before departing for India where he learned of a pending Bill that would disenfranchise Indians. He urged his colleagues to take a stand against the infringement upon their rights, but they responded that they had inadequate leadership to see them through this battle. They subsequently convinced Gandhi that he must stay another month to lead the opposition. Once momentum picked up in the resistance, he was then persuaded into delaying his departure for about another year. After a six-month return to India in 1896, he was again prompted to return to South Africa, at which time he returned with his family.

Despite his initial agreed upon one-year commitment, fate led Gandhi to spend twenty years in Africa leading the struggles against various racist laws. Besides the abuses from European citizens, they faced discrimination in the form of unfair taxes without representation, denial of citizenship and restrictions on land ownership. One Act rendered marriages performed prior to coming to South Africa as illegitimate. Time after time, their property and basic human rights were taken away with the stroke of a pen.

Gandhi was charged by his compatriots to lead them in the battle for their liberties. However, to the dismay of many, Gandhi had no intention of using violence against their adversary. His studies of the philosophies of intellectuals such as Tolstoy convinced him of the power of truth and love when combined with civil disobedience through peaceful resistance.

The term *Satyagraha, truth and love force,* which described his style of nonviolent resistance, was coined while confronting the Black Acts. Gandhi taught activists that they should love their enemy but that they also had a moral obligation to ignore unjust laws. They should be willing to accept any consequences for their civil disobedience without retaliation, even when met with imprisonment, violence or death. The concept of using nonviolence, openness and love to resolve human rights violations was almost unheard of. Although his supporters were very skeptical, this turned out to be the key to winning the struggles in South Africa and later in India.

Introduction to Pioneers Addressing Racism

With these disciplines in place, the government's wrath perpetrated on this peaceful movement exposed ruthlessness and immorality to a level that their society could no longer tolerate. This led to public pressure, which factored into ending the government's practice of violence and negotiating more equitable legislation. The Satyagraha movement proved that pure truth and love combined with action will always, in time, overcome fear, hate and injustice. Satyagraha was thus the model for the ideals and actions mirrored by King and the Civil Rights efforts.

While much of King's inspiration came from Gandhi, Gandhi's inspiration and ideology came in large part while reading Leo Tolstoy's book *"The Kingdom of God is Within You"*. Tolstoy examines the contradiction in the Old Testament doctrine of "An eye for an eye" and Christ's rejection of that philosophy, replacing it with ideals of unconditional love. Tolstoy also advocates the merits of pacifism and peaceful resistance. These teachings that aligned with Gandhi's Hindu beliefs became the foundation with which he built upon for the Satyagraha movement that led to their freedom and government independence. Gandhi's adherence to peace inspired the world, setting the example for many great leaders that followed.

Jo Ann Robinson, Rosa Parks and Dr. Martin Luther King Jr.

In the 1950s, the bus system in Montgomery, Alabama became a microcosm of segregated society. Blacks faced daily indignities on their commutes to work, going shopping or anywhere else that would require bus transportation. Protocol required African Americans to enter the front door to pay the fare, but they were then forced to exit the front door and re-enter through the rear to get to the black-section. They were not even allowed to walk through the front of the bus, which was reserved for Whites only. If the black section filled, incoming Blacks had to remain standing even if there were no white passengers. If the white section then filled up, African Americans at the front of the black-section were forced to forfeit their seats to the incoming white passengers.*

---

* Juan Williams, *Eyes on the Prize,* (Penguin Books Ltd. 1988), p. 60.

Over the years, a few African Americans defiantly challenged the rules and were either kicked off the bus or arrested for violating Jim Crow laws. In 1944, Mrs. Rosa Parks was thrown off a bus, without a refund, for refusing to re-enter through the back door. In 1949, English professor Jo Ann Robinson boarded a bus with arms filled with gifts from her Christmas shopping. She was now rushing to make a flight to Cleveland when she absentmindedly sat in the front section. The angry driver walked to her and raised his hand as if to strike her. When he began yelling at her, she ran off the bus in tears dropping packages and was so distraught that she cried all the way during her flight to Cleveland.

After the holiday, Mrs. Robinson returned to Montgomery and recounted her experience with the Women's Political Council. She was disappointed when met with the same unmoved responses that Gandhi had met when he described to his compatriots the abuses he encountered when arriving in South Africa. The women told their friend that this was simply a fact of life in Montgomery.

Over the following years, both the Women's Political Council and the NAACP closely monitored the abuses separately and began watching for a case that they can get behind in order to challenge the system. In 1955 the WPC put a plan together to initiate a boycott of Montgomery buses. The opportunity to put the plan in place came that same year.

On Thursday, December 1, 1955, eleven years after Mrs. Parks was thrown off the bus for refusing to re-enter through the back, she found herself on the very same driver's bus. When the white section filled and started overflowing to the black section, she refused his demand to forfeit her seat to a white male passenger. Mrs. Parks had been active in the Civil Rights Movement for about a decade now and was a secretary for the NAACP, in addition to her trade as a seamstress. She had grown intolerant to the unfair treatment and was compelled to stay her ground. She remained in her seat and resolved not to allow herself to be mistreated in this way any longer.

Introduction to Pioneers Addressing Racism

Mrs. Parks was following the footsteps of other Civil Rights proponents from her past and present. Due to having to face sexism* on top of racism, most female activists played background roles in the movement, but women such as Mary McLeod Bethune and Septima Clark played a pivotal role in blazing the trails until the movement gained traction. Their activities required sacrifice that sometimes put their personal wellbeing at risk. Because Mrs. Parks' courageous act was in defiance of the unjust and demeaning bus segregation rules that were enforced by Jim Crow laws, the driver had Mrs. Parks arrested and thrown in jail. Supporters rallied to her defense and the historic bus boycotts were ignited.

The Women's Political Council immediately sprang into action with their plan that very same day. Jo Ann Robinson stayed up all night long printing 35,000 leaflets with a note urging African Americans not to ride the buses that following Monday. Her students distributed the fliers on Friday and local ministers were approached to see if they would hand out leaflets to their congregations over the weekend. There was no guarantee the ministers or congregations would participate. The Women's Political Council thus took a big gamble in executing the plan without knowing if the community would be supportive. Although some ministers felt the boycott was too radical and would not participate, many ministers agreed to give their support.

To provide organization to the protest, church and community leaders gathered to form the *Montgomery Improvement Association*. Although new to Montgomery, a twenty-five-year old pastor in his freshman year was unanimously voted in as president and asked to take the lead in organizing the boycott through this assembly. The newly arrived Reverend King was taken by surprise, but was honored to fill this role.**

The committee who chose Dr. King was able to see this young man's great potential. Dr. King was a well-educated, humble servant who was eager to make a contribution of service to the Movement. He entered college at age fifteen and received his first bachelor's degree at age nineteen. He received his second bachelor's in theology at age twenty-one and his PhD in philosophy at age twenty-six.

---

* Betty Collier-Thomas; V.P. Franklin "Sisters in the Struggle", (New York University Press, 2001), p. 11.

** Williams, *Eyes*, p. 67-74.

It was in September of 1954, when at the age of twenty-five, Dr. King moved from his birthplace of Atlanta, Georgia to Alabama. He and his new wife, Coretta, were living in Boston where Whites treated Blacks with more respect. But they opted to leave their safe haven to answer the call they heard coming from Montgomery, where Dr. King would take up the pastorate for Dexter Avenue Baptist Church.

Dr. King had started his involvement in the Civil Rights Movement, prior to the boycott. He soon started combining his service to the church with Civil Rights activities. He had become active with the NAACP and then with the Alabama Council on Human Relations. This latter, multi-racial group focused on improving race relations through education. Some felt his affiliation with this council was in conflict with the NAACP. King however, knew early on that the vital works of organization seeking legal remedy to resolve injustices of discrimination were not going to be sufficient to bring about lasting change. Reconciliation and true integration always stayed at the forefront of King's dream.

The hope of reconciliation was driven by his faith as well as the lessons of love he learned from Gandhi. Early on during King's college education, he was introduced to the philosophies of Gandhi and David Thoreau who provided the framework for the movement. King studied, adopted, and further developed Gandhi's philosophy of Direct Action through nonviolent resistance and unconditional love. He established what seemed to be an unshakable faith in God and the human spirit. He lived by the faith in the power of love for overcoming fear and transforming our world. King was absolutely committed to this belief and he never strayed from these values. His conviction was based on ideals that transcend basic human instincts and he was able to see the good in even those filled with hate. No one was excluded from his compassion.

From the very first sermon given at the start of the bus boycott, Reverend King began to instill these ideals in the other activists. He suggested that they had a moral obligation to resist the immoral treatment they were receiving, but that they must act with love and dignity.

His leadership allowed them to navigate the roadmaps architected by Christ, Gandhi and Thoreau. After a very long and difficult struggle, victory was eventually achieved through the boycott

Introduction to Pioneers Addressing Racism

resulting in the Supreme Court ruling declaring bus segregation unconstitutional. This success came on the heels of the Brown vs. Board of Education decision, sparking the Civil Rights Movement in which King's visionary leadership evolved.

In 1957, shortly after the victory in Montgomery, King helped establish Southern Christian Leadership Conference to continue the struggle where the boycott left off. Integral in his vision and incorporated in this organization was the idea of the *Beloved Community*; a truly integrated brotherhood.

King presided over SCLC and stayed active for the remainder of his life. SCLC worked in parallel with other organizations such as the NAACP, CORE and SNCC, taking a lead role in the Civil Rights Movement. Although these organizations were sometimes unable to close gaps in methods and ideology, they succeeded in collaborating during key periods to focus their efforts towards their common objective. King also discusses Malcolm X for whom he had much respect. Although their relationship was contentious, they were both completely dedicated towards finding solutions for overcoming oppression. King acknowledged that throughout Malcolm's life, he experienced much greater extremes in poverty, violence and hatred, accounting for their differences and for Malcolm's cynicism towards the Civil Rights leaders. In the end though, they shared a common dream of liberation, for which they sacrificed their lives.

For the next thirteen years of his life following the bus boycott, Dr. King's leadership became the guiding light that led activists through the dark times of the movement. The hardships faced during their struggles would test movement participant's most basic values. Over time, the exposure to hatred and violence became too much for many. Some reached their limits of tolerance, finding it hard to forgive and began clamoring for retaliation. King too struggled with the pain, stress and seemingly hopelessness of the cruel and senseless attacks, but he helped others to understand that submitting to the instinct of anger and sinking into bitterness was all the power needed to keep them oppressed. Choosing love over hate was their only hope for keeping their hearts free, that they might overcome their bondage.

In spite of the bombing of his home and continuous death threats, the murders of several Civil Rights leaders, and a church bombing that killed four innocent little girls, King continued to advocate peace.

He passed these ideals along to thousands of others suggesting the victims of bigotry turn the other cheek and return spiteful violence with forgiveness. Proposals, that at first seemed incomprehensible, turned out to be the path to freedom. His humanitarian message was widely embraced, giving courage to all who followed him on this path.

King's example of unconditional love transformed hundreds of thousands of lives and changed the perception of millions. His humility and optimism became powerful examples of what we can all become. His vision for the possibility of all races growing together into a harmonious society inspired a renewed hope that reached around the world.

Malcolm X

Malcolm X started out on a path in stark contrast to that of Gandhi and King, which is partially attributed to the harshness of his early life. As a child, he suffered burdens that no human being should have to bear. His family was tormented by the Ku Klux Klan and his father and four of his uncles were killed at the hands of white men. After his father's murder, their hardships rapidly intensified. Under the extreme pressure of her struggles to provide enough food to feed her four children while living in abject poverty, his mother was hospitalized for insanity, where she remained institutionalized for the remainder of her life.

Along with the violent acts of overt racists, Malcolm had to contend with the prevailing supremacist attitudes from even those whom he had respected. He was particularly hurt when his favorite teacher rejected his dream for practicing law. This trusted mentor advised that he was reaching too high for a Negro and that he should set his sights on more realistic aspirations, such as becoming a waiter at a country club. This vote of no-confidence was much more painful coming from those he believed would support him in his ambitions.

Persistent negative portrayals of Blacks, personal rejection and the denial of his dreams had a devastating effect on his morale. Bitterness consumed him and by his adult life he had given up. Repeated frustrations were turned inward into self-destruction, ultimately leading to the addiction of drugs and alcohol. He became a gun-carrying sociopath resorting to scamming, conning and exploitation of others to feed his addiction. He was convinced that he would be murdered; fears that came very close to reality, as he carelessly stepped on the toes of associates who were ready to kill in order to preserve their reputation. As fate would have it though, the police were to uncover his burglary ring and he was sent to prison where his life would be forever set on a course in search of spirituality, self-analysis and personal transformation.

While in prison, he became acquainted with a fellow-inmate who was part of the "Nation of Islam". He introduced Malcolm to this religious movement that adapted an American-born version of the Islamic religion, teaching him the disciplines that freed him from his addiction and mental torment. Some of Malcolm's siblings had already converted and although skeptical at first, Malcolm eventually converted as well. Through his mentorship, he had a profound spiritual experience that saved him from immanent self-destruction. Such psychic transformations are miraculous for anyone who has fallen to these depths. Although in prison, he was free for the first time in his life.

The NOI advocates many positive aspirations including independence for African-Americans, psychological healing, and economic and spiritual growth. They denounce the use of drugs and alcohol and the abuse of women. Their ideology and their very strict codes of discipline provide a strong sense of identity to those who embrace these ideals. However, during that time years ago when Malcolm converted, they flatly rejected the idea that Blacks and Whites would ever be able to unite. They preached that Caucasians are inherently evil, that they can never be trusted and that lying and exploitation are innate characteristics of their nature. The historical treatment of Blacks by Whites around the world was the proof of their cynicism.

The claim that all Whites are evil by nature seemed more plausible as he examined the experiences he had throughout his life. He eventually became completely sold on this idea. Armed with this new perception, he was able to redirect his self-destructive internal strife into mistrust and resentment towards Whites. Malcolm had suffered so much at the hands of Caucasians but with the shift to this new perception, he now gained a new sense of freedom. He was able to escape their oppression and restore his self-image.

Upon his release from prison in 1952, three years before Martin Luther King, Jr. started gaining influence as a leader in the Civil Rights movement, Malcolm united with NOI where he rapidly became one of its most prominent ministers. For the next 12 years, his gratitude was exhibited by becoming the most vocal advocate for the NOI. He aggressively disseminated the message that Caucasians are "the white devil" and that the only way African-Americans will ever be free is to segregate. They believed they must separate completely from Whites and form their own state so that they may take control of their own destiny. *

Contradicting Messages

Between the Black Nationalist and the Civil Rights movement, two opposing paths had been paved. While Malcolm X was following the ideology of Marcus Garvey and the NOI, King instead followed the path of Gandhi and Thoreau. Malcolm, the NOI and the Black Nationalists focused on mistrust of Whites and planned to achieve independence for African Americans through separation, resorting to any means necessary. King and the Civil Rights Movement, on the other hand, were advocating nonviolence, unconditional love and integration of all races. Although the Black Nationalists had a three-year head start for building momentum under Malcolm's leadership, their ideology was now being seriously challenged.

Malcolm accused African-Americans, including King and the Civil Rights leaders that advocated nonviolence, of being brainwashed-uncle-Toms. To Malcolm, the accusation that they had blinders on concerning the Black Nationalist's belief that integration was impossible was evident to them by the violent responses of white racists towards the Civil Rights Movement.

The Black Nationalists and the Civil Rights Movement now became rivals that fundamentally had the same goal of liberating Blacks from their oppression, but extremely opposing ideas on how to achieve it. Both groups provided much strength to a multitude of individuals, but the conflict between them increased over time, causing confusion in African-American communities and resulting in erosion of solidarity.

* Nation of Islam; http://www.noi.org/about_beliefs_and_wants.shtml

Introduction to Pioneers Addressing Racism

Re-converging Philosophies

The tension between the Black Nationalists and the Civil Rights Movement carried on for several years, but in the end, Malcolm X had a falling out with the NOI followed by a life-changing experience during a pilgrimage to Mecca that set him on the road towards amending his previous twelve years of divisiveness. He was able to see Whites in a new light that enabled him to conclude that racism was a learned malady and not a natural part of one's makeup.

Although he maintained a deep mistrust for Whites in the United States, he came to believe that King and the Civil Rights Movement's pursuit of nonviolent change was the right course. He made public statements apologizing for his misperceptions, taking the first step towards aligning himself with the Civil Rights Movement. Unfortunately, Malcolm was soon to be assassinated and a full reconciliation never took place between these two factions. Yet, much doubt was lifted from the Civil Rights philosophies by those who followed him.

King's and Gandhi's examples of nonviolent Direct Action and unconditional Love have proven their effectiveness in transforming the individual and the potential for changing the world. While Unity Initiative has adopted these values, we can benefit by educating ourselves and understanding the issues leading to opposing views as well. For if the frustrations of the oppressed, the mistrust of the separatist and the hatred of the bigot are to be effectively addressed and rooted out, we cannot be afraid to hear them and understand their fears. This is done in the spirit of courage, truth and unconditional love.

Our ultimate aim is to provide an environment for those wanting to live in peace and harmony. This is the only effective course of action in every aspect of our lives. Little can be gained in trying to force ideals on those rigidly holding onto their opposing views or even in fighting the overt racist. Such battles are a waste of energy that can be better spent helping those with the desire to become free from their fear-driven misperceptions. Plenty of valiant organizations have already been established with the vital role of overturning unjust laws while promoting legislation to protect against the enumerable manifestations of bigotry. Unity Initiative will give us a venue to detoxify from the poison produced by racism, allowing us to discover the true spirit within each of us.

Chapter 4: Origins of UI Principles

The Sources

Principles are the fundamental rules or codes of conduct of an individual, group, organization or institution. They directly shape our morals. The principles of UI are primarily a combination of the ideals in the philosophies of the movements led by Gandhi and Martin Luther King, Jr. combined with the principles adopted from 12-step programs. Furthermore, invaluable education and growth can be gained through the ideals of "anti-racism" courses and training. Where available, they will give comprehensive understanding of all facets of racism that are not fully covered in this text.

Although the principles from these dissimilar sources were by no means mutually exclusive, they did address very different issues. The level of emphasis placed on individual values therefore varied from one organization to the next.

Principles emphasized in the Civil Rights Movements

Gandhi and King were both leading oppressed societies to overcome the attitudes of their oppressors. The skills and principles they needed to develop were abilities meant to ultimately induce a change in *others* for overcoming hate and callousness by awakening their loving compassion. More than anything, the principles they advocated were unconditional love, truth, self-sacrifice, discipline and Direct Action.

Their movements embraced the principle messages of *nonviolence* and *unconditional love* that originated from lessons taught during the *Sermon on the Mount*. Previous to this ideal, the world largely subscribed to the philosophy of "an eye for an eye". With that doctrine, seeking vengeful retaliation becomes a justifiable means for violence or other forms of harm that would normally be against our morals. But to the astonishment of the audience that day, revolutionary ideals were presented contradicting this world standard.

Here are the words that were used to rebuke such rationalization for using these destructive means for addressing disputes.

> *Ye have heard that it was said, an eye for an eye, and a tooth for a tooth. But I say unto you, resist not him that is evil: but whosoever smiteth thee on thy right cheek, turn to him the other also. And if any man would go to law with thee, and take away thy coat, let him have thy cloak also. And whosoever shall compel thee to go one mile, go with him two. Give to him that asketh thee, and from him that would borrow of thee turn not thou away.*
> Mathew, 5:38, KJV

No matter what our beliefs are on religious or other spiritual principles, we will surely be inspired by these humbling ideals. In this world-changing message, our actions are directed away from retaliation, leaving little room for violence regardless of the circumstance. Attempting to fight evil with evil is pointless. We are also advised to avail ourselves to the service of our fellow man; going beyond their expectations. The teachings then challenge us even further by recommending we love our enemies.

> *Ye have heard that it hath been said, Thou shall love thy neighbor, and hate your enemy. But I say unto you, Love your enemies, bless them that curse you, do good to them that hate you, and pray for them which despitefully use you, and persecute you; That ye may be the children of your Father which is in heaven: for he makes his sun to rise on the evil and on the good, and sends rain on the just and on the unjust. For if ye love them which love you, what reward have ye? Do not even the publicans the same? And if ye salute your brethren only, what do ye more than others? Do not even the publicans so? Be ye therefore perfect, even as your Father, which is in heaven is perfect.*
> Mathew, 5:43, KJV

These words challenged society in a way that was contrary to common attitudes. These ideals don't even seem to make sense on the surface. Shouldn't we defend ourselves and others if we are violated? Should we not retaliate to teach them the lesson that they cannot get away with such acts? Why should I love the person who wishes me harm? The surface answer is that hate and violence are self-destructive, even when rationalized as retaliation. Those who resort to such offenses are victimized by their own poisoned heart. Hatred will eventually create further wounds as well as resentments in others, so both parties end up losing. A deeper meaning transcends our human instincts into a higher spiritual plane. We are challenged to look at the perfect core of every human.

Similar ideals of forgiveness, unconditional love and humility can be found in other religions. Here is an example found in Islam:

Forgive him who wrongs you;
Join him who cuts you off;
Do good to him who does evil to you;
And speak the truth even if it be against yourself.

(Hadith said to be inscribed on the sword of the Prophet Muhammad)

Certainly, these high ideals are not always easy to live by, but King would echo Gandhi's statement that the philosophy of an eye for an eye "leaves everybody blind". Only unconditional love has the power to effectively eliminate these maladies. Loving those in your life that love you is certainly invaluable, but the practice of loving your enemy gives us the power to transform.

The next principle, *self-sacrifice,* was essential for exposing the hatred of the oppressors, awakening their conscience and opening up their hearts. Both leaders and followers of these movements sacrificed not only time and money; they physically put themselves directly in harm's way. Although their marches and demonstrations were meant to be peaceful, they exposed themselves to racist assaults and police brutality. Individuals were frequently attacked and several were killed. Along with the rest of the activists, King and Gandhi both faced arrests and beatings, sacrificing themselves and putting strain on their families.

The principle of *truth* was practiced in their commitment to openness, their continual self-analysis, as well as public admissions of mistakes. The principle of *discipline* was taught and practiced first through unwavering patience and willingness to stay the course. Each initiative was like an uphill battle with considerable roadblocks and setbacks. The Montgomery bus boycott lasted just over a year requiring men and women of all ages to endure many hardships.

Discipline was also practiced in avoiding retaliation for attacks against the movement. As they sacrificed themselves on the front lines of their cause, facing hostile mobs, they had to refrain from responding with any forms of negative aggression. When faced with violence, the response of these men, women and children was to forgive; to turn the other cheek.

This reaction sometimes had a profound effect on the perpetrator of the assaults, but the greater effect was in galvanizing the moral resolve of community observers that were not directly involved in the conflict. Those who tried to stay out of the middle were moved to take a stand against the oppression. The overall positive impact on the conscience of the communities and government proved the practical effectiveness of the movement's philosophy.

Along with the disciplines practiced in movement activities, forms of discipline were exercised in the personal lives of the activist. Gandhi encouraged healthy practices in all other areas of life including diet, sex relations, physical exercise and financial responsibility. His experimental commune on Tolstoy Farm during his *Satyagraha* campaign against the black Acts in South Africa helped Gandhi and movement participants enjoy a simple, healthy and humble life free from ego-feeding habits. This lifestyle further added strength to their cause by allowing the participants to maintain a clear conscience of their motives while avoiding possible criticism of opulence from their detractors.

The principle of *Direct Action* was another crucial component of these movements. Their philosophies did not end at pacifism. Nonviolence was merely the starting point; rejecting ineffective methods that relied upon the guaranteed destruction of human life. These activists viewed all life as being sacred and invaluable. Harming others was fundamentally against their morals. Instead, the organizations behind these movements focused their efforts on bringing people together, raising the confidence and esteem of the oppressed, and touching the hearts of their oppressors.

Principles emphasized through the 12-Steps

In contrast to the issues faced by Gandhi and King, the members of 12-step programs have typically faced oppression largely of their own making. When an individual is suffering from personal shortcomings, the skills they will need to develop are ones that will allow them to escape the clutches of a destructive ego. The fundamental principles emphasized in the 12 steps were formulated to recover from fear and self-hate, which is masked by over-inflated pride. The principles needed to overcome these maladies are humility, self-examination, self-disclosure, personal responsibility, amendment of past wrongs, spirituality and service to others.

The 'principle' of *humility* is in actuality the fundamental attribute we seek, which is at the opposite end of the spectrum from egotism. The importance of this attribute cannot be over-emphasized. It can be equated with self-truth or pure honesty and is the ultimate personality change being sought by taking action towards all other principles.

Self-cleansing in 12-step programs begins with an acknowledgement or admission of a problem or a shortcoming. This is part of *surrendering* our ego, which is a very difficult, but crucial step. Further steps require much more in-depth self-examination of past mistakes, as well as personal character flaws. The actions involved in these principles inevitably expose many defects in our make-up, as well as the harm that ego-driven actions have caused others. After becoming honest with ourselves about our defects of character, this *self-examination* is followed by *self-disclosure* to another human being. This humbling act is usually very difficult, but serves many purposes including helping us to purge ourselves of the pain of our suppressed past.

The next step is to take *personal responsibility* for our own suffering as well as any possible harm we may have caused others. If such wrongs were discovered and disclosed in the previous steps, we then follow up by amending past infractions by acknowledging mistakes to those we harmed, paying off debts, recommitting to relationships with friends and family, or doing whatever is necessary to make things right. With these changes, we have done the best we can to continue our lives with a clean slate.

Origins of UI Principles

From the beginning stages of the efforts towards these values, members pursue a *spiritual* path based upon their own belief system. This very personal experience of discovering and establishing his or her own ideals is left up to each individual. The final principle the members must follow is becoming of *service*. The action involved in seeking our spiritual beliefs, in rigorous service work, as well as further efforts for continually keeping our slate clean have proven to be very effective measures for replacing egotism with humility. These are personality changes that guarantee a happy, meaningful life. Details about these values are discussed in the chapter *Establishing Concepts for the Principles*. The suggestions for putting them into action are then presented in the section on *Principles in Action*.

Commonality of Principles

Although the emphasis on the ideals by these sources differed, they both naturally included the same fundamental set of standards. The 12-steps don't explicitly discuss discipline, but you won't make it very far past the first step without it. The movements for racial equality were not as emphatic about self-examination, but they were given no choice but to look deep inside themselves, root out selfishness and reach for a higher state of consciousness as they faced overwhelming circumstances. Both required the extensive development of humility attributes.

All humans are challenged by these concepts to some extent. In the case of those struggling to be freed from an oppressor and for those who are spiritually, physically and emotionally bankrupt, adopting these principles is often a matter of survival. They are highly motivated by the life-threatening consequences of not embracing these disciplines. But these practices are not intended to be exclusively for those in life-and-death struggles. They are for anyone wanting to live a full and joyful life. All that is needed is a desire to grow and the willingness to choose to put them into practice. We then take the necessary action to improve our lives and to give to others.

Putting it altogether, below is a condensed list of principles and practices we strive for as individuals and as an organization. These are the values we wish to bring back to our communities once we have adopted them into our own lives through Direct Action. Although they are perfect ideals that we may never fully achieve, they are the beacons of light for which we continually strive.

GUIDING PRINCIPLES

UNITY
TRUTH
LOVE

SPIRITUALITY
HUMILITY
SERVICE

DISCIPLINE
SELF-CLEANSING
SELF-SACRIFICE

NONVIOLENCE
DIRECT ACTION

The Three Legacies

It may be observed that the first three principles are the three *legacies* of Unity Initiative. A legacy is defined as something handed down from the past, as from an ancestor or predecessor. Our legacies were passed down from generation to generation and best exemplified by the sources mentioned above. *Unity*, *Truth* and *Love*, are the fundamental principles that make up the three sides of the triangle of the UI symbol. They are the essential values that are at the core of all other principles that when practiced result in humility. These principles go hand in hand. Where one can be found, you will find elements of the others, and where one is lacking, you will likely find that all have deficiencies.

Chapter 5: Establishing Concepts for the Principles

Unity

Unity is a state of harmony; a state of oneness. Most of us have experienced this kind of connection with others at some time in our lives whether in close family ties, a sports team, an academic, social or work group, or a unified community or organization. As we grow closer together, we learn to understand, trust and care for each other. When we are with others that we share these bonds with, we feel safe, secure and accepted. We get energized by their love. Our self-esteem increases and we are able to tackle life's challenges a little easier. The unified group will hold us accountable, challenging us to grow. When we are provided with good living-examples, we are more likely to emulate their behavior and adopt those traits.

When we are separated from such associations, living the life of a caveman, we are robbed of basic human needs. Isolation cuts us off from vital nurturing, and our growth is inhibited since we don't get the opportunity to learn from the experiences of others. If deprived for too long, we can become drained of energy and consumed in fear. Most of us have experienced life in this state as well; the experience of being so disconnected that we ironically seem to feel loneliest when surrounded by others. We feel like they are judging us, so as a defense, we judge them in return. We become over-sensitive and blame them for our problems. We are often confused by the behavior of others, and we are easily agitated. Our life can potentially completely unravel and seem meaningless if we don't become reunited.

All too often, people in this vulnerable state connect with others with similar problems by finding and identifying a common 'enemy' to direct their negative energy. Without sufficient self-knowledge and understanding of what they are feeling, they find relief in focusing their attention outside of themselves and onto someone else. An unhealthy camaraderie then grows among these individuals in their common feelings of fear-driven resentment. They isolate themselves from anyone who challenges their divisive points of view. They allow themselves to assimilate then perpetuate the myths and misperceptions of those that are not like them.

This exclusive protection mechanism may give short-term relief but guarantees long-term suffering. The price is living with perpetual animosity, sinking deeper into an ever isolating groupthink mentality; eventually deteriorating into hate that prevents peace of mind. They never get to experience unconditional love nor absolute freedom from fear.

Hate and happiness are incompatible. To extract from life all that it has to offer, we must overcome our fears of all people and search for common ground.

So much of our world is unfortunately suffering from lack of unity. We are divided by so many physical boundaries manifested by our psychological barriers. These barriers are the result of our misperceptions accumulated from our biases based on race, ethnicity, religion, gender, beliefs and class. Fear of those different from ourselves is passed down from previous generations. Misperceptions are fed to us from early on in our childhood. We hear critical-minded observations of the behaviors in others on top of observing already established racist constructs. Negative labels placed on those groups reinforce those misperceptions making racial-unity a virtual impossibility.

Unity primarily refers to the oneness we wish to achieve with the fellowship to overcome this division. The unifying efforts that we will be undertaking are meant to bring us together by sharing our lives with each other through dialogs at meetings and other events, as well as socializing with each other in our daily lives. By first breaking down the physical barriers in this form of Direct Action, we expose ourselves to the truth about each other. We begin to view others with a clearer perspective; that we are all alike in so many ways, yet it is our differences that make life so interesting and enjoyable. Although the years of distortions that we were exposed to won't be rooted out of our consciousness overnight, our persistence in pursuing unity with diverse individuals will immediately give a sense of joy and replace disconnectedness with a condition of harmony.

The unity with others discussed above is what probably first comes to mind when contemplating this principle, especially when considering the name of our organization. There are two other contexts of unity that may not be as obvious. These are unity with ourselves and unity in the realm of spirituality. Just as our misperceptions have caused division in our personal relationships, distorted self-perceptions have kept us from experiencing true self-love founded on humility. As a result, many of us suffer from an inability to feel comfortable in our own skin.

We may feel a disconnection in spiritual matters as well. Even if we have spiritual or religious beliefs, we may still have perceptions or feelings of apartness. The activities outlined in the twelve steps are the Direct Action we will take to address these deficiencies. Their practice will restore our relationship with ourselves and strengthen our spiritual connection.

Truth

Truth covers all things that are factual and real and is practiced through efforts to be honest in our perceptions, action and communications. At one end of the spectrum we have honesty, openness, integrity, understanding, clarity and personal responsibility, while at the other end we have dishonesty, confusion, misinformation, distortion and denial. We apply truth to many levels of our lives. On the surface, these qualities are simply applied to avoiding dishonest behavior such as lying, cheating or stealing. At this level, facts are relatively easy to discern and agree upon. On a deeper level, these qualities can be applied to our internal beliefs, emotions and perceptions. But when communicating and acting at this level, ambiguity brought on by the complexity of our personal experiences blurs the line between facts and opinions. We may also be apprehensive due to feelings of vulnerability. Yet by building intimate relationships and sharing ourselves with others, we begin to get a clearer picture of who we are as well as an appreciation for those around us.

In Shakespeare's Hamlet, Polonius gave this advice "This above all: to thine own self be true, and it must follow, as the night the day, thou canst not then be false to any man." To be truthful with others, we must first be honest with ourselves. This prerequisite is the starting point for this principle. This requires self-analysis and an open mind. If we are unable to be honest with ourselves, then our action and communications will be distorted and counter-productive and can possibly become harmful. Our perception of others will be inaccurate and our relationships can become strained. To overcome self-deception, we must first be willing to take a deep look at ourselves. We will need to look at our past to see how the events of our lives have shaped our views and how they have fundamentally affected our relationships. We must also be willing to stay open-minded to the ideas, experiences and knowledge of others to ensure the broadest perspective in order to avoid tunnel-vision.

As we will see, the 12-steps are designed for this kind of thorough self-examination. Starting with an acknowledgement of a need or desire for change, we examine our lives looking for accumulated debris that may be blocking us from growth and happiness. After analyzing these facts about ourselves, we take the necessary action to clear away the negative thoughts and feelings we've held onto. Most find the steps intimidating since our pride will not readily submit to such self-examination and retribution. James Garfield observed "The truth will set you free, but first it will make you miserable." Of course we should expect a certain amount of discomfort as we overcome the fear of dredging up our innermost thoughts and feelings, then exposing them to another human being. This fear is so great for some that they will simply refuse to take these steps. Every imaginable rationalization for denial has been conceived for avoidance. But if we decide simply to continue carrying around this baggage, we are choosing stagnation, while the reward for cleaning our slate is happiness, self-esteem and improved relationships.

Truth can also be practice through step-work by incorporating daily self-examination and communication with others. We avoid stuffing our feelings to prevent them from re-accumulating. When we become hurt, angry, frustrated, envious, or disturbed in any other way, we take responsibility for these emotions while sharing them with a trusted friend. We look at what our part was in the disturbance to see what action we can take to shed sunlight on those feelings, processing them before they fester into resentments, self-pity or depression. To the extent that we practice these disciplines in our lives, our heart and our mind will become free allowing us to experience life with peace and joy.

In this state of honesty, we can then apply these principles to our opinion of others of diverse groups. However, we will only gain clear insight when we are provided factual information. This is not so simple since misunderstanding and misperceptions are frequently perpetuated through stereotypical myths, which cause distortions.

We are sometimes exposed to vicious comments directed towards particular gender, religious, ethnic or racial groups such as "These people are lazy and just want a 'free ride'"; "That group is greedy and has no morals"; "Women are over-emotional"; "Men have no feelings"; and the list goes on. Stereotypes are also reflected in the media or may be passed along through friends and family. As children, we don't usually question these portrayals nor do we have built-in psychological filters to prevent biases from infiltrating our perceptions. As a result, we are adversely influenced by these negative images.

Compounding the difficulty of learning the truth are certain psychological protection mechanisms of our ego. When we live through periods of insecurity or our self-esteem is low and we are experiencing fear in our lives, our egotism is vulnerable to distortions. Our ego is alternately telling us that we are either worthless or that we are superior to others. In this confusing state, the discomfort of our inferiority complex will drive our ego to find shortcomings in others in order to try to re-inflate itself. It will feed on these stereotypes as a means of avoiding self-examination and continue feeling superior. By the time we are adults, they are deeply engrained in our conscience and our mind will not just simply let them go. They become real for us.

We often wind up repeating stereotypical statements, spreading our distorted perceptions, which are then passed on to the next generation. The destructive outcome of these stereotypes is the objectifying of our fellow human beings. Such portrayals erode our ability to view others as humans equal to ourselves, so our conscience and emotions become disconnected from them. In this state, we are vulnerable to getting caught up in hatred and condemnation. When we objectify a person or race as subhuman, our moral resolve becomes weakened and we can rationalize inequality of opportunity or exploitation. We can even disregard the use of violence. But more likely, we are simply apt to ignore, reject or exclude them from our lives. This exclusion is essential for keeping stereotypes and other distortions intact.

Negative stereotypes are frequently formed as opinions based on personal observations mixed with non-factual hearsay. These opinions are then transferred through communications to others as if they were undisputed truths. So how do we end these distortions? Ultimately, *we are responsible*, but if we don't know how to counter such negative forces in our lives, what are we to do? Truth is the principle, but how exactly do we replace distortion with truth? Seeking truth takes action based on courage, compassion and love. The 12 steps will lay down the groundwork to launch us on the path of a committed pursuit for the truth of our own nature. Combining this with direct contact with our fellows of diverse groups, we will melt away our fear and misperceptions of others.

Love

Love is patient, love is kind. It does not envy, it does not boast, it is not proud. It does not dishonor others, it is not self-seeking, it is not easily angered, it keeps no record of wrongs. Love does not delight in evil but rejoices with the truth. It always protects, always trusts, always hopes, always perseveres.
1 Corinthians, 13:4 - 7, NIV

The last of our three legacies is love, and more specifically, unconditional love or *Agape*. While it may seem like a sentimental value to hold as a fundamental principle for an organization, love is nothing less than the powerful gift we were all given that can reshape our world. It has the capacity to overcome any fear-driven emotion.

In his book "The Greatest Thing in the World", Henry Drummond declares that love is even greater than faith or hope. Without love we are nothing. This virtue nurtures us when we are weak, inspires us when we are strong, and is the glue that is capable of uniting us regardless of our differences. When we put love into action, we naturally fulfill the spirit of all principles.

Love encompasses strong feelings of deep affection, liking, compassion and warmth towards others. When we love someone, we value who they are as an individual. We feel blessed to share our lives with them and we are concerned with their well-being. It is the base for the principles of fairness and justice. We practice love by devoting our time and attention, strengthening our connection. We give recognition for each other's value and we are patient, tolerant and forgiving of each other's human frailties.

Martin Luther King, Jr. observed three distinct forms of love, using terms found in the Greek language. The first is *Eros* which is the romantic love based on aesthetic beauty and attraction. The next form of love is *Philia*, which is the love of family or friendship or some other mutual bond. King notes the beauty in both of these forms of love. But then he goes on to describe *Agape*, which he like Drummond, proclaims to be the greatest of all human attributes. Agape is unconditional love seeking nothing in return. King believed it to be "the love of God working in the lives of men."

Without unconditional love, we place requirements on our affections, respect or compassion. We may expect others to return these feelings or act in a specific way. When our expectations are not met, we reciprocate by withholding kindness or ending tolerance. When we love unconditionally, we eliminate these contingencies, looking for the good at the core of every human being. Having our expectations met is no longer a prerequisite for holding interest in another's wellbeing. When another is immersed in selfishness or filled with hate, we maintain hope for their personal recovery.

Nurturing this attribute transforms ourselves as well as those around us. Our hearts and souls are strengthened as we become able to experience love in the most contentious environments. When we are verbally or physically assaulted, unconditional love protects us from bitterness poisoning our heart. We are able to overcome initial instincts for revenge, avoiding destructive, ego-feeding reactions. Freed from the bondage of hate, we find compassion for our enemies. In this state, they are often compelled to change as well.

The human response to love is so powerful that Gandhi and King absolutely relied upon it for winning over hearts in their battles for Civil Rights. Facing violent attacks that threatened their lives, they fearlessly marched on, armed only with their faith in love. Even when faced by opposition from their own supporters, they never wavered from these values. Although Gandhi and King frequently yielded to the inspired ideals of others, backing down from a position earnestly based on love and justice were out of the question when it meant compromising principles.

Both these men faced growing pressure from many who were fed up with waiting for change and were willing to resort to violence to protect their communities and to achieve their rights. Some viewed Gandhi as a coward, while some labeled King a foolish Uncle Tom for his nonviolent convictions. How could they love those who meant them so much harm? Many desired retaliation, but the vision that came from their education and experience gave them choices that opened up a path excluding the use of fear-driven acts of destruction. Their understanding of the power of love to overcome fears and alter hearts gave them the faith to lift the movements above reactive propensities for revenge.

The consistent effectiveness of the use of love solidified their morals. They were neither for sale, nor vulnerable to compromise through intimidation. These men stayed true to this value, even when faced with risks to their lives. Both men received repeated death threats and encountered several instances of violence long before they were finally assassinated; yet neither they nor their fellow activists retreated from these ideals. They were heavily burdened by the vicious methods, in which they were forced to withstand; but they were still able to find compassion and forgiveness for their assailants. By looking beyond the violations, they were able to view their rivals as misguided children of God whose disillusioned sickness of hatred could be transformed through the inevitable healing brought on by love and truth. This perception made their unconditional love possible and the power of their unending compassion did indeed change many hearts.

In the end, both of these men along with many activists were killed in their unyielding pursuits. Gandhi and King both predicted this would be their fate, but they were willing to die for these principles. They believed that the societal impact of their efforts was more important than their very lives. Their example of this unyielding commitment to love and truth are indelible in the minds of all who shared in their sacrifices.

In contrast to the unconditional love practiced by the Civil Rights participants whose love was often simply rejected and sometimes returned with hate, the recipients of the love practiced in 12-step programs are usually actively seeking help. As we will soon see, the twelfth step involves carrying the message of hope and recovery, as well as serving our friends, our families and our communities. Men and women working on this step make themselves readily available to anyone seeking this path. In many cases, this service work requires sacrifice of time and other resources. However, those who have worked at this step found what King and Gandhi and the movement participants had discovered: *happiness and self-love grow proportional to the expansion of their love for others.*

Spirituality

The next three principles directly align with the three legacies. Spirituality aligns with unity, humility with truth, and service with love. A wide variety of definitions for the term spirituality can be found. However, it almost always includes some concept or experience of synchronicity or power in our universe that goes beyond the limits of our five senses of sight, hearing, smell, taste and touch. We present these ideals with the very broadest of meaning. It involves an awareness of a higher level of connectedness of our world that is not easily explained, defined or understood.

This organization embraces the principle of spirituality but does not exclusively promote the beliefs or practices of any particular faith. We in fact wish to open the door to everyone, regardless of his or her views. All personal belief systems are highly encouraged to be pursued and strengthened.

Because of its mysterious nature, spirituality is by far the most ambiguous of all our principles. This value is a highly personal set of beliefs and experiences based on a lifelong journey. Finding our own spiritual path may be the primary purpose of our existence. But no two people will hold the same exact ideas. On the contrary, if we compared all our sets of beliefs we will inevitably find concepts that are in stark contradiction. When terms and views are expressed in this book or by other members that do not coincide with your own beliefs, feel free to modify them to your own understanding or even disregard them altogether.

Our fellowship follows the custom of other programs that subscribe to the concept of a 'Higher Power' or 'Power greater than yourself'. Seeking such beliefs is an integral part of the steps. Some of us who have difficulty with the idea of an intelligent Supreme Being have viewed the loving group conscience of the fellowship as their Higher Power. The combined experience of the united group provides an invaluable resource for strength and guidance. For most of us, our beliefs are continually changing as we pursue our own understanding.

Others come from different backgrounds that use varying spiritual names for this Higher Power, such as God, Vishnu, Allah or Great Spirit. The rooms of the many 12-step organizations include people from a wide variety of religious and spiritual backgrounds. The aggregate of these groups are composed of Christians, Jews, Buddhists, Muslims and other religions. They include atheists and agnostics as well. All who embrace love, tolerance and unity, rejecting hateful divisiveness are welcome. Our sets of beliefs are highly diverse, yet we hold a sincere mutual respect for each other without criticism or judgment. Every individual must be free to seek his or her own spiritual path and stay faithful to their beliefs.

Humility

Humility is a frequently misunderstood virtue. It is often mistakenly associated with weakness, but in actuality, this virtue requires great strength in character. We define humility as the opposite of egotism. Humility is grounded in truth and includes an accurate self-perception, while egotism is the result of a distorted image of ourselves. This distortion carries on to all our relationships resulting in a self-appraisal of 'less than' or 'greater than,' but never 'equal to'.

Egotism is often characterized by conceit, pride, arrogance, bloated self-importance and selfishness. Conversely, egotism is exposed by low self-esteem and negative feelings projected towards others. Although one of these extremes may be dominant, they are usually present simultaneously.

At the core of egotism are insecurities resulting from fear. Our ego will always seek money, power, property, prestige or other gratification through *external stimulation.* But because these are ineffective solutions for overcoming fear, the unresolved anxiety can put us in a state of constant alert where we perceive normal activity around us as a potential threat, even though no such threat exists. Among other consequences, this can inhibit trust, preventing us from forming healthy relationships or feeling connected to others.

A humble person, on the other hand, is unpretentious and is distinguished by peace and joy brought about by internal or *spiritual growth*. Humility is sometimes equated with honesty and, in this respect, directly aligns with the principle of truth. *It is a true sense of self with a compassionate understanding of others.* A humble person has a high self-esteem and because all are equal, views him or herself as neither superior nor inferior to anyone else. This perception is a key factor in facilitating and building bonds in relationships.

The effects of humility are as beneficial as the consequences of egotism are detrimental. Many religions and philosophies understand humility as the path to liberation from suffering. Ego is never at rest. It causes emotional instability because its answers to life's problems are ineffective. Fear is simply masked instead of conquered. Humility is at peace with its place in the world, and it is content. Fear is subdued. Although a humble person may share their experience, strength and hope with someone seeking guidance, they neither judge nor criticize. And while they stay open-minded to the appraisals from others to see how they can improve, they are not shaken by unwarranted criticism. A phrase often used to put this concept into perspective is *"What others think of me is none of my business."*

In the purest sense of *perfect* humility, negative feelings towards oneself, towards others and towards any other aspect of life are all but eliminated. Complete contentment comes through acceptance. This does not mean humility is blind to problems or injustices of the world, but that it is not encumbered by negative emotions. Humility is motivated by hope rather than despair. Of course, we are all human and our ego is part of that humanness, but humility gives us emotional stability, which makes us less vulnerable to negativity in our environment and more effective in dealing with life on life's terms.

Humility is also frequently tied to the negative connotation of humiliation. Humiliation is the painful feeling that one experiences with the apparent lowering of their self-image or the shame one feels when something embarrassing is revealed about themselves. But as mentioned above, having pure humility and a complete void of egotism would make one impervious to humiliation. However, as long as we are human and have fears, we will have ego. And as long as we have egotism, we will inevitably experience the bruising of our pride. *Humiliation is simply the exposing of those remaining parts of our ego that are still clinging to an untrue or inaccurate perception of ourselves or of others.*

Without this understanding, we may react negatively to these feelings with resentment or self-pity; our ego's defense mechanism taking over. But armed with this knowledge, humiliation can be a very positive experience in our lives despite the pain. It has the potential force to evoke a clarifying adjustment in our perception without a direct effort on our part. We can minimize the sting by recognizing our ego is the source of our suffering and immediately surrender to humility. We maximize the benefit of surrendering by responding to these prideful setbacks with self-examination and a deliberate adjustment in our perception. Practicing the principle of self-examination and discipline in this way will turn our experience of humiliation into humility. Our discomfort will turn into a sense of contentment.

The following table of personality attributes is an adaptation of the "Off the Beam / On the Beam" signs that list positive character attributes and their opposing character flaws. Note that the traits on the ego side are essentially the converse of the traits on the humility side. Each pair of traits represent opposite ends of the same spectrum. Instead of spending energy *battling* the ego-oriented traits, we can reduce them by setting focus on the humility end of the spectrum and walking in that direction. Aligning ourselves with the above principles will be fulfilled by taking action to develop these humility traits. We will see later how the 12 steps are part of the fundamental Direct Action we will take.

Establishing Concepts for the Principles

Table of Personality Attributes

Driven by Ego	**Guided by Humility**
Prideful	Humble
Dishonest / Deceptive	Honest / Truthful
Self-Centered	People & Spiritually-Centered
Selfish	Generous / Giving
Hopeless	Hope-filled / Faithful
Negative / Cynical	Positive
Apathetic	Caring
Judgmental / Condemning	Compassionate / Empathetic
Hateful	Loving
Unreceptive	Open-minded
Divisive / Exclusive	Uniting / Inclusive
Blaming	Accountable / Responsible
Slothful / Compulsive	Disciplined
Gluttonous / Impulsive	Restrained
Hypercritical	Encouraging
Easily Disturbed	Emotionally Strong / Mature
Resentful / Merciless	Forgiving / Merciful
Impatient	Patient
Controlling	Accepting
Obsessive / Greedy / Lustful / Jealous	Contented
Skeptical	Trusting
Fear-controlled	Courageous
Obstinate	Willing
Self-Pity	Grateful
Agitated	Calm

Some may respond to the proposed principles and humility attributes with thoughts such as, "This is too much! I can't possibly live up to such high expectations. These standards may be possible for the likes of spiritual giants such as Gandhi or King, but they're just not realistic for the *average* person." But we do not need to worry. As so aptly put by the AA *Big Book*, "We are not saints. The point is that we are willing to grow along spiritual lines. The principles we have set down are guides to progress. We claim spiritual progress rather than spiritual perfection." (*Alcoholics Anonymous*; pg. 60)

We cannot possibly meet all these perfect ideals one hundred percent of the time. Keeping in mind that the matching qualities on the opposite sides of the above table are each extreme ends of a spectrum, we can only do our best to walk *towards* those perfect attributes on the humility side. As fallible humans, we may make improvements towards them for the rest of our lives, yet never reach and maintain perfection with any of these standards.

As we continue on, we will certainly backslide from time to time. We will catch ourselves being dishonest or judging and controlling others. We will occasionally become consumed with resentment, fear, jealousy, skepticism and self-pity. We will get caught in subtle traps such as self-righteousness, rationalization, justification and victimization, in which we find all kinds of excuses to abandon accountability and discipline. These mental twists cause us to make mistakes and to get off the beam. When we do, our feelings will be our barometer. When we are feeling upset or disturbed in *any* way and experiencing emotions such as anger, jealousy, anxiety, fear or disappointment, our inclination may be to point the finger at someone or something else and blame them for our disturbance. But this is not only a distortion, it is essentially allowing others to control us, which leads to unnecessary suffering. Through the 12 steps we practice accountability by taking full responsibility for our lives. In doing so, we find we are less dependent on the behavior of others for our own peace and happiness. We become freed from our voluntary bondage by others and we do our best to reach for these perfect ideals.

King and Gandhi were far from perfect. Both openly acknowledged their shortcomings, admitting making many mistakes. They too wanted to preserve their right to be human, expressing their wish not to be placed on a pedestal. Throughout their lives, they stumbled repeatedly, but they never completely succumbed to their human frailties. They were never derailed from doing the next right thing. When they fell, they got back on their feet and continued their journey in the desired direction. Gandhi viewed his life as a series of experiments, which he readily conceded had occasionally resulted in failure. King too admitted he made numerous mistakes and said that we all have a civil war raging within us. This battle seems to be non-ending. Forces of temptation within us constantly try to draw us towards the ego-feeding traits. For some reason, we seem to have been wired this way. Analyzing the challenges posed by these internal driving forces will give us a better understanding of our own nature.

This force drawing us towards our ego-based attributes seems to be instinctual. Trying to resist is like swimming upstream against the currents of a powerful river. The effort is difficult and it sometimes seems pointless. But to simply give up and let ourselves get carried away by indulging in unhealthy behaviors brings us to destruction. If we don't put up adequate resistance to the pull of these desires, we will be smashed into all kinds of stumps and boulders in the form of damaged relationships, missed opportunities, and the loss of health and self-respect. And downstream, at the end of this river is a treacherous waterfall that crashes onto sharp destructive rocks that cannot be survived.

We know that at the upstream end of the river lies a lake of tranquility and abundance. That is where with little effort, we can flourish in our relationships, our jobs, our homes and our communities. But to succeed in these areas, we must pay a price by replacing a life of hedonism with discipline and sacrifice. Most are fortunate enough to experience this simple living to varying degrees in the innocence of our childhood, but many of us did not gain sufficient knowledge and respect of the insidious currents of temptation that are constantly pulling at us towards the mouth of the river. We let ourselves drift into the currents where it started to carry us away.

At first, it seemed very exciting as we were living on the edge! But then, we hit those first couple of painful rocks and stumps. For some, it taught the necessary life's lesson concerning the dangers in the allure of life's indulgences. They clearly saw that the excitement of such behavior exacts a high price. It can be destructive and will pull them away from the life they love. So in order not to drift too far off from the calm waters of the lake, they accepted the responsibility to work against the gentle drift of the current and incorporated into their lives the necessary disciplines to prevent themselves from straying too far.

Then there were those of us that thought those first couple of boulders we hit seemed like a fair price to pay for the exhilaration and sense of freedom. It made us feel alive with excitement. We laughed at those who tried to warn us of the dangers of the currents and scoffed at their seemingly naïve lifestyles. And although the accruing injuries started taking a toll on us as well, the speed of the river was picking up and we continued to get thrilled with the rush! As time went on, we needed more of that exhilaration to keep ourselves preoccupied in order to keep our minds off of our wounds; so we indulged further in unhealthy behavior, disregarding the opposition of our loved ones. Inevitably for all of us though, the pain becomes too great and no amount of thrill can overcome the misery that has become our life. We had a real dilemma here. We could not possibly continue on like this. Not only was it becoming increasingly destructive, but there was very little joy left in our fantasized free-spirited lifestyle.

On the other hand, the tranquil life appeared stiflingly boring and foreign. If we've gone this far, we may now feel a sense of doom that we may never make it back. For most of us though, survival instincts kick in and we begin to swim against the current back towards safe waters. At first it seems so impossible, so unnatural for us. We are being forced to take action in ways that we have rarely experienced. But the more we exert ourselves, the more natural it becomes. The further we get upstream, the wider the river grows, making our struggle easier. Soon we start gaining strength as we lose the fear of the treacherous dangers behind us. We begin to reap the rewards of our struggles with self-respect and the love of others. Our conscience clears as we untangle from the debris that kept us from enjoying our lives and experiencing a union with the world around us.

When we make it back, we realize we must not ever take for granted those forces that drew us so close to annihilation. We will need to adopt the disciplines in our daily lives that will keep us on the right path and out of harm's way. This will certainly require exercising discipline in all areas of our life: physically, mentally and spiritually. We will need to change our attitudes towards the lives of those we childishly rebelled against and become open-minded to where they were right. We can extend this humility even further by taking the initiative to seek the knowledge of others, then following their example. With these practices in place, we will be able to maintain a clear head and a free heart.

Establishing Concepts for the Principles

Discipline

Why were we made in this way; to be constantly swayed by temptation as described in the previous section? Most things we usually crave are almost always bad for us, while the things that are healthy and beneficial are so frequently less appealing. Why do we seem to have natural desires to be slothful and gluttonous instead of being motivated to exercise, eat healthy, read material to help us grow or volunteer in our community to help others? And why is it that most of those things that give us instant gratification often result in low energy, less self-respect or harmed relationships? Long-term happiness seems to only come slowly as the result of forcing ourselves to take healthy action that we sometimes dread doing. To avoid suffering and to find balance and joy, we use discipline in all areas of our life.

Discipline is the sustained use of self-control in overcoming instinctual impulses or emotions in order to achieve a higher purpose. It is the controlling of our action, our thinking and our emotions for the sake of self-improvement. The key word is 'control'. Exercising discipline often involves purposefully exerting oneself over a natural, intuitive or instinctual tendency.

First we may practice discipline in the form of *self-restraint*. Here we are avoiding temptation and ending impulsiveness. This involves resisting the urge to act in selfish, unhealthy or destructive ways. We may have to force ourselves to avoid indulging in overeating, smoking, excessive drinking, drugs, unhealthy sex behavior and other destructive habits. We may also need to use restraint in our relationships to avoid lashing out, criticizing or gossiping. This form of discipline helps us to avoid a painful existence by keeping us out of trouble.

To go further, we exercise discipline through *self-exertion*. Whereas self-restraint is avoiding or resisting negative temptations, behaviors, thinking and emotions, this form of discipline is in the use of willpower to exert ourselves into positive action. For our physical wellbeing, we may force ourselves to exercise and to eat healthy. Few of us get to the point of enthusiastically maintaining physical fitness or a well-balanced diet; it seems more natural to choose the life of a couch-potato gorging on junk foods. Most of us, however, certainly prefer the health benefits of the former over the latter.

For our relationships, we exert ourselves for the sake of *giving*. We give our time and attention. We make an effort to communicate with kindness and love. We listen when they need to express themselves. We validate their feelings when they are in pain. When asked for advice, we do so in a gentle, non-critical, non-controlling manner. We can also exercise discipline in our relationship with our Higher Power. We read spiritual books, make time to pray and meditate and talk to others interested in our beliefs.

For our psychological health, we can use discipline to transform negative thoughts, perceptions and emotions. We make a habit of regularly opening ourselves up to others. We use discipline to stay open to new perspectives and positive thinking. When we are upset we can journal to explore ourselves in self-analysis and we can reach out for help. When we catch ourselves dwelling in negativity, skepticism or critical thinking, we take responsibility for processing and resolving these feelings, instead of blaming other people. We can sometimes move ourselves into seeing the positive aspects of a "bad" situation, as well as seeing virtues in those who are the object of our scorn.

Sometimes simply making a decision to turn our resentments into compassion, our anger into forgiveness, or our worry into faith is all we need to get ourselves out of our misery. If that's not enough, we use discipline to whatever extent is needed to change our thoughts and emotions. *We let our actions shape our emotions rather than letting our feelings and desires control our behavior.*

Although we all understand the benefits of a disciplined life, the temptation of the short-lived instant gratification of unhealthy practices is sometimes too great for us. We become child-like, easily distracted from reaching a higher goal. "We want what we want when we want it!"

Discipline requires a willingness to sacrifice that comes with maturity. Undisciplined actions usually require minimal mental or physical effort, while we usually have to force ourselves to exercise healthy behaviors.

Discipline also requires endurance, since life's blessings and life's difficulties can create impediments by taxing our time and enticing our subconscious to abort our efforts. The tendency to rest on our laurels, using our past accomplishments as an excuse to end our healthy practices, as well as the temptation to quit when our efforts become challenging, must also be overcome. Over time, exercising these practices becomes more natural and we find that our mind and body decrease resistance to this lifestyle as we reap the rewards of healthy living.

Finally, we must use discipline towards taking the necessary action for achieving our primary purpose of transforming ourselves and advancing unity. In the section on humility, we presented the table of humble attributes and opposing ego attributes. Because our instincts pull us towards these ego-based characteristics, which are corrosive to healthy relationships, we must use discipline in order to progress towards the humility-based traits and to live within the realm of our guiding principles. We must be *rigorous* in our search for truth, our service work and our spiritual pursuits. Our goal of unity is thus entirely dependent on our individual use of discipline for taking the steps for personal growth.

Self-Cleansing

Self-cleansing is directly aligned with the principles of truth and humility. This category of discipline is concerned with freeing ourselves of toxic memories and feelings by embracing honesty on the deepest, most basic level. As we go through our lives, starting from an early age, we accumulate emotional garbage that we carry around for many years. The refuse continues to plague us, as long as we let it fester without taking the necessary action to effectively process and eliminate it.

Our lives can be visualized as having a glass slate, which is between us and the sunlight that nurtures us psychologically. The refuse we collect throughout our life piles up on that slate blocking us from the light, suffocating our inner-being. The most insidious example of this refuse is resentment, which is usually coupled with self-pity. Starting from childhood, if we held unreasonable expectations of those around us, our disappointment may have turned into frustration and anger. If we continued to perceive those who let us down as responsible for our anger, we will unlikely do anything to change our attitude. We can become judgmental, hypercritical and cynical.

As children, we simply did not have the maturity to comprehend the consequences unless we were gently guided by our parents or mentors who had the necessary level of emotional balance. Even as adults, we are naturally going to get angry from time to time. We are only human. But anger simply masks other feelings such as fear, insecurity, envy or hurt feelings. If those emotions are not addressed starting with an acknowledgement, the anger can grow. It can mushroom into a full-fledged resentment where we repeatedly put others on trial in our mind, inevitably finding them guilty and prosecuting them to the "fullest extent of the law."

To our thinking, the judge and jury are fair and impartial. But when we are in this state, how can we possibly be just? What part of our thinking is honestly representing the other party? Do we allocate time to closely examine our own behavior to discover our role or question if our judgments are being overcritical? Do we ask ourselves if our expectations are fair? Is the other person truly as evil as our imagination makes them out to be? The honest answer to these questions is almost always 'no'.

Upon close examination, we find we are frequently quite unfair in the criticism we can conjure up. Whether their misdeed was real or imagined, our mind will usually demonize the other, even for small infractions. When we dig deep enough, we can often see where we played a role in the offense, even though our defense mechanism tries to block our taking personal responsibility. We sometimes find that our own misbehavior caused a reaction that contributed to the misdeeds of others we are now condemning.

But what about so called *justified* anger? How are we supposed to handle cases, where we have unquestioningly been wronged? For example, a parent who abandoned us, or even a family member or acquaintance who abused us when we were innocent children, too young to fend for ourselves? Or what if someone cheats us, attacks us, steals our property or harms us, or our loved ones in some other way, without provocation? And what about self-righteous and arrogant people, who seem to go out of their way to hurt others just to re-inflate their ego? Don't we have the right to be resentful towards such people? The answer is yes, we do have the 'right' to be resentful, but then you are allowing yourself to be victimized twice. First you are violated by the act of the offender, and then you are harming yourself with your resentment. Of course the adrenaline-rush of a burst of anger sometimes feels like a pleasurable elixir at first; it's like a drug. Anger may overcome your pain or fear in the short term, but bitterness will soon turn toxic. They can potentially even lead to health problems. Possibly the best analogy of holding on to resentments is that *it is like drinking poison, expecting the other person to get sick.*

When we hold onto a grudge, we may think we are holding that person accountable. We are punishing them for hurting us. Or we may believe that it is a defensive measure and we are keeping them in check because we are afraid they will harm us again if we let our guard down. But is self-destructive bitterness really necessary or effective as a safeguard? And as far as our intention to punish or to hold them accountable, the targets of our scorn are often oblivious to the extent of our resentments, let alone suffering from them. They are not the ones tossing and turning at night, unable to sleep because of the unending trials in our heads; we are!

And when it comes to justifiable anger, don't we really believe *all* our resentments are justified? Why else would we be angry if we didn't think there was good rationale behind it? But how much of our animosity is based on misperception? Have you ever been angry and lashed out at someone only to find out you absolutely had the facts wrong? Perhaps you were angered because you didn't receive an expected communication from someone, only to find out later that communication was impossible for one reason or another. Maybe in a panic you accused someone of stealing or misplacing your property only to find it later where you left it? Or maybe you have been the one accused of something based on someone else's misunderstanding. We've all had similar such experiences. The fact is that *all* of our resentments are to some extent rooted in fear-based misperception and fueled by selfish expectations. We cannot possibly have a crystal clear perception without the ability to read other's thoughts, feel other's feelings and know their life history.

But animosity is not the only clutter blocking us from the sunlight. Many of us are plagued by fear, guilt and shame. We are all human and we all make mistakes. Whether our mistakes were small lies we told to someone for selfish gains or something more serious, we hold on to guilt for our wrongdoings.

Then there are those of us who have gone much further than simply lying or stealing. Some may have cheated on a loved one, or hurt or abused someone who is innocent or defenseless. Some may have committed crimes causing themselves and others so much pain they can hardly live with it, and plan to go to their grave with those secrets. But if we continue to keep such skeletons in our closet we can never heal, so we are more vulnerable to repeating wrongdoings. We are likely to grow sicker and possibly sink to even worse behavior.

Others among us may also be plagued with shame for not living up to the expectations of our family or for some perceived failure or shortcoming. And just like resentments, guilt and shame are manifestations of fear. But we may have fear for many other reasons as well: fear of failure, rejection, humiliation, and so on. We cannot live joyful lives and be truly emotionally available in our relationships, as long as we hold on to all this baggage. We must clean house. We must clear the glass slate above us, clearing our conscience so the sunlight can shine down on us and make us healthy again.

The practice of self-analysis is an essential facet of this discipline. Such exercises allow us to become aware of what makes us tick. Because most of our thinking is done at a subconscious level, we are not fully cognizant of our own opinions and perceptions. Internal examinations will bring these thoughts and feelings to the surface, allowing us to better understand our own makeup. Whether taking a self-survey or examining ourselves for our current state of mind, anytime we contemplate our subconscious thoughts, we are searching for a deeper truth about ourselves.

In chapter eleven, the twelve steps are described, laying out the foundation for resolving the root causes of our own prejudices. The first step may require such self-examination if we have not already explored ourselves for our biases. Steps Four through Ten are then designed for further examination and self-cleansing. We first clean up all the wreckage of our past in steps one through nine. We then continue to rigorously practice our housecleaning disciplines in Step Ten to avoid a re-accumulation of debris.

No doubt these efforts take an enormous amount of faith, courage and discipline. We will not work through them honestly without these key attributes. But when the strength comes and we are able to fearlessly take them, we will find a path to freedom from the bondage of self. We come to know life as we did not dream possible. When worked rigorously, we give ourselves the clean slate that allows us to find peace. The effects of these steps are something that must be personally experienced. After getting the first taste of the fruit that these disciplines bear, some become willing to risk any consequence to become free of their self-imposed prison. With our efforts being driven by this level of faithful willingness, we are guaranteed to find absolute freedom.

Surrender

When we find ourselves caught in the struggle between the temptations of our instinctual desire for instant gratification and our need for healthy living, we will find little peace until we surrender. Living a life of constant self-restraint will prevent us from destructive action in the short term, but the psychological energy required to continually fight our ego in this way is neither practical nor sustainable. What we need is for our ego to end its fight so that we can be at peace.

To surrender is to stop fighting or to give up. What we are really talking about is a complete surrender of old ideas and behaviors, wholeheartedly embracing new values and practices. But we are likely to acquiesce only when we either see a benefit to concede defeat, or the consequences of not surrendering becomes too perilous; in other words, when we have hit a bottom.

For those who live a disciplined life, the benefits of a healthy lifestyle are clear. They have little problem surrendering to humility. However, although the painful repercussions of an unhealthy lifestyle are equally clear to those of us who have lived without discipline, those consequences are not usually enough to bring about change. Without arming our altruistic selves with the necessary tools and understanding to convince us that the payoff for surrendering will not result in even greater pain, this suffering may not be a sufficient deterrent. But once we are shown alternatives and are able to observe others who had benefited from surrendering, the link between letting go and happiness brings us sufficient hope to make this leap of faith.

The third step of the twelve steps of action is designed for helping us make this transition. Prior to this step, we first become aware of the changes we need to make. We then gain the necessary faith that the Power of our spiritual beliefs, combined with the fellowship, and the suggested action in the remaining steps will provide joy that far exceeds the pleasure in our unhealthy practices. To surrender, we make our best effort to turn our thoughts and our actions over to the source of our highest ideals. We abandon old ideas and behaviors and commit to a set of disciplines that directly align with our values.

When we do this, the temptations of our ego drop off dramatically, since we have resolutely pledged to live within the realm of the new principles we have adopted. We decisively eliminate the option of undesirable habits. We will still need to practice discipline, but we will find our ego putting up less resistance. As we start exercising healthy behaviors, we quickly start reaping the rewards that bring happiness and peace of mind. This ultimately keeps our ego at rest. *All that was needed was clear direction to the path towards liberation and a willingness to change our course.* Once we start taking the first steps in this new way of life, we begin to experience the paradox that we must surrender in order to win.

After applying the principle of surrender to our own behaviors and practices, we can next apply this principle to personal relationships. We take a look at the way we treat friends, family and colleagues to see if we are selfishly trying to control the behaviors of those around us. We can examine ourselves for critical-minded judgment, selfishness and impatience and how such attitudes affect our interactions. Are we demanding? Do we use guilt or shame as tools to try to get others to "act right"? Have we ever resorted to forceful aggression instead of relying on gentle assertiveness? Have we rebranded our coercive manipulation as charismatic persuasiveness?

For all our relationships, we must be ready to evaluate whether our interactions are in the spirit of love and service versus crossing boundaries, which deny others the right to make their own choices. In those cases where we see we are trying to dominate or manipulate, we make an effort to step back and surrender control. We give everyone their due respect. When we offer suggestions, we do so without forcing our ideas; prepared to accept it if our advice is not taken. Likewise, when we want something from someone, we make our request fully ready to accept an answer of "no."

Under these conditions, trust will grow and our relationships will flourish.

Establishing Concepts for the Principles

With widespread agreement on a healthy set of guiding principles, surrender can also be applied to healing diverse relationships between disputing groups. They can help in addressing conflicts with peace and unity, instead of resorting to divisive measures that could lead to violence. When discord arises, a community needs only to agree on applying the same principles towards the other community that we would practice in our own relationships with individuals. We would certainly never incite violence, nor launch a personal attack. Instead, we would make every effort to be respectful and fair.

Ideally, we would be kind and patient, listen to their grievances, then try to understand their perspective to acknowledge where they are right. We would strive towards the goal of a united "win-win" outcome, but we never sacrifice our morals for our personal advancement. Keeping our principles in tact must be at the forefront of our priorities, as we will surely suffer the consequences of our conscience if we forego our values simply to get our own way. To keep our own self-respect and peace of mind, we must commit to this unconditionally. Our principles are not for sale and not to be controlled or compromised based on the behavior of others.

Having likened community interactions to individual relationships, let's visualize two groups that are caught up in a multigenerational feud. They justify their own resentment- fueled behaviors by the wrongdoings of the other. They both engage in distorting the truth to further their personal cause and hurt their adversary. Pride prevents each side from conceding good points of the opposition or admitting their own faults. Perhaps there are plenty of present-day examples you can draw upon that fit this description. You may have more sympathy for one side or the other, but you see both sides adversely contributing to the conflict and compounding the problem.

Now imagine, motivated by a widespread desire for change, a new leadership rises within one of these two groups and completely redirects the course for their segment of that society. They come together as one voice and unconditionally commit to a fundamental set of moral principles based on truth, love and unity. They surprise outsiders with their announcement of a unilateral commitment to work towards reconciliation. The shock grows when they go further by admitting they have been wrong in their own hateful attitudes and in their participation in divisive behaviors. They vow to immediately stop such actions and instead try to make reparations for their part of the conflict. They express a desire to better understand and serve their adversary and try to promote a common bond.

The listening world can't believe what they are hearing and are waiting for the other shoe to drop to see what demands they make on their opponent. But no such demands come. When they mention the wrongdoings of the others, it is noncritical and they make it clear that their changes are not contingent on any action on the part of their rivals. Instead they persist in their commitment to truth, unity and service, restructuring government to be more open, thus enabling a partnership with their opponents. From beginning to end, the announcement reveals no sign of deceit. They truly appear to have had a miraculous turnaround in their philosophy that has resulted in absolute humility.

What kind of impact would such a standpoint have on the opponent? What would the perception of the world be on such a turnaround in philosophy? What would your perception be? Surely many would be skeptical or cynical, possibly even writing them off as fools. But even from the start, wouldn't such humbling intentions possibly melt away years of mistrust in the minds and hearts of many, generating hope of reconciliation?

Then the world observes that over the next year they live up to their commitment of peace. While they still continue to pursue most of their original goals that were at the heart of the conflict, they abandon all methods that are not aligned with their adopted principles. Undeterred by their opponent's persistent divisive responses preventing unification, the transformed group re-affirms they are doing this unconditionally. Continued attacks by the opposition are met not by vengeful retaliation, but by reaffirmations of their resolve to stick to their principles and calls for reconciliation.

As time goes on, the transformed group persists in adherence to their principles. They amend their mistakes to the best of their ability and continue to extend unconditional love and service to everyone in their communities including groups and individuals in the opposition. They are now living with a clear conscience and an ever-growing compassion for their adversary.

Establishing Concepts for the Principles

The impact of the transformation becomes increasingly significant on the opposition. Many are finding it impossible to stay resentful. They in fact, have a growing admiration for those they once detested. The communities of the opposition start emulating the activities and programs of the transformed group and start opening up regular dialogs with their counterparts. Unified gatherings from both sides start meeting to build mutual respect and to find common ground. Over time, they grow more united with a diminishing gap in their differences.

After the first decade, the transformation is now overcoming the rivals. A growing number of government representatives formally of the opposition have opened their minds and hearts to the transformed group, embracing their philosophies; and they are now gaining strength in numbers. Only a few years earlier they were labeled as unpatriotic fools, but they are now considered to be of the highest moral standard. The remaining dissenting governing voices seem so out of touch with current values and political climate.

Eventually, the two sides overcome so many differences that they form a partnership to explore how these principles could be extended to resolve conflict beyond their borders. Could these values that have been so effective in domestic policy be as effective in foreign relations? Collaboration begins between the two groups for exercising these ideals abroad. Using programs such as "Peace Corps" as their model, they commit to redirecting overseas military resources towards diplomatic solutions. Because of the sincere respect and compassion expressed from these former rivals, they are welcomed with open arms. Massive armies of goodwill are then mobilized to start building bridges of peace and a new era of reconciliation has begun.

Only one side decided to surrender and to unconditionally embrace these principles, but because they were rooted in a power so pure, their adversary could not resist the change and both sides won.

"But this is a fantasy scenario!" you may exclaim. But finding examples of leaders who have initiated similar policies of goodwill resulting in long lasting positive changes is not too difficult. Most notably were the Civil Rights movements led by Gandhi and King. Gandhi and his follower's love-truth force philosophy brought reform to South Africa and then India. King and the Civil Rights Movement's adoption of this philosophy allowed them to achieve an enormous degree of success with legislation and social reforms in the United States.

In 1990, Mikhail Gorbachev received the Nobel Peace Prize for his valiant efforts at political and social restructuring within the Soviet Union. His implementation of perestroika and glasnost as well as his enabling the reunion of East and West Germany were initially viewed with great skepticism, but his commitment to the reform marked the end of the Cold War. Another example that was initially met with skepticism was the unilateral disarmament by the Irish Republican Army led by Sinn Fein president Gerry Adams. Many had doubts about their resolve, but their actions indeed resulted in much peace and goodwill.

These are all examples of sacrifices through unilateral surrender based on high moral principles. Without exception, they resulted in meaningful improvements in the relationships of the disputing communities. Although none of these historical events resulted in the Utopian society idealized here, King, Gandhi and movement followers did have glimpses of it and led us all further in that direction. Moreover, their personal lives were wholly transformed. Gandhi was simply driven by the intuitive forces of the fundamental truths he read about in other's philosophies. The accomplishments of Satyagraha were largely done without any historical example of what was to be expected. *They simply accepted that love is the most powerful of all human attributes.* Their actions were experiments based on that hypothesis.

The experimental practice of these principles on Tolstoy Farm gave the Satyagraha movement vital strength. They succeeded in reaching a significant level of self-purification while making the above-described transformation. Their discipline won the respect and admiration of their adversaries including government officials who later helped them obtain their rights. In the end they were granted the very change in laws they were seeking; but the true success was the deep level of love they experienced, self-respect for themselves and compassion for their rivals.

Those who sacrificed in the Civil Rights Movement had the same experience. Starting with the participants of the Montgomery bus boycott, King and other ministers preached the use of non-violence. They were soon visited by ministers from the *Fellowship*

Establishing Concepts for the Principles

of Reconciliation who counseled the boycott leaders on the methods used by Gandhi. King became an ardent student fully embracing Gandhi's techniques. Most of the participants of that boycott were devout Christians many of whom were parishioners of King's Baptist church. But the extent of humility, honesty and unconditional love that they attained through the movement brought their faith to a new level. As with the activists of Gandhi's era, many had a difficult time comprehending the concepts of self-sacrifice and unconditional love. Many still hung onto the justification of 'an eye for an eye' and were very skeptical of the outcome. But King won the confidence of most, while many others who remained doubtful joined on blind faith.

King and the others went about the business of purifying their hearts with continued discussions in their meetings. As new activists joined their ranks, they were quickly introduced to these philosophies. Their participation was contingent upon surrendering the option of violence, then thoroughly adopting these values and practices. Their motives and actions had to be beyond reproach. These training seminars turned out the well-disciplined soldiers of peace who filled the ranks of the movement. The rare veering from these values was usually from those who did not go to the training sessions. In some of these cases, participants exhibited lack of discipline by retaliating against verbal and physical confrontations. For those who stuck to the nonviolent principles, the rewards were great. They experienced the transformation of their very being that included self-respect and love for their enemies. Their fears began to vanish and were eventually replaced by hope and confidence.

Many Whites who were once their adversaries or simply apathetic, were overcome by a sense of respect and admiration. The closer the movement held to these principles, the more hearts they won over. And like the Satyagraha movements, the Civil Rights Movement enjoyed great success in achieving its aim. Also like the Satyagraha participants, the Civil Rights activists discovered the most valuable prize was their own psychological and spiritual transformation, which occurred much sooner and deeper than the physical liberation experienced by the addition of the Civil Rights acts.

So although the effect of these large scale efforts in adopting these principles have not yet resulted in the eradication of bigotry, they forever altered the policies and perceptions of societies around the world. More compelling were the transformations that allowed the participants to experience a deep and everlasting freedom. Their unilateral commitment to these concepts allowed them to reach a state of self-actualization without reciprocation from their opponents.

This is crucial for true comprehension of the value in embracing these principles. Although the peace and joy we experience may be enhanced and made stronger by others uniting on this spiritual plane, their participation is not a requirement of us reaping the benefits. We can open the door for others to join us in our transformation, but our ultimate commitment to transform unconditionally will allow us to grow, regardless of mutual acceptance of these ideals.

Service

Being of service is the act of contributing to another's welfare. We have all had some experiences of serving in our jobs, our families and in our communities. Of course we sometimes do these things with self-serving objectives. At work, we are naturally motivated by the expectation of receiving a paycheck or some other compensation from our employer. We may even have ulterior motives for performing a service, subconsciously masking self-serving expectations with seemingly altruistic intentions. In most cases, we have a mixture of selfless and selfish drives.

Then there are services performed out of pure unselfish love such as the caring for a person unable to care for themself, the helping of a person in need or the volunteering for your community. These services come with invaluable rewards of self-love, joy and peace of mind. They give life meaning. Furthermore, although expectations of external rewards will frequently result in frustration and dissatisfaction, expectations of internal compensation such as self-respect and happiness do not seem to block those benefits from coming to fruition.

Giving with only the expectation of internal rewards is the meaning of this principle. It is love, unity and humility in action. Service is directly aligned with the principles of love and self-sacrifice. The actions that are involved in service can be anything from small acts of kindness, to a short-term commitment of helping others, to a long-term or even lifelong commitment of service to family, places of worship, organizations or institutions. We sometimes do these services with very little notice. Some feel it detracts from their experience when attention is given to their efforts. Some will even go to lengths to hide their efforts of goodwill to ensure their motives are purely for internal rewards.

This is a truly selfless practice and one that must be experienced. We certainly don't want to always go around boasting about our good deeds, but on the other hand, there is something to be said about the goodwill produced when we observe the acts of kindness by others. How much joy is generated when we notice someone else's generosity? Not wanting to advertise your service work is a necessary part of humility that will enhance personal rewards, but hiding every act of giving will prevent occasional opportunities of multiplying the benefits. We directly help those we provide our service to, we help ourselves as recipients of internal rewards and we help those that observe our example of love in action. Especially when we are in a mentoring role, our action sets the example.

When first starting involvement in service work, we should be gentle on ourselves. Our ability to give effectively is developed over time and we should not be hard on ourselves if we feel like our efforts are not producing measurable results. Just hang in there and your effectiveness will grow. We simply take the action and we leave the results up to the power of our spiritual beliefs.

Self-Sacrifice

When we forego our own self-interest or wellbeing for the benefit of others, or for the advancement of a cause we believe in, that is self-sacrifice. This is the act of heroes and is the highest form of discipline and an integral part of service. This attribute is practiced daily by parents rearing their children; by teachers and mentors teaching their students; by soldiers, police, firefighters, rescue workers and others who put their lives on the line to save and protect anyone who is in need. Self-sacrifice is practiced, at some point, to some extent by every human being who has ever given their time, energy or any other imaginable resource to preserve or promote another's wellbeing.

In 12-step programs, many members often sacrifice unselfishly in giving of themselves to help those seeking recovery from their ailments. Some go to hospitals, jails, prisons and other institutions reaching out to those who are still suffering.

In the case of Gandhi and King and movement followers, self-sacrifice became integral to their daily lives. They were willing to die for their cause. They suffered everything from imprisonment and violence to death so that their vision of love and freedom could transform a society sickened by fear-driven hatred. They sacrificed themselves so that future generations might have a better life. We are all the beneficiaries of the principles they worked so hard for. As a result of their efforts, our world is filled with more peace, compassion and equity. We have a clearer understanding of the problems they exposed along with solutions they developed. We are able to reach greater depths of truth and deeper levels of love because of their example.

Our present challenge is to take responsibility in keeping these ideals alive so that they may be passed on to the next generation. But what kind of self-sacrifice might we expect in the realm of uniting diverse groups? As mentioned in the introduction, discussions and actions addressing racism will likely stir emotions of fear, resulting in rejection, scorn or criticism. We may even find that some close friends and family members won't understand what we are trying to do, resulting in strain on those relationships.

In our service work, we will mainly sacrifice time. Once we go through the process of working through the steps and take action to incorporate the principles in our lives, we will have the experience necessary that allows us to guide others through the steps. This service work requires spending much of our energy passing on what we have learned along with our strength and hope. Desperate calls will inevitably come in when someone we are helping is going through a rough time and needing the strength of a friend. We will occasionally need to make room for such calls that cause interruptions while we are enjoying a leisure moment, busy at work, eating meals, trying to unwind from a stressful day, or turning in for the evening.

Although these inconveniences can take a toll on us in extreme cases, the benefits greatly outweigh the sacrifices. The growth and happiness we observe in others, partially as the result of our own unselfish acts provide us with joy and self-esteem. Intimate relationships will develop with an unshakable trust. Over time as our effectiveness increases, we find that we gain more energy and what we at first perceived as burdensome sacrifices, we come to view as blessings of opportunity for getting out of self.

Nonviolence

Violence is a contradiction to all UI principles. Gandhi's and King's embracing of nonviolence was often misinterpreted as being the "choice of weaklings"; that they were merely cowards who were afraid to fight for their convictions. King and Gandhi rose above such antagonistic rhetoric. They were able to demonstrate that on the contrary, applying these principles in the course of Direct Action took immense courage and discipline. They did in fact fight for their rights and faced bloodshed and death while confronting their oppressors, but they were so faithful to their values that they did so without weapons of destruction.

Because they were not encumbered by fear-driven ego controlling their life, they were largely free from feeling threatened by their opponents. This made it unnecessary to react with hate and instead, enabled them to love their enemy as a parent would love their angry child. They knew that physical aggression only led to more destruction and was fundamentally an act of fear. Fear is a prerequisite for violence. It is an expression of that fear. Violence in the animal kingdom is the result of survival instincts; reactions to the fear of their demise. Whether for obtaining food, defending territory, competing for mating rites, or reacting in 'fight or flight' mode when backed into a corner, it is always a matter of survival. Humans, on the other hand, can be controlled by their insecurities and false pride. By allowing the fostering of hatred with these frailties, they become the primary driving force in their pursuit of violence.

In contrast, Gandhi and King pursued values that allowed them to greatly reduce fear and keep their respect for their opponents intact. The disciplines they exercised enabled them to bravely face those who threaten them without reacting in fear. Their faith in the power of unconditional love led them to find constructive solutions for the problems faced by the movements. They continually relied on self-appraisal and listening to the feedback of both critics and supporters to keep their motives in check. Whereas propensities for self-promotion or concerns for preserving one's image increase susceptibility for letting opinions control our behavior, Gandhi's and King's practice of humility helped guard them from these frailties.

Their philosophy was not simply one of passivity. They did not believe we should merely put our head in the sand in hopes that our society's issues will magically disappear. They challenged us to the highest level of courage; courage based on love and humility instead of fear and arrogance. They wanted both sides of each conflict to find a win-win outcome through reconciliation, and to prosper. Under this state of consciousness they were able to formulate and execute strategies based on integrity, reshaping perceptions to the benefit of our whole society. They demonstrated that by eliminating fear, we reduce the need for aggression.

The level, to which the Fellowship of Reconciliation, SCLC, CORE, SNCC and other followers of nonviolence kept to this value, set them apart from other factions who would not renounce the use of physical force. To take part in marches, the freedom rides, sit-ins, and other demonstrations led by these movement leaders, unilateral commitment to this value was a requirement. Activists had to be willing to "take blows" without reprisal.

Most militant individuals and organizations flatly rejected this vow. Anger often arose in them simply at the thought of letting their oppressor mete out such abuse without striking back. But somehow, those following King and Gandhi were able to rise above the human element of the violent acts. They were telling the racist, *"You can hurt my body, but you cannot hurt me. I will not stoop to the use of violence and allow the diminishing of my soul."* Their willingness to sacrifice themselves was only made possible by the absolute inner strength and security of those who kept to their pledge. The courage, humility and capability of rising to this spiritual plane were unsurpassed by any other organization.

There is no question about the outcome of their sacrifice. They peacefully changed the world. Along the way, they set the example for countless others so that we too could grow beyond being driven by negative emotions.

Establishing Concepts for the Principles

Direct Action

Direct action is the physical application of all other principles. This was the term used by Martin Luther King, Jr. for communicating that their movement was going beyond passive resistance that might allow injustices to go unanswered. They were indeed answering back decisively with action fortified by these principles. That is, they answered back with action based on love and courage instead of hate and fear. They simply rejected any option that did not align with these values; even when it assured material gains. Evil means can never be justified in the pursuit of a moral end.

Direct action is the crucial force required to give all other principles life. For what good are any principles if they are not backed up by efforts to put them into practice? To only speak of love, truth and unity will only get us so far. Passive knowledge alone will not bring about the transformation and the joy that action will. In and of themselves, the principles do not spell out specifically how we can integrate them in our lives. They are simply fundamental ideals that can be used as our guide. Likewise, the humility traits in the table of personality attributes do not specify or recommend any course of action. They merely represent the components of the composite transformation we hope to achieve.

To incorporate these principles in our lives and to acquire the desired attributes, we must make a deliberate effort to change. This is the ideal behind the adage *"Faith without works is dead"*. The actions we take lead to the desired personality traits that allow us to live within the realm of the principles. For example, the house-cleaning *actions* of self-analysis and opening ourselves up to others develop *personality attributes* such as honesty, integrity and trust allowing us to live within the realm of the *principles* of unity and truth. The *act* of listening to someone unload their burdens develops *personality attributes* such as patience and compassion. These allow us to live within the spirit of the *principles* of love, unity and self-sacrifice.

Along with these examples, the actions we will take are the suggestions specified in following the 12 steps. We will also work at directly breaking down the physical barriers of our diverse groups by joining in the fellowship and participating in the efforts of our organization. Details of these activities are presented in the section *Principles in Action*.

Principles Conclusion

To the extent these principles can be accepted, they should be used as the litmus test in weighing the integrity of *our own* personal beliefs. For any ideas or efforts we engage in that we want to examine, we can ask ourselves, "How does this perception or action align with compassion, justice, or unity? Is there anyone I would feel uncomfortable sharing these concepts with and if so, why? Are these ideals beneficial to everyone, or do they come at someone else's expense? Are these values my ultimate intent or do I have an agenda based on perceptions that I have not yet scrutinized under these magnifying glasses?" If we cannot satisfactorily align them with these standards, we should discard or refine them so that they fit flawlessly. We should not have to rationalize our ideals or motives. They should be as pure as our humanness will allow.

Because the issues of racism we are facing are very sensitive and can evoke strong emotional opinions, opposing views will inevitably emerge. When conflict or contradictions occur, these same questions can equally be applied in evaluating other's beliefs and behavior. Topics of disagreement can be broken down to basic elements and each one scrutinized to ensure it does not go against our agreed upon principles. They can then be used as the building blocks for expanding on ideals in our communications.

During these analyses, we can ask the same questions we ask of ourselves concerning the alignment of action and beliefs with these standards. In many cases the obvious result may be that we will see flaws; that their views contradict these principles. We may see divisiveness instead of unity. We may see a lack of compassion, truth, humility and so on. In cases like these we can easily fall into self-righteousness and become judgmental and indignant. But this is obviously not the intent of this exercise and this attitude in itself is against these principles.

Instead, in those cases where we are in disagreement with others, we can try to present a warm and loving new perspective by bringing our conversation to the level of these values. We can suggest weighing each other's perceptions and actions against this backdrop. We can explain that we are trying to live up to these ideals and that if they are in agreement with using this set of precepts for evaluating beliefs, you would like them to help you see where their concepts meet these standards.

Learning from others is a key part of our growth, so we should be open to other's views if they can help us change and improve our own perceptions by clearly demonstrating how their beliefs are more closely aligned with these principles. Discussions should be in the spirit of finding the higher truth; not in winning a debate. Ultimately, we should be most interested in our own transformation and only exert ourselves in helping others in their conversion when they request that from us. We must avoid attempting to force self-righteous ideas on others since this is a form of ego-filling-control and will likely only inflame resentment. If our discussion becomes heated or argumentative, we should consider ending the discussion until we are able to communicate peacefully.

Finally, this very organization should be observed through the lenses of these principles. The contributors to this book are only human. We are not unaffected by prejudice, nor are we perfect at practicing these ideals. Without the benefit of the gift of omniscience, our observations will occasionally reflect a biased picture. Although this text was written with a sincere attempt to be fair in the assessment of the historical events that led to our problems, we must concede the difficulty in this goal. Because these perceptions are based on personal experiences, some views will certainly be partial and may possibly seem unfair, contrary to our earnest desire to avoid such divisiveness. As the fellowship grows, a broader perspective will mature. This text is simply the starting point for the discussions that will lead to a wider view.

Our very foundation: our literature, philosophies and actions should be scrutinized by the test of these principles. As this organization expands and matures, some of the ideals will surely be improved upon. Present contexts may become outdated. Some perceptions, in light of more information, may prove to be inaccurate or incorrect.

We all have the individual duty to weigh these concepts out for ourselves to determine their meaning for us personally. Ideas should be discarded that cannot be reconciled with personal morals. Each member of our fellowship bares a responsibility to voice perceived contradictions with the principles or with the 12 traditions. The group conscience or its representatives can then decide on what further action is required. If we all accept this role of safeguarding our primary purpose, Unity Initiative will continue its transformation as an organization as we do as individuals.

SECTION II:
Observing Racism in Our Society

Chapter 6: Historical Review

Historical Racial Events: Snapshots in Time

In the previous section we discussed the fundamental principles we wish to incorporate as the foundation for this organization and the basis of the action suggested for personal growth and uniting our communities. Because they touch on the most fundamental aspects of our lives, disagreement will likely arise as we get down to the details of exactly what specific action these principles prescribe. Individually we must determine for ourselves what we feel we can or should do. Still, we believe our unity will be much stronger if we can agree upon a fundamental understanding for these precepts regardless of race, religion or political affiliation. With these standards filtering our perspective, our next step is to review our history and use these principles as a measurement of our past and present racial climate.

By the end of this section it will hopefully not only be obvious that we still have problems of racism in this country; but it should also reveal why none of the efforts made so far has sufficiently resolved these issues. It will hopefully be clear that to this date, we have only addressed the symptoms of the problem and not the root cause.

Here and in subsequent chapters, we will highlight some of the key periods in our history to try to understand the origins of our ongoing problems with racism. Examining these events that have shaped the American racial landscape and acknowledging our country's transgressions is crucial for healing our society. By facing our past and gaining a clearer understanding of how we arrived where we are today, we are first living up to our legacy of truth. A solution cannot effectively be defined if the problem is not fully understood. Part of our nation's recovery will require us, as individuals, to directly confront our demons so we can purge them from our lives.

To the extent we examine and understand the problem, will we be able to effectively formulate, accept and apply viable resolutions. Furthermore, by examining these events together, it will hopefully put us all on the same page so that we can unite and strengthen our resolve. This is an essential element for our effectiveness in dismantling racism.

So to get a better understanding of how we have arrived at

the difficulties we face today, let us start off by reviewing a brief summary of some key historical events that have shaped our racial landscape and revealed the mindset of our country. Keep in mind that many important events are not included, and although the focus of this history is on the relationship of Blacks and Whites in America, we must remember that atrocities were committed on American Indians, Asians, Hispanics and other racial and ethnic groups during this history. Women too have suffered abuses as the result of the same underlying issues.

- Slavery believed to date back over 10,000 years on almost every continent.
- **Slavery of Native-American Indians** and nonwhite **Africans** begins in the US around the time of the settlement of the first Europeans and is practiced until 1865.
- Over two centuries of war against the newly arrived Europeans, along with the diseases they import, devastate the **Native-American** population. Their societies are ravaged and the white American government, forcing them into ever-shrinking reservations, takes their land.
- **1650**: The original slave population in the US includes a large percentage of White European indentured servants. The establishment of nonwhite slavery is formalized with the **slave codes** of Virginia and Maryland. Slave owners legally whip, brutalize and even kill their slaves. Rapes and killings are all too common with insufficient moral or legal checks to prevent this inhumanity. These atrocities carry on for nearly two and a half centuries.
- **1775:** The first **abolition** groups are forming to end slavery originally driven by religious beliefs. Their moral compassion earns them the label of radical extremists.
- **1776, July 4th:** The **Declaration of Independence** is adopted by the Continental Congress. Expressing desire to be free from tyranny, this document exclaims: *"We hold these truths to be self-evident, that **all** men are created equal, that they are endowed by their Creator with certain unalienable Rights, that among these are Life, Liberty, and the Pursuit of Happiness."* The institution of slavery, however, is ironically granted an exemption from these inspired ideals.

- **1789:** The **U.S. Constitution** is amended nearly two years after ratification with the addition of the **Bill of Rights,** establishing individual freedoms through the highest laws of the land. It will take a civil war and nearly another decade of struggles before these rights are granted to people of color.
- **1816:** The **American Colonization Society** is established with a mixture of noble and ill-begotten intentions of establishing the African settlement **Republic of Liberia (Land of the Free)** in West Africa. In **1821** the first 88 settlers are sent and 13,000 more are sent by 1867.
- **1822:** Birth of **Harriet Tubman**. After her escape from slavery, Tubman acts as a spy for the North, risking her life in the *Underground Railroad* to help set other slaves free.
- **1830, May 28th:** The **Indian Removal Act** is signed into law by President Andrew Jackson. The bill authorizes the relocation of Native-Americans to territories west of the Mississippi. Native-American leaders were sometimes forced under pressure to sign removal treaties. Their evacuation makes way for the expansion of European settlers.
- **1831:** The weekly newspaper *The Liberator* is published for over three decades by American abolitionist William Lloyd Garrison in which he exposes the hypocrisy of slavery in a democratic society.
- **1838:** Born a slave, **Fredrick Douglass** escapes captivity and becomes active in the abolitionist movement. Famous for his oratory skills, Douglass becomes a counter-example to those perpetuating myths that slaves were not intellectually capable of independence.
- **1852:** Abolitionist Harriet Stowe's antislavery book **"Uncle Tom's Cabin"** is published, helping raise compassion for the plight of slaves, awakening the conscience of White Americans.
- **1857:** After his owner brings him to Free states for intervals stretching several months, slave **Dred Scott** petitions the US Supreme Court for freedom for his family. However, America's leading authority of justice rejects his appeal, sentencing his family to a life of continued oppression.
- **1859:** Abolitionist **John Brown** leads an attack on the arsenal at Harpers Ferry, West Virginia, in an attempt to spark a slave rebellion. The attempted seizure fails with Brown being hanged for treason, but the incident helps ignite the Civil War.

Historical Review

- **1861:** The **Civil War** starts between northern and southern states partially based on issues of slavery.
- **1863:** Construction begins of the **First Transcontinental Railroad**. Labor shortages lead to heavy reliance upon Chinese immigrants who face years of racial discrimination on top of deplorable working conditions.
- **1863**: Lincoln's **Emancipation Proclamation** is established to abolish slavery in confederate states. While some refuse to comply, other states immediately free their slaves. This executive decree becomes a goal of the Civil War and is later formalized with the 13th Amendment.
- **1865, April 9th:** General Lee surrenders to Ulysses S. Grant, marking the beginning of the end of the **Civil War**.
- **1865, April 15th:** President Abraham Lincoln is assassinated and succeeded by Andrew Johnson. Johnson's lack of will to match Lincoln's commitment to the rights of the freedmen severely dilutes the effectiveness of reconstruction.
- **1865, June 19th: Juneteenth** commemorates the date that federal troops force Texas to end their resistance of the Emancipation Proclamation and to proceed with the liberation of its slaves. Most states already yielded to the Presidential order that had been enacted two years earlier but it was largely ignored by Texas until this forced compliance.
- **1865-1877: Reconstruction** period. After Lincoln's murder, his bold vision of reconstruction is severely hampered by a country that is exhausted, bitter and still overwhelmingly racist. During this period, lynching and other forms of brutality continue against the freedmen. Many of the provisions planned to give the former slaves a chance at life are nullified, leaving no other possibility than a life of abject poverty.
- **1865, December 18th: 13th amendment** formerly abolishes legal slavery.
- **Civil Rights Act of 1866** gives further rights to freed slaves countering the slave codes.
- **1868, December 6th: 14th amendment** provides for citizenship, due process and equal protection under the law for all persons born or naturalized in the US. This amendment essentially reverses the Dred Scott decision.

- **1869, October 2nd:** Birth of **Mohandas K. Gandhi** who's philosophy of **Satyagraha**, (truth-love force) and actions of civil disobedience towards unjust and immoral laws is to become the model for Martin Luther King, Jr. and the Civil Rights Movement.
- **1870: 15th amendment** provides for the right to vote regardless of race or color. However, it will be nearly another 100 years before the Voting Rights Act in 1965 is signed, giving the required protection to fulfill the spirit of this amendment.
- **Civil Rights Act of 1871** targets violence of the Ku Klux Klan by giving protection to people of color through legal redress.
- **Civil Rights Act of 1875** provides for equal treatment to people of all races in public accommodations.
- **1876: Jim Crow Laws** to be practiced for nearly 90 years, formally institutionalizing **segregation** by excluding Blacks from equal access to most resources available to Whites. The dehumanizing laws foster an environment of disrespect for nonwhites that make it impossible for their white peers to view them as equals. The friction from this division leads to abuses that culminate in violence. Such practices are first made unconstitutional in public schools by the 1954 decision **of Brown vs. Board of Education**.
- The **Civil Rights Acts of 1964** then targeted restaurants, hotels, stores and private schools. **The Voting rights act of 1965** removed barriers to voting polls.
- **1882, May 6th: Chinese Exclusion Act** places a ban on Chinese immigration to appease European animosity over competition for employment. The **Scott Act of 1888** expands the Act by denying reentry after leaving the country. Only intended to last a decade, the Act is not repealed until the **Chinese Exclusion Repeal Act of 1943**.
- **1893 - 1915: Gandhi** dedicates over 20 years of his life fighting racist laws in **South Africa** while honing in the ideals of the Satyagraha philosophy of Love-Truth Force.
- **1896, May 18th: Plessy vs. Ferguson** Supreme Court decision upholding Jim Crow segregation laws under the doctrine of "separate but equal". The decision waters down the Fourteenth Amendment by ruling these rights only apply to the federal government and not to private citizens or entities. The ruling re-enforces racial segregation within private communities.

Historical Review

- **1909, February 12th: National Association for the Advancement of Colored People** is founded by a mixed racial group to provide a vital voice for racial discrimination issues and to promote Civil Rights for all citizens. Early efforts are directed towards overturning Jim Crow laws. Their effort towards legal action against racist legislation results in much success for advancing rights and their critical role continues to this day.
- **1927, March 30th:** Birth of **Cesar Chavez.**
- **1929, January 15th:** Birth of **Martin Luther King Junior.**
- **1930, April 10th:** Birth of **Dolores Huerta.** A high school teacher of the 50s, many of Mrs. Huerta's students were children of migrant workers who often came to school hungry and were sometimes unable to even afford their own shoes. Moved to take a stand against economic injustice, she begins a life of community activism and later joins forces with **Cesar Chavez** to establish the **UFW (United Farm Workers)**.
- **1941: Executive Order 8802** is signed by President Roosevelt, creating the **Fair Employment Practices Committee** which is meant to bar racial or religious discrimination in government and defense industries. The act does little to curb discrimination in the South and the benefits seen in the North are mostly lost with the end of World War I.
- **1942: Executive Order 9066** forces the relocation of **Japanese-Americans** into internment camps. Along with their loss of liberty, many of these American citizens faced loss of property, lack of medical treatment and death. The hardships continue for two years until a ruling in 1944 by the Supreme Court.
- **1947 Community Service Organization** is founded in California to address problems of discrimination and police brutality of Latinos. Founded by Antonio Rios, Edward Roybal, and Fred Ross, CSO becomes an important training hub for Civil Rights leaders such as **Cesar Chavez** and **Dolores Huerta.**
- **1948, January 30th:** Assassination of **Gandhi.**
- **1952: Malcolm X** unites with Nation of Islam. After being released from prison, he spends the next 12 years as their most outspoken minister.
- **1954, May 17th:** Supreme Court case **Brown vs. Board of Education** overturns **Plessy vs. Ferguson**, outlawing Jim Crow

segregation practices in public education facilities. This ruling paves the way for the Civil Rights Movement to extend integration in the remaining parts of our society. However, many Whites remain unwilling to cooperate with this decision. Twenty-two months after the ruling, 100 United States congressmen sign the **Southern Manifesto** as a protest against the decision and during his inaugural address eight years later, Alabama's Governor George Wallace expressed Southerner's defiance in his quote, *"segregation now, segregation tomorrow, segregation forever"*.

- **1955, August 28th:** Fourteen-year-old African American **Emmett Till** is brutally mutilated, murdered and then dumped in a river for reportedly directing a flirtatious comment at a White woman.
- **1955, December 1st: Rosa Parks** is arrested in Montgomery, Alabama for her refusal to comply with Jim Crow laws sparking the **Montgomery Bus Boycott** led by Martin Luther King. The boycott lasts a year resulting in much hardship for the activists, but their determination results in a federal court ruling that the bus segregation laws in Alabama are unconstitutional. As a final symbol exemplifying the fierce resistance to extend Civil Rights to Blacks, the decision is reversed by an appellate court. In the end though, justice prevails and the Supreme Court later upholds the ruling of the federal court.
- **1955-1968: Dr. Martin Luther King Jr.** dedicates the rest of his life to the Civil Rights Movement followed by hundreds of thousands of supporters. During this period, activists are subjected to all forms of violence driven by racial-hatred, but their efforts successfully influence the passing of several Civil Rights laws that patch many of the deficiencies not addressed during the reconstruction period.
- **1957:** Birth of **SCLC (Southern Christian Leadership Conference)**. King becomes president and presides over SCLC leading the way in the Civil Rights Movement until his assassination eleven years later.
- **Civil Rights Act of 1957** establishes the Commission on Civil Rights to primarily act as a watchdog committee to protect voting privileges for people of color by investigating allegations of voting rights violations. The **Civil Rights Act of 1960** then extended voting protection by establishing federal inspection of

voting stations as well as penalties for interference with the voting process.
- **1960: Lunch counter sit-ins** are initiated by a small group of African-American college students taking seats in a section reserved for Whites. The small demonstrations explode into a multi-state protest involving tens of thousands of students. To provide leadership and nonviolence training, **Ella Baker** of SCLC helps arrange a conference for the students to organize. From this convention, the **Student Nonviolent Coordinating Committee, SNCC**, is born and becomes a key organization for the fight for Civil Rights.
- **1961: Freedom rides,** mostly led by CORE and SNCC, test the Supreme Court's ruling in the case of Boynton vs. Virginia (1960), declaring segregation in interstate bus and rail stations unconstitutional. The campaign exposes much of the South's unwillingness to cooperate. Activists are severely beaten and a bus is set on fire and burnt to the ground.
- **1962: National Farm Workers Association (NFWA)** is founded by **Cesar Chavez** and **Dolores Huerta;** later to become the **United Farm Workers (UFW).** In an effort to gain rights for migrant workers vulnerable to abusive labor practices, this organization adopts the nonviolence principles taught by Gandhi and King.
- **1963, June 12: Medgar Evers Assassinated.** The Civil Rights activist is shot in the back as he exits his car at his home. Nine days later, the murderer is arrested, but is acquitted by an all-white jury. Thirty years pass before he is finally convicted and sent to prison.
- **1963, August 28: March on Washington for Jobs and Freedom.** People of every race join with African Americans, totaling nearly a quarter of a million, to unite in Washington DC for a march led by Civil Rights leaders. King presents his inspired *I Have a Dream* speech.
- **1963, September 15**[th]: Ku Klux Klan bombs the **16**[th] **Street Baptist Church** in Birmingham, Alabama. Four young girls are killed in the blast and twenty two others are injured. The sermon this day is entitled "The love that forgives". King later conveys the Civil Rights Movement's vow to stick to their nonviolence principles.

- **1963, November 22ⁿᵈ:** John F. Kennedy is assassinated. His administration was instrumental in enforcing Civil Rights by going as far as sending federal marshals and National Guard troops to troubled areas that were not complying with Civil Rights legislation.
- **1964, January 8ᵗʰ:** President Lyndon B. Johnson declares a **"War on Poverty"** backed up by legislation as part of his vision of the **Great Society**. Many successful programs are established to give vital assistance to poverty-stricken citizens of every race. However, between high pressure resistance from opposition and the cost of the Vietnam War, most initiatives are abandoned. Before being cut, these efforts help in lowering poverty levels from 19 to 11 percent.
- **1964, June 1ˢᵗ: Freedom Summer** campaign in Mississippi takes place combining the efforts of CORE, SNCC, NAACP and others with the goal of registering black voters. On June 21ˢᵗ, one black and two White Jewish young volunteers from CORE are arrested by a police officer who is a member of the Ku Klux Klan. The next morning, James Chaney, Michael Schwerner and Andrew Goodman are released, only to be ambushed by waiting Klansmen, tortured then murdered.
- **Civil Rights Act of 1964**, enacted in July, made illegal discrimination based on color, race, gender, religion or national origin.
- **1964: Malcolm X transformed** by his trip to Mecca where he sees Caucasians in a new light. Prior to his death, he expresses regret for divisive statements made towards Civil Rights leaders and opens the door to reconciliation and alignment with the movement's ideology.
- **1965, February 21ˢᵗ: Malcolm X assassinated** preventing a full reconciliation with the Civil Rights Movement.
- **Voting Rights Act of 1965.** This act outlaws the use of discriminatory voting practices. Requirements to pass literacy tests were racist tools designed specifically to discriminate against African-Americans at a time when they were being denied adequate education.
- **1966, June 30ᵗʰ: National Organization for Women (NOW)** is established to address issues of discrimination.

Historical Review

- **1968:** Inspired by the African American and Latino Civil Rights efforts, the **American Indian Movement (AIM)** is founded in Minneapolis, Minnesota. The organization works to tackle problems of poverty, housing discrimination, police harassment and treaty violations.
- **1968, April 4th:** After living with death threats for over a decade, **Martin Luther King, Jr. is assassinated.** The final Civil Rights act he worked on is successfully passed the following week.
- **Civil Rights Act of 1968** is signed, extending the 1866 and 1964 acts. Prior to his assassination, King represented the Civil Rights Movement in working with President Johnson to shape this legislation. The act prohibits discrimination in housing and provides for enforcement of these laws.
- **1972: Shirley Chisholm** becomes the first African American to run as a candidate for the President of the United States. Chisholm advocates for Civil Rights, is elected to the New York state legislature in 1964, and helps establish the **National Organization for Women**.
- **1989:** Former Grand Wizard of the Ku Klux Klan, David Duke, is elected to the House of Representatives in the state of Louisiana. Referring to himself as a racial realist, Duke urges the voluntary separation of the races.
- **1990: Nelson Mandela** freed after 27 years of imprisonment in South Africa. In 1993 the racial segregation policy of apartheid is dismantled and in 1994 Mandela is elected as the first black president of South Africa in the first fully represented election of that country. The symbolism of this progress sends a message of hope around the world.
- **Civil Rights Act of 1991** strengthens the rights of employees seeking justice in discrimination cases.
- **1991:** African-American **Rodney King** is severely beaten with batons and stomped on by four LAPD officers after being chased for speeding. Racism is believed to have been a factor in the excessive force used. The public outrage leads to indictments, but riots break out in 1992 when the police officers are acquitted. A year later, two of the officers are sent to prison for Civil Rights violations.

- **1998:** African-American **James Byrd** of Jasper, Texas is brutally murdered in a racially motivated attack, so heinous that it shocks the nation. *This is one of many hate crimes occurring each year.*
- **2001, September 11:** Muslim extremists attack targets on U.S. soil. Although denounced by mainstream Muslim groups, this event ignites across-the-board anti-Muslim sentiments, discrimination and violence.
- **2004:** Senator Sam Brownback proposes joint resolution 37 to compel the U.S. government to make a formal apology for the atrocities committed against American Indians. However, to this date, the government has taken no action on this resolution.
- February **2007**, the House and Senate of the state of Virginia unanimously pass a resolution to express regret for the state's role in slavery. A small number of courageous states soon follow their lead with their own apologies, but an official federal acknowledgement has yet to be made.
- May **2007**, African-American presidential candidate, Senator Barack Obama is placed under Secret Service protection after receiving racially motivated death threats.
- **2008**, November 4th, presidential candidate **Barack Obama** wins the general election clinching 365 out of 538 Electoral College votes. President Obama becomes the first nonwhite to win the office of the Presidency of the United States.
- **2008:** Over 100 current and former African American secret service agents join together to take legal action for discrimination in employment practices.
- **2010:** Controversial anti-illegal immigration legislation, Arizona Senate Bill 1070 is signed into law. Perceptions that the regulation is conceived out of bigotry and concerns over racial profiling and human rights abuses spark controversy around the world, exposing our continuing struggle with racism.
- **2011:** Unveiling of the Martin Luther King, Jr. Memorial. Dr. King becomes the first African American honored within the National Mall.
- **2012:** November 6th, presidential candidate **Barack Obama** is voted in as Presidency of the United States for a second term.
- **2013:** February 27th, Rosa Parks becomes the first African American woman to be depicted in a full-length statue in the U.S.

Capitol's Statuary Hall. The nation's most powerful politicians, led by President Barack Obama honor Rosa Parks with the unveiling of her statue.
- **Present:** While progress continues slowly towards a unified country with equal rights and opportunities, incidents of racial discrimination and hate crimes continue to be reported each year.

Unity Initiative

Historical Events Summary

To summarize further, government-sanctioned slavery was practiced in the U.S. from around 1619 to 1865; nearly 246 years. The untold damage from such prolonged abuses had a devastating effect, crippling the economic, social and psychological welfare of those generations. With Lincoln's assassination, the plans for reconstruction, our country's effort to make amends, heal these wounds and reunite the country was quickly squashed leaving ex-slaves with no resources to prevent a bleak future. Except for remaining Indian territories, white Americans controlled the vast majority of our country's assets. There was very little sympathy for the plight of the freedmen who were in fact, widely viewed with contempt.

To heal, they would need our nation's unyielding, determined support. We would need to have atoned for the past with earnest efforts to undo the damage, but that never happened. Instead, they faced a slow and bitter battle for legislative reform to close gaps and loopholes that kept our country from honoring basic Civil Rights. This took over another 100 years when counting the Civil Rights Act of 1968 - about 350 years of open oppression by the country as a whole. The injustices for the duration of most of that period were sanctioned by the U.S. government, which all but ended with desegregation starting with the ruling on Brown vs. Board of education.

In 2007, the first official apology is given by the state of Virginia but only a few other states followed their example. Yet these actions were bitterly criticized by many Whites who cannot accept that a problem still exists or that amends are still due for acts committed by past generations. But the fact is our country was severely scarred by over 12 generations of abuse without as much as a national acknowledgement of the harm done. There were no reasonable reparations made to adequately ameliorate the astronomical disparity in economics or to re-architect the unfair power structure. As a result, we have never in our history reached a point of complete absolution, mutual respect or understanding. The rate of the progress that has been made has been like trying to save a blazing building with a garden hose; the effect of each advance has seemed to be too little, too late.

Historical Review

Concerns about the shortfall in our country's efforts to amend our past are reflected in the below excerpt from President Lyndon Johnson's commencement address at Howard University.

"Freedom is the right to share, share fully and equally, in American society, to vote, to hold a job, to enter a public place, to go to school. It is the right to be treated in every part of our national life as a person equal in dignity and promise to all others.

But freedom is not enough. You do not wipe away the scars of centuries by saying: Now you are free to go where you want, and do as you desire, and choose the leaders you please.

You do not take a person who, for years, has been hobbled by chains and liberate him, bring him up to the starting line of a race and then say, "*you are free to compete with all the others*," and still justly believe that you have been completely fair.

Thus it is not enough just to open the gates of opportunity. All our citizens must have the ability to walk through those gates.

This is the next and the more profound stage of the battle for Civil Rights. We seek not just freedom but opportunity. We seek not just legal equity but human ability, not just equality as a right and a theory but equality as a fact and equality as a result." *

* PBS Website: http://www.pbs.org/wgbh/amex/eyesontheprize/sources/ps_bakke.html

When comparing the current state of our country to the climate of a century ago, we can see that we have certainly come a long way in accomplishing these ideals. Many battles were won against racism in the public sector, but the slow progress that has been made has not translated to the private lives of the individual. The gains made by the Civil Rights Movement only addressed the most visible symptoms of racism that were exposed in the government regulated quarters of our society, not the underlying cause. We continue to put inadequate bandages on gaping racist wounds, but the social issues, perceptions and constructs that allowed the damage to take place have never been treated.

We have only lived one full generation since the bitterly won Civil Rights Act of 1968 so those memories are still fresh. Most Americans readily acknowledge racism is prevalent, yet concerning racism's victims, some cannot understand "why they don't just get over it." This view is often heard from individuals who consider themselves nonracist, yet truly believe the answers to the implied accusations lie at the heart of the problem. These perceptions seem to be rooted in a frustration that somehow the obstacles are not real; that the barriers are only in the minds of those who refuse to use their psychological capabilities to push them aside. "They need only to exercise willpower to succeed in life."

Such sentiments expose a lack of understanding of the destructive power of racism and a disconnection from the communities who have to deal with it. They disregard the inequities in opportunity, allowing us to wash our hands of the responsibility of a problem that seems too big by convincing ourselves the suffering of others is self-manufactured. If our heart and mind are truly free from the racist doctrine that Whites are superior, we cannot accept the notion that people of color are not reaping proportionate benefits from our country because they are too lazy or lacking social or work ethics. We have to ask ourselves, *what is wrong with our society that we are still blocking equitable quality of life for all.*

For 246 years our country dug an economic hole, in which former slaves were placed. We then erected a barbwire fence of social rejection around them for over another century, ensuring their continued isolation; a social-malady that has yet to be overcome. We must accept that despite having forced integration in education and employment, the efforts made so far to resolve these problems have not been sufficient.

On the other hand, although we obviously have a long way to go, we can also see hope in the positive changes that our country has made. They could not have been accomplished without the growing support and cooperation of all races and an awareness of the problems that still exist. Besides the strides in legislation that have reduced abuses and improved opportunities for minorities, our tolerance for bigotry has decreased while growing numbers of individuals are connecting with people in diverse groups. The media is doing a better job of removing gender, ethnic and racial stereotypes and providing more positive portrayals. We are seeing signs of growing respect for those who led the way to positive changes, including the establishment of a national holiday and a monument to honor the accomplishments of Dr. King.

Historical Review

Finally and most remarkable was the presidential campaign and election of 2008. The democratic primaries included an African-American, Barack Obama, and a woman, Hilary Clinton, competing for the democratic nomination. Both candidates received an enormous amount of support, but Obama clinched the nomination. The republican candidate John McCain chose a woman, Sarah Palin, as his running mate. This set up a race that guaranteed that either a woman or an African American would be elected to the White house, breaking the exclusivity of the historically white-male office.

Along with the fierce competition that produced sometimes bitter reactions from sectors of the American public, excitement energized the country that we were turning a corner in history; that the scales of equality were indeed slowly moving in the direction of balanced opportunity.

On November 4th, 2008 Barack Obama won the election to become the first nonwhite president of the United States of America. This historical milestone brought hope to millions across the political spectrum. In a hopeful sign of conciliation and unity, Senator John McCain spoke for most Americans during his concession speech in his recognition of the pride felt for the symbolism of how far our country has come with respect to racism within the last few generations.

McCain stated: "America today, is a world away from the cruel and prideful bigotry of that time. There is no better evidence of this than the election of an African-American to the Presidency of the United States." McCain went on to make a pledge to the Obama administration to help lead the country through the difficulties being faced. He then requested his supporters to offer their goodwill and earnest effort to work together in bridging the gap of their differences.

This scene was repeated on November 6th, 2012 in the Presidential race between Mitt Romney and Barack Obama. Romney too gracefully expressed his hope for President Obama's success in guiding our country in these difficult times. The message sent across the country by the election results and ensuing reaction of jubilation, which reverberated around the world, was clear; we are changing.

Chapter 7: Assessing Our Past

Difficult Hurdles for a Split Society

All races are made up of such interesting cultures with beautiful people who are filled with common hopes and dreams. We all share the same basic values and morals. Although it seems these common values should bind us altogether, there seems to be fundamental characteristics in our human make-up that have prevented the races of our communities from evolving together as a unified civilization.

Possibly driven by the theoretical "reptilian brain" instincts for survival, this division seems to date back to the time of the formation of early tribes fighting for resources. Some hold that these deeply subconscious drives have resisted millions of years of evolution and cause us to act unjustly aggressive. Impulses to expand, then defend territory have progressed over several millennia into the competition of rivals jockeying for their position in the human race.

Like today, those participating in this competition likely perceived each other as inferior or superior, based on victory in battle, material gain and technological progress. Sadly, higher-conscience attributes such as compassion and community-cohesion did not evolve as the valued characteristics of an advanced culture. Those not participating in the race, those humble, quiet societies content with the simple lives, in which they were born, were likely judged to be inferior.

Did such divisions between aggressively materialistic and non-competing tribes lead to perceptions of racial superiority? Did that ultimately factor in to the justification of exploitation of other races perceived to be inferior? This is a broad brush to paint such a complex picture, but these generalities seem to be pieces of the puzzle that formed our civilization.

The exploitation through enslavement had been practiced for over 10,000 years, so understanding the exact roots of such crimes of humanity can only be theorized. But as the "human race" gained momentum, slavery spread across the globe. The observations of dominance amongst races and tribes perpetuated as twisted perceptions of inferiority versus superiority. Americans, Asians, Africans, Europeans, Arabians, all participated in these atrocities. The horrific acts that were committed in this abuse were demonstrations of some of the most barbarous crimes in human history.

Although most races are guilty of these practices, Caucasians pushed the envelope in the degree of their exploitation with few moral restraints. They brought slavery to new levels with the lucrative *transatlantic slave trade.* The importing of slaves had a major impact on the birth of the United States agriculture and economy as well as the economies of Great Britain and other European countries. Ancestors of European descent sailed to Africa to find slaves to provide for the hard labor needed in developing our agriculture. They abducted innocent men, women and children from harmless tribes that were certainly of no threat. They were hunted down and treated like animals. To maximize profit on these raids, slave merchants would pack in hundreds of innocent souls into the cramped cargo hulls of their ships. Imagine being packed in like rats and tightly chained down to one hot tortuous spot for an entire week's journey through the rough seas without fresh air. They were given very little food or water. Disease and unbearable stench were the consequences of inadequate efforts to maintain sanitary conditions. The mortality rate was extremely high. Only the strongest were able to survive the treacherous voyage. Those who did make it were sold like cattle in the slave market. Families were ripped apart; men were forced into hard labor and battlefields while women became servants to work in the fields or the slave-owner's household. They sometimes wound up as sex slaves to the barbarians who destroyed their lives. The violent demoralization of innocent lives, resulting from these immoral practices, continued in the United States for nearly two and a half centuries.

The overall effect of these crimes against humanity can be traced to many of our culture's biggest problems. How could a nation born on exploitation, hate and shame possibly avoid the pains we are now experiencing? The monumental hurdles for healing our nation's wounds at the end of the Civil War would require considerable effort. Yet, the United States' abrupt abolition of slavery was carried out without adequate means for transitioning freedmen into their new life. Provisions for protecting newly gained rights under the 14th and 15th amendments were not enough to overcome bitter opposition. Lincoln's intentions for addressing some of the economic problems largely died with his assassination.

As a result of not providing sufficient financial and moral support to former slaves to become integrated into our society and acclimating them to their new life, the success of the black communities and the health of our country's resulting race relations has been as only can be expected. Psychological wounds continue to fester. Poverty and unemployment of minorities is still extremely high. Fear and resentment still divide our communities. That is the state of the American racial climate. Our country is still sickened and dysfunctional because we have never taken the necessary action to recover.

When slaves were freed, they made up about ten percent of our population. The other ninety percent of the nation continued to treat them as social pariah, excluding them from most resources. So many generations of innocent lives were destroyed while many more continue to deteriorate. The emotional scars of an entire race were never given a chance to heal, resulting in a breeding ground for fearful disillusionment for our whole society. Hearts are poisoned by resentment and mistrust. We spend much of our time blindly blaming each other for our continued suffering, without holding ourselves accountable, by investigating how we can personally make a difference by getting involved in solutions of direct action.

In addition to the inadequacy of care given to tend past injuries, many overt racists actively work to keep those wounds fresh. At the extreme end of the spectrum from the overt racists are those who truly desire recovery with an end to racism. A small fraction of these people actively participate in the healing process, but many others fear the situation may be hopeless.

In between these two extremes are countless others who are frustrated because they can't understand why this issue doesn't just go away. They refuse to believe the problem is significant enough to warrant a continuation of expending our resources. This denial is much easier when you are the economics and power beneficiary of systemic racism. But without properly addressing these crimes against humanity, they cannot simply be forgotten. How could they? As a compassionate society, we should be trying to understand the reasons our country's wounds have not healed. We must come to terms with the unlikelihood of progress being made, without widespread personal involvement.

Looking at statistics that highlight inequities, it is not surprising that people of color are more sensitive to these issues than their Caucasian brothers and sisters. But very few Whites are completely blind to the reality of racial problems. Growing numbers are becoming more willing to face these truths and stand up for what is right. They are eager to make a difference for future generations.

However, many hurdles must still be overcome. Fear and misperception are our biggest obstacles. A large portion of our nation is not ready to concede that present day Caucasians bare any responsibility in resolving our country's racial economic imbalance. Three major roadblocks stand in the way. The first issue is overt racism. Many are still afflicted with bigotry. Second is the fear of blame. Many fear that such an acknowledgement will result in their being forced into taking responsibility that will result in humiliation or an undue burden for acts that "they did not commit." When pressed about the injustice of current racial inequities, many will throw up the defense that it's simply not their problem. They claim they are not racist, they certainly never owned slaves, and that those abuses all happened in the past, long before their generation.

Such arguments are a smokescreen for denying responsibility of the problems we all inherited. They allow us to avoid participation in perceived burdensome solutions. Unfortunately though, like the national debt, this is a problem each new generation will suffer from, even though it did not originate from their generation.

We only need to look at our local communities and distribution of wealth to see our economic prosperity is not fairly shared. Caucasians have clearly been the primary recipients of our lucrative economy, whose foundation was dependent on slavery - extorted labor. This wholesale stealing of life, liberty and labor may have occurred many generations before present-day Caucasians received the benefits, but time alone does not launder the injustices of the unfair advantages. Ex-slaves were excluded from the fruits of their labor and their descendants now face systemic barriers of racism that prevent them from fully participating in economic privileges made possible by their ancestors.

The final roadblock is that many perceive the suffering of so many people of color who are below the poverty line as being there by their own undoing. The perception is based on the principle of *personal responsibility*. This is the value that each individual should be responsible for his or her own well-being and that we must work hard if we are to succeed in life. We must take care of our health, study for our education, work hard at our jobs, plan for our future and save for a rainy day so we are not dependent on others. Based on this understanding, any aid to those who are not succeeding is viewed skeptically as unfair special treatment. The recipients are stigmatized by criticism of being undue victims.

Each individual's practicing of discipline and taking responsibility for his or her action is certainly important. The gray area here is the implication of equal opportunity. This argument ignores the fact that Whites have received unfair advantages to the detriment of people of color for centuries. The level of hard work required to achieve success in every area of life is prohibitively greater when deprived of adequate resources with a supportive culture. *Equal opportunity is still a theory that has not yet been realized.* This idealized state requires equitable access to resources, but fear, bigotry and social structures prevent exclusionary barriers from coming down. A person exposed to established racism is indeed a victim. Although this legitimate claim does not absolve anyone of personal responsibility, it does put them in a class that deserves compassionate understanding along with moral support.

When fully educated on American history, while embracing the principles of truth and justice, we cannot deny the reality of these problems. Our society that created this environment of injustice has the responsibility to examine the root causes of continued oppression and find solutions to bring it to an end. Finding a resolution is part of the package we must all accept for living in this great country, regardless of the depth of your family's roots in its soil.

Racism and Past Politics and Economics

President Lyndon B. Johnson was a great man who faithfully carried out the legacy of John F. Kennedy by facilitating in the establishment of many effective social programs, frequently responding to the prodding of Dr. King and the Civil Rights Movement. He brought the Civil Rights Act of 1964 across the finish line and led the way to the passage of the Civil Rights Act of 1968. Johnson took the initial steps to move forward on the vision of rebuilding decaying cities into healthy communities with strong infrastructures of schools, healthcare, housing and most important of all, an atmosphere of respect fostering the building of relationships between all cultures. His administration architected the *Great Society,* which included the *War on Poverty.* This legislation included successful programs such as Head Start and Job Corps. Over the next decade, poverty levels dropped from 19% to 11%, going a long way in addressing deficiencies of health and education, as well as mending race relations.

But despite Johnson's great deeds and intentions, instead of a decisive War on Poverty and racial injustice, we were derailed by the war on Vietnam that deeply scarred many countries around the world. Some reports estimate that millions of people were killed and millions more wounded. The moral and psychological scars continue to take their toll. Despite the successes of the War on Poverty, it struggled to compete for funds that were choked off by this conflict. Met with powerful resistance from opposing forces, its effectiveness was severely hampered. The result was a short life for many programs and continued delays of amending our past.

Questions may now arise concerning corrective steps for our government in addressing ongoing economic issues that trace back to past racial injustices. Should monetary compensation be established similar to amends made to American Indians? Is it possible that a comprehensive economic stimulus package could be created that would ameliorate the inequities that have not been righted through the changes in legislation to this date? Although seeking such retribution may be a merited course of action, these pursuits are simply beyond the scope of this organization. Our focus is solely on breaking down the social barriers, which are at the root of the issues that perpetuate these disparities.

However, ignoring such topics presents an incomplete picture. Although we do not want to become embroiled in the volatile passions evoked by the controversy in these politics, we can approach it from the angle of personal introspection, as well as gain more insight to our current racial climate. We can start by asking ourselves questions such as "Where do I stand on economic policies like welfare and Affirmative Action?" "How do I perceive beneficiaries of such regulations?" "What are the good points versus the bad points of these programs?" and finally "Do my perceptions flawlessly align with my most basic values?"

If we are opponents of such policies, what is the right thing to do to amend and alleviate the suffering of those who are still in the grips of racism? Many opponents attack such legislation, stating that setting quotas is nothing but "reverse-discrimination". They argue that these programs are contradictions to the free enterprise system and corrosive to our systems of democracy and capitalism. Others say they provide loopholes that allow for too many abuses, cause destructive dependencies and are counter-productive to our economy.

Proponents on the other hand defend that such regulations directly address issues of racism that past generations have failed to resolve; that doing nothing only results in prolonged oppression. They counter the charges of "reverse-discrimination" by contending that while legislation such as Jim Crow laws were based on fearful divisiveness and intended to exclude, these policies are based on justice and compassion with the intention of broadening inclusion. They point out that every government program has such shortcomings but that we have a moral obligation to atone for past atrocities and current inequities by guaranteeing a portion of our resources to those who are being denied equal access.

Whatever our perceptions are concerning such clashing views, we believe that we will improve our ability to make the right choices when we let our ideals be shaped by the founding principles discussed earlier. Someday we may be able to help heal enough wounds and help pave the way for enough trust so that the continued gaps in economic and educational prosperity can be addressed by the organizations that have made that their advocacy. But as long as our communities remain segregated, a financial solution alone will not be enough to resolve our problems.

For now, what can be learned from these ideas is more a question of personal than of national responsibility. "What can I do to make a difference?" Our personal responsibility starts with freeing our heart of our own prejudices and simultaneously sharing love and compassion with our brothers and sisters of all diversities. We can make an enormous difference by simply extending the unconditional love and respect that all humans deserve.

Our Dysfunctional Society

As wonderful as this country is, it is clear we have inherited a dysfunctional society plagued with social issues from the festering wounds of our past. Generation after generation they are swept under the carpet. Criticizing our forefathers for not resolving these issues is easy in hindsight, but in all fairness we should try to understand the mindset that had to be overcome. When exposed to racism as a cultural norm from birth, the slow acclimation to distorted views can numb our sense of justice. Most who grew up with them rarely even questioned their morality. When challenged, they defended it was simply a part of their heritage and nobody else's business.

Past generations had great difficulty mustering enough support of individuals with the resolve or clarity of how to address these problems to gain the necessary traction needed to promote reform and reconciliation. The trailblazers who did have the vision for healing our society have always met overwhelming resistance by those disillusioned by the myths of supremacy and clinging on to the past.

Many centuries of bigotry made the myth a "reality" in the minds of most Whites and many nonwhites. But as a result of the heroism and sacrifice from pioneers such as Harriet Tubman, Gandhi, Lincoln, King, Fannie Lou Hamer, Kennedy, and Johnson in challenging these views, progress is being made. These relatively rare voices opened enough eyes to start making a difference in many of our major institutions. While the path to healing is still being paved, efforts to effect changes on a personal level have yet to be established and the relationship between Whites and nonwhites that has evolved over the last four centuries continues on like a dysfunctional family.

Our society now exhibits some of the same behaviors and symptoms that are reported by members of 12-step programs who came from abusive homes. In some of these families, a child could be singled out and more severely victimized by abusive and controlling parents than their siblings. Let's imagine an extreme case of such a family having a child grow up in an environment where they are repeatedly ridiculed. They are put down with sometimes subtle, other times painfully overt messages that they are unworthy of being part of the family; that their contributions don't count; that they will never measure up. In every stage of their development towards adulthood they are continually berated. They are abused physically and psychologically. They are deprived of the love and nurturing that is essential for basic mental health and psychological growth, as well as resources needed to advance in life. We all know people who have lived through some degree of these types of abuses. Some may even have firsthand experience.

Now imagine that those same family members, who abuse this child, nurture their siblings with positive attention. As children themselves, they don't know any better, nor do they have the power to intervene in their sibling's mistreatment. They are likely to avoid challenging assertions that their sibling is inferior and will wind up taking on these beliefs; and subsequently they become perpetrators of their abuse. They are neither inherently evil, nor naturally hateful. Their prejudice and mistreatment against their sibling is taught by their family's abusive conduct. They are in the trap of the groupthink mentality.

Institutional racism plus *white privilege* set up just such an environment on a global scale. Relatively speaking, Whites play the role of the nurtured children; lavished upon with abundant opportunities and advantages while exempt from negative social judgment. Our country's forefathers were in the role of the parents; paving the way of opportunity for most, while passing along stereotypes and setting the example of unfair treatment for others. People of color are frequently put in the role of the abused child; excluded from many opportunities, deprived of a supportive culture, stigmatized by the perceptions established by our ancestors, then held in ridicule when they are not able to overcome the hurdles stemming from oppressive stereotypes and practices, in which their critics are often collaborators.

Now let's say that after the children of the imagined dysfunctional family become adults, the abusive parents pass away and one of the children becomes conscious of the wrongs committed on their abused sibling. Maybe a close friend makes comments about their unkind words, challenging the groupthink mindset and exposing their abuses. From then on, they have made an effort to stop saying hurtful things.

Although the majority of the overt abuse has now been removed from their sibling's life, some continue to either sit on the sidelines doing nothing to stop the abuses, or they persist in reinforcing negative perceptions with belittling statements such as "Ok, so they had a rough childhood, so what's their problem now? Why don't they stop feeling sorry for themself and pull themself up by their bootstraps and do something with their lives?"

As the non-abused sibling matures, they become more aware that their family set up an environment guaranteeing their sibling's failure, then blamed them for failing; reinforcing the perceptions of their inferiority. Considering their exclusion from opportunities, as well as the damage inflicted without any means to counter the stigmatizing effects, pulling themself up by their bootstraps is highly unlikely. Their sibling's bootstraps had effectively been cut off.

They become aware that for years they rationalized that they had no responsibility in their sibling's plight since their role paled in comparison to the abuses of others. They also see that, although they stopped participating in the mistreatment long ago, they never made direct amends for their role or for the years of non-action as they watched the continuation of abuse. *They come to realize that they are now a perpetrator by proxy.*

Even if their abused sibling were to liberate themself without changes by others, would that absolve them of their role in the suffering? What is their responsibility here if any? If they love them, they will want to do anything they can to amend their past behavior and to help them attain the life they deserve; a life in which they themself have enjoyed, but in which their sibling has been deprived. They see years of built up animosity, fear and confusion and feel ashamed, helpless and afraid. Their sibling's suffering now causes them pain, but what can they possibly do to help them heal?

Using the analogy of an abused child is of course an oversimplification of the challenges of racism and the personal effects of living in a hostile environment. Most African Americans were made stronger by the centuries of adversity they faced. Families and communities bonded together forming a shield of strength that enabled them to endure extreme abuses. Characteristics of individual fortitude and determination were forged over the generations, allowing communities and individuals to make great strides in all areas of our society.

However, besides the economic hindrances that devastated nearly an entire race, many individuals did indeed also suffer the emotional and psychological problems as described in the above analogy. The self-images that were damaged in these cases and the related problems of stress cause a reduction in happiness. * Black children and adults alike eventually will face situations where they are rejected or treated unfairly, solely because of the color of their skin.

With this awareness, what can we do as a society to help heal our country? Invaluable lessons can be learned from 12-step programs where the rooms are filled with people who were simultaneously both victims and perpetrators of abuses. The aggregate of our misdeeds run the gamut of every imaginable mistreatment. Some were more active as abusers while others suffered more frequently by the selfishness of their offenders, but most of us have experienced each role to some extent. The difficulties we face closely parallel some of these same issues that continue to plague our society.

Those who were severely abused found themselves in a predicament similar to this symbolic mistreated-child, raised in an environment with nearly impossible odds of a healthy life. Those among us in this category usually suffer from depression, resentment and low self-esteem. Relationships are frequently strained. These difficulties often led to isolation and destructive cycles that may include prisons, mental sanitariums and other institutions.

When we take on the role of the abuser we are neglectful, controlling and hypercritical. When abuses are carried to the extreme, we are plagued with remorse, disillusionment and personality disorders that can lead to the same destructive ends. The transgressor will find protection in the use of blame and denial. The denial makes it possible for us to avoid responsibility for our own defects and contribution to the plight of others, while blaming tactics are employed as a smokescreen defense.

* Based on studies effects of racism on self-image from Social psychologist Kenneth B. Clark (1950s Brown vs. Board of education), Klonoff & Landrine, 1999", Nyborg VM, Curry JF. 2003, CNN report "Kids on Race"

Assessing Our Past

Not surprisingly, just as victims of racism can assimilate to the ideals of the racist, many of us who were victimized by abuses can likewise eventually become perpetrators, not realizing or caring that we are repeating the behavior of those who wronged us. We are thus allowing the perpetuation of our afflictions.

Our future seems hopeless until we are introduced to predecessors who found effective solutions to these problems. When we enter the fellowship, we are given a chance to recover from the wounds of abuses and help ourselves and others heal from the suffering brought on by our abusiveness or neglect. The process of recovery is the same for both the oppressed and the oppressor.

We are first nurtured back to health by members of the group with ample supplies of compassion, combined with the sharing of group member's experiences, strength and hope. This does not mean unhealthy coddling. On the contrary, it involves helping each other take full responsibility for our lives, but it is backed up with abundant love and support, as each of us walks through our own personal struggles.

Once we have gained enough strength with the support of the group, we begin to look at our own wrongdoings. If we want to fully heal, we are left with no choice but to look in the mirror. We become painfully aware of the suffering we have caused as the result of our own selfishness, and become motivated to set things right. We do this while working the 12 steps with the help of those who came before us. We clean up the wreckage of our past, by first taking a thoroughly honest look at our shortcomings, while searching our past for any harm we may have caused. We usually discover that we often justified our wrongdoings by pointing out the violations of those we hurt. But when faced with destruction we found we had to pardon others for their role and only focus on our own behavior.

We are then ready to make amends for our wrongs. In some cases these amends will last a lifetime. For example, when it comes to family members that we have neglected or abused, we happily commit to being good-loving sisters, brothers, husbands, wives, daughters and sons. We avoid criticism, release control and make an effort to end our neglect by allocating time to contribute to these relationships. When the damage to others manifests in misbehavior on their part, we must be careful not to dodge our own responsibility by solely focusing on their flaws. We must consider that this is likely partially a symptom of our own abuses or neglect. In the spirit of unconditional surrender and self-sacrifice, the primary focus must always be on what and how *"I"* can change. Under these conditions we can all become healthy and flourish.

For our organization, this will also include focusing on our own contribution, collusion or inaction to racism. Regardless of our race or background, we first take the necessary steps to change our attitudes and behaviors while looking for any debris lingering from our own past personal lives. We remove the wreckage that blocks us from happiness and keeps us in fear of others. Along the way, we develop bonds of unity, building intimate relationships in our diverse community by spending time in group discussions and one-on-one dialogs.

When we get to the twelfth step, we start helping anyone else interested in starting on this journey. Many of us make ourselves available to those facing difficulties, to talk anytime, day or night. We are willing to do this because we all understand what it is like to suffer and many of us were given this same compassion when we most needed the support. We do this also because it is mutually beneficial. Not only is giving a vital part of our growth, it feels good to give away what was so freely given to us. To watch lives be restored and return to happiness the same way our life was is equally joyful. At the same time, we are buying more insurance for our own mental state. The more we give, the more we receive.

Although we will surely experience significant healing by our integrated activities, we will be especially effective in helping others of our own race in matters of addressing their issues of bigotry. Whites and people of color do have slightly differing roles in dismantling racism and recovering from its effects. Whites will be able to help other whites to: 1) expose and work through their own prejudices, 2) become aware of the level of racism in all our major institutions, how they contribute, and what they can do to change or reject those practices, and 3) break down social barriers to other diverse groups.

People of color will be most effective in helping people of their own race or ethnicity to: 1) expose and work through their own prejudices, 2) determine if and how they collaborate with racism, and 3) strengthen their own racial identity while breaking down social barriers.*

*Adapted from the conclusions in chapter two of "Teaching/Learning Anti-racism"

However, this does not mean we won't be helping others outside our race. It simply means that we are not qualified to give advice on solutions that are beyond our own experience. Through integrated activities we will start chipping away at institutional racism by removing fears and mistrust.

These acts of compassion provide nothing less than the essential nutrition that all humans require for spiritual and psychological growth. Intuitively we all know this. We have all experienced the power of love as well as the corrosive destruction of hate and neglect. Yet these ideals have not been applied to the healing of our country's racial problems. As a result our whole society has been sickened and we must all endure the effects of our turbulent past. Each new generation is left holding the bag of mistrust, fear, questioned integrity and compromised morals. We all inherit the scars from the wounds of our predecessors.

Certainly there have been many heroic white Americans who worked hard and risked their own wellbeing, sometimes paying a high price for doing the right thing. They fought for the emancipation of slaves. They joined forces with people of color, assisting in abolishing government-enforced segregation, overturning discriminatory laws and securing constitutional rights. Taking these stands are some of America's most shining contributions to our history. But beyond that, our society missed so many opportunities to change. Too few took the necessary steps to heal from the hateful destruction of so many decades of slavery, segregation, violent abuses, exploitation and neglect.

As already discussed, the private social efforts to change hearts have been scarce and public-governmental efforts to resolve symptoms of institutional racism have had minimal effect. Marginal support for change pitted against overwhelming resistance for the status quo resulted in all initiatives falling short. To grow beyond our dysfunction, we will all need to change our mindsets to gain compassion. We will need to pick up the pieces of the fractured society we inherited from our ancestors, acknowledge our current problems and take Direct Action to truly integrate our communities.

The Missing Acknowledgement

Racism is a form of insanity similar to the phenomenon in Nazi-Germany that allowed the degradation of a society to the depths of fostering an environment producing the nightmare leading up to the holocaust. At its peak, racism held our whole country in a state of delirium that allowed the unconscionable practice of slavery to persist for centuries, followed by continued oppression and human rights violations.

After being freed, Blacks were left to fend for themselves with scarce resources to get started with their new lives. They were left to scratch and claw to find food and shelter as their means for eking out some kind of existence. Practically no provisions were made available to integrate them into the American society and economy that would enable them to become self-sufficient. Under these conditions, how many generations should it take to make something out of nothing; to rise out of the depths of poverty and dependency without adequate resources and without moral support? What has been done to heal these deep wounds? Where was the necessary widespread compassion needed by our Caucasian siblings to strengthen their spirits?

The freeing of slaves at the end of the Civil War created a state analogous to the environment endured by the previously discussed fictitious abused child when their abusive parents pass away. The child is left to contend with this legacy being carried forward by other less-abusive, yet no more compassionate clan and society members. The victim is not suddenly made whole simply because the violations are measurably reduced. For sure, they are given a sense of hope, but they are still considered to be inferior and treated unfairly. They are "kept in their place." And God forbid if they somehow get the impression that they now have a right to a piece of the estate their ancestors left behind.

Sometime after the emancipation or the abolishing of laws promoting segregation, wouldn't it have at least been the right thing to do to include a public statement of apology by all state and federal representatives? Of course the end of the Civil War did not bring an end to our country's delirium. The union was in a very fragile state and our nation's leaders were exhausted. They were wary of any further action that might give rise to more bloodshed or cause further friction between the North and South, resulting in continued deterioration of loyalty to the union. Former slave owners were resentful that their 'property' and livelihood was forcefully taken from them. Many of those who didn't even own slaves were still under the delusion of superiority and were resentful of their standing in the social pecking order with rise in status of those they regarded as inferior. So instead of throwing more salt in the wounds of vocal countrymen, reeling from the upheaval of their lives, we instead allowed the continued victimization of those who were innocent and without power.

Maybe it wasn't realistic to have expected our country's leaders to face the personal consequences of stirring more resentment and risking further alienation by trying to provide additional support. Most left at the helm after Lincoln's assassination were certainly not free of racism themselves, nor did they share the same level of resolve for alleviating the suffering of the freedman. The minority of congressional members who were anxious to commit the necessary action and resources to full reconciliation were labeled as radicals.

The priorities of most were still disproportionately influenced by the pain of fellow Caucasians. But in hindsight, we can see the effect this had on our whole country. Not acknowledging a wrong inhibits healing. When we falter as individuals, we go a long way in correcting our mistake, starting with an acknowledgment along with an expression of regret. Applying this humility at a public level can accelerate the recovery process.

As an example, Germany has made apologies for the holocaust, taking a definitive stand against such atrocities while validating the pain of the victims. Another example was in India where officials showed much wider public support for ending discrimination of the untouchables.

In contrast, many of our country's leaders during the Civil Rights era publicly committed themselves to the blocking of efforts towards integration. With the exception of a few states prompted by the Virginia apology in 2007, no such official acknowledgement has been made for slavery or segregation. Wouldn't it have helped our healing for our country's representatives to address African Americans with a statement similar this?

Unity Initiative

"We the people of the United States wish to end the suffering of our country's racist past and to unite our society. For many generations our country has treated African Americans and American Indians with immoral savagery. Our country's economy flourished at the cost of the blood and sweat of their ancestor's inhumane enslavement; the fruits of which they have been excluded. What was done was regrettably and unjustifiably reprehensible. All people of this country are deserving of first-class citizenship and have an equal right to peace and happiness. We regret the past atrocities and commit to taking the necessary action to heal those wounds and right those wrongs in order to unite our nation."

Imagine what would have been the effect if sometime soon after the Civil War our country had taken this courageous step, following it up with committed action to amend the wrongs of our country's founding colonies. What would our lives be like today if we had immediately integrated our communities? If we had honored the victims and acknowledged the pain with which they had to process. If we had given them compassion to heal, quality education plus economic resources to become independent, and protection to exercise their voting rights to help set the path of their own destinies. How different would our country be now? Imagine the harmony, as well as the spiritual and economic prosperity we would all be experiencing. Surely we would continue to have problems, but how could poverty, hatred and our other social ills exist in such a society to the extent it does today?

But this was not the course we chose. On the contrary, our abused siblings were continually treated contemptuously for the next several decades, while our whole country did little to protect this already wounded segment of our society. Very few Caucasians showed support or took action for Civil Rights. Some of the more abusive Whites continued on with violence nearly unabated. Those that were nonviolent still usually treated our colored siblings as inferior outsiders and did little to stand in the way of our more abusive white brothers and sisters because they were either too afraid or simply preconditioned for inaction. They rationalized that they were not responsible since they were not the ones committing the offenses. They would thus continue to turn a blind eye or wait for government intervention to resolve these issues.

But if we want to amend these wrongs, action will need to start with us as individuals. Our government, which oversaw the rise and fall of slavery, acting as our representatives might have been the best institution for taking the lead role in such amends. However, the responsibility to do the right thing falls on the public's shoulders when our standards for justice are not met

Regardless of the role the government plays, we are not cleared of this responsibility. The American public has a rich history of rising to the occasion in helping those victimized by tyranny and injustice, but we have so far largely missed our opportunity to do that here within our own borders. Now is the time to hold ourselves accountable and take the action that will heal our country. It is never too late to do the right thing. Are we ready?

Black Nationalist Ideals for Resolving Racial Inequality

A number of African Americans courageously still hold hope that healing will occur someday; but for now, most have been able to move forward without earnest cooperation from Caucasians. Meanwhile, others grew weary of waiting for their white brothers and sisters to change their perception of superiority and show some real sign of inclusion. Thus, they have rejected the possibility of social integration and have turned their weariness into defiance against a society that seems unwilling to change their mindset.

While Dr. King and the movement participants sacrificed unwavering love, patience and nonviolent action to bring about reconciliation, Black Nationalist organizations such as the NOI were gaining strength based on the conclusion that Whites were simply unwilling or unable to transform. Some became convinced that if change in economic opportunity were to occur, it would possibly require violence or at a minimum, segregation on their own terms. Such organizations found strength in setting a high moral standard for themselves and removing all dependencies from Whites. Black separatists began envisioning a separation of the races.*

*http://www.noi.org/about_beliefs_and_wants.shtml;
   http://www.splcenter.org/get-informed/intelligence-files/ideology/black-separatist

To a great extent, these movements gave a vital sense of identity that allowed them to find liberation; not unlike that experienced by King and the Civil Rights activists. But the sometimes angry messages of Black Nationalist leaders who would not renounce violence were understandably viewed as threatening.* The perceived abrasiveness of those such as Marcus Garvey, Elijah Muhammad and Malcolm X caught many Whites off guard, who were accustomed to Blacks "staying in their place." Those fears were magnified by the guilt and powerlessness Whites felt for the ills caused by generations of sweeping old crimes under the carpet.

Unfortunately, our society did not have the psychological fortitude to concede the truth of some of the accusations that led to their divisive elements. Their defiant independence obscured the positive facets of these movements. We couldn't see beyond our own fears so the attitudes they adopted in challenging the status quo were used to label them as anti-American racists. But is it so inconceivable why the voiceless would find hope in their empowering message? Those in the ghettos feeling abandoned and suffering from the full weight of oppressive racism were especially lifted by the opportunities made possible by such organizations.

Through studying the history of American race relations, we see generations of persistent noncooperation of many Whites in participating in the progress of change. They have resisted extending respect, let alone surrendering a fair share of resources to fully integrate nonwhites into mainstream society. When our awareness is raised to the hopelessness being experienced today through the withholding of mutual respect, understanding how frustrations have led to individuals embracing the beliefs of such organizations is not too difficult. Yet it is also not too hard to imagine that if the separatists had it their way, we would at best create a situation similar to the volatile Israeli-Palestine relationship; a breeding ground for fear, hate and violence. Some may argue that such a state would be better than the current unjust system we now live in, but many see real signs of change and maintain a hopeful faith that we can do better.

*http://www.africanamericanquotes.org/violence.html

Assessing Our Past

To find a solution that unites our country and ends divisiveness, we must try to empathize with those who see no other option but to rebel. Past and ongoing racism is a valid reason to be disturbed. All Americans should be dissatisfied with the disparities in which we continue to live. To feel fear, sadness, hurt and frustration is only natural. These emotions can in turn develop into anger and even rage; especially for the victims. What else can be expected? As a society, we haven't taken any action to acknowledge these feelings let alone provide the means for individuals to resolve them on a personal level. We should all be striving not only for equal opportunity, but also towards the compassion needed for amending the current inequities brought upon by the inherently unfair system.

Unfortunately, the fact that we "should" be willing hasn't resulted in any changes. Only through the arduous efforts of those who persisted has change occurred.

How can we take the energy and motivation produced by our frustrations and turn them into positive results, while avoiding divisive measures? History reveals that the most meaningful and lasting changes made were brought about, not by bitterness, but by a steady, levelheaded determination.

When we use unbridled rage as the fuel to drive us, it may feel like a welcome relief to release our raw emotions, but we open the door to a myriad of other problems that will likely end in the failure of reaching our objectives. Our actions are inherently destructive. At a minimum, we become divisive, but at the extreme, we cause harm to innocent people. We will likely project negative perceptions and skepticism on those who might otherwise be our allies. What are our motives and what is the true source of our anger? Have we allowed personal feelings unrelated to our cause to creep in, pollute our motives and drive our actions? Are we using this important occasion as a venue to vent our masked personal problems? Has ego-driven self-righteousness become our guiding intuition? Do we believe "the ends justify the means" so that we will rationalize bending or violating basic human morals in order to achieve our objective regardless of the destruction?

This is no way to bring about change. King and Gandhi inspired reform, not by forcing the body to go against the will of the mind, but by transforming the mind so that the body would naturally comply with the ideals of doing the right thing.

Urging activists to rise above anger-driven reactions and steering clear of the seductive allure of the intoxicant of resentment, Dr. King made this appeal during his *I Have a Dream* speech.

> "Let us not seek to satisfy our thirst for freedom by drinking from the cup of bitterness and hatred. We must forever conduct our struggle on the high plane of dignity and discipline. We must not allow our creative protest to degenerate into physical violence. Again and again, we must rise to the majestic heights of meeting physical force with soul force." *

This ideal requires us to examine ourselves for raw emotions that might derail our efforts. To the best of our ability, we must free ourselves of all negative feelings in order to keep our motives pure.

The movements led by King and Gandhi proved the effectiveness of bringing about social change without being controlled by fear driven anger. They were never forced to compromise their principles. These emotions were certainly factors in the motivations of the activists, but they were trained to be disciplined and not bring that energy into movement activities, so they processed them within private venues. They took personal responsibility of their mental state, taking away control from their oppressors. They embraced the principles of nonviolence and opened the door for everyone to join the fight for freedom and equality. Many thousands of eyes were opened and millions of perceptions were shifted. The gaps of social divisiveness as well as the extremes of inequity were greatly reduced. Although we have a long way to go before our nation can be satisfied that we are doing all that is possible to resolve our problems, these examples have pointed us in a direction that may one day help us reach that destination.

---

* *Reprinted by arrangement with The Heirs to the Estate of Martin Luther King Jr., c/o Writers House as agent for the proprietor New York, NY. Copyright 1963 Dr. Martin Luther King Jr.; copyright renewed 1991 Coretta Scott King*

Assessing Our Past

Civil Rights Movement Efforts for Ending Discrimination

While the government has only been in the position to resolve the manifestations of racism through legislation, King and the Civil Rights Movement advocated principles that would address the root issues that created the symptoms.

Dr. King was a rare individual who seemed to excel in every area of his life. Although his parents were able to afford their family opportunities that many others did not have, they were still unable to avoid the ever-present tribulations of racism. King however, was not deterred by these obstacles. He was able to transform his pain and resentments towards Whites into love and hope.

Prior to its gaining traction in the fifties and sixties, torchbearers such as W. E. B. Du Bois, Ella Baker and Rosa Parks paved the initial path for the movement. With Dr. King's extraordinary vision and charisma, he crystallized the ideals of the movement and combined them with Gandhian principles. He was able to articulate their message in a way that elevated the confidence of the participants, galvanizing their resolve. His speeches and personal involvement were key components in changing perceptions of the movement from being the instigation of a few radicals to a noble cause worthy of widespread support. His leadership accelerated participation such that the rare involvement in this activism quickly mushroomed into a crusade of mainstream ideals.

Without King, the Civil Rights Movement would not have embraced nonviolence principles to the extent that it had. With this peaceful foundation, he led campaigns to secure democratic rights guaranteed by our constitution to extend to people of every racial identity. The ideals King derived from his Christian beliefs and from the teachings of Gandhi were passed onto his parishioners and other movement followers. They were imbued with ideals of discipline, love and respect. The accomplishments they achieved while overcoming their difficulties were monumental.

However, instead of celebrating and supporting those noble efforts to overcome our nation's plight, their courageous movement was mostly met by vicious cruelty that often turned violent and frequently led to the murder of innocent activists. The few Whites who joined in to participate or support the movement were not nearly as vocal as those who resisted their efforts. The majority of our white ancestors may have been against the violence, but they did little towards taking a stand to let their objections be known. Time after time, most Whites let these peaceful demonstrators get verbally and physically abused by mobs of racist citizens. And the police, that very institution ordained "to protect and to serve" would sometimes unleash vicious dogs on protestors or attack them with nightsticks. In Birmingham, the city leaders ordered the fire department to turn high-pressure water hoses on crowds that included children. Demonstrators were thrown in jail by the hundreds for having the audacity to assert their democratic rights. Simple privileges, such as eating with Whites at the same counters, drinking out of the same water fountains and enjoying the same seating precedence on busses were vehemently resisted.

But the movement kept their faith and stayed the course till the juxtaposition of hatred of the opposition against the backdrop of the loving campaign became more than that of the conscience of the white majority could tolerate. They saw that King and the peaceful activists were neither provoking the violence nor retaliating. Like Gandhi and those who embraced Satyagraha, they simply let themselves be the recipients of the brutality in order to expose the viciousness of their racist opponents.

It was a credit to our society that we could no longer sit in paralysis watching the attacks. Our conscience forced us to acknowledge the cruelty of our citizens and to take a stand against the unprovoked aggression. The federal government finally intervened and then created legislation that started a trickle of rights extending to people of color.

However, unlike most of their contemporary brothers and sisters of European descent, this movement found that no rights would ever be simply handed to them. They had to face many battles to receive these benefits. Each new effort of the movement was met with the same criticizing question "When will *they* ever be satisfied!?" This question was raised after slaves were freed, but later generations wanted an end to segregation and mistreatment. The question was raised again after segregation was overturned, but later generations wanted the right to vote and an end to racist laws. This question is raised even now that most unfair laws have been patched, but institutional racism continues to result in exclusion from so many parts of our society. How can anyone ever be satisfied as long as we are not all equally valued and respected?

We never proactively stepped up to the plate to extend these rights. Each one had to be pried from the resentful claws of the racists in our country as most moderates stood on the sidelines paralyzed into non-action. Laws are still changing because we continue to live in a society plagued by bigotry. The necessary healing of our country simply has not taken place. The multitudes of wounds were left unattended over these many generations. So as new loopholes are exploited, our legal system must do its best to shore up those gaps. This is the best we can do, until the root of the problem is resolved.

Yet, those who followed King and adopted his ideals always fought these battles with love through nonviolence. They were not simply interested in changing laws or in gaining rights; they wanted to unite people of all races. They wanted to help our country find a path to healing the root of our problem; our own tainted hearts and minds. They even extended their love to the racist, faithful that love was stronger than hate when coupled with Direct Action.

Through their efforts they made enormous gains for our whole society. We have historical proof of the power of such faith. We learned that change does not come easy, but that if your ideals are based on high moral principles, you will transform your life while impacting the lives of others.

Unfortunately, much of our country viewed their efforts with the narrow perspective that they were only working towards the advancement of colored people. Most could not comprehend that extending democracy to the lives of the oppressed would benefit the country as a whole. Fearful-disillusionment prevented the sharing of King's vision of uniting *all* people. The efforts to alleviate the symptoms of racism received the majority of the focus. With most of those battles accomplished, we hope to now breathe new life into the ideals of forming a Beloved Community.

Overwhelmed by Racism

We have so far only focused on two paths that have been followed for enabling large numbers of individuals to make progress in their life in overcoming racism: those subscribing to the ideology of the black Nationalists, rejecting the possibility of integration and the followers of nonviolence, promoting love and harmony through direct-action. Many others have found liberation through their religious pursuits. There are also those who have extraordinary inner strength and drive that helped them find their way out of hopelessness; those remarkable souls who defied all odds and were able to rise above the depths of poverty and despair on their own natural resources.

For all these cases, individuals have found measures of success in life, in spite of the barriers of racism. These exceptional examples unfortunately do not however lend proof that efforts to end racism or provide equal opportunity have succeeded. They are simply extraordinary stories of the ability of the human will in overcoming any obstacle. Apart from these multitudes, a number of families have proven to be much more vulnerable and have been unable to make it over the daunting hurdles. A large portion of minority communities is still suffering from the legacy of our racist past, losing the struggle against oppression. They are still excluded from opportunities that would make it reasonably possible to break free and they are often significantly affected by the stigma from persistent negative stereotypes.

Like the conceptual abused sibling, most people exposed to such problems will become overwhelmed and suffer substantial adverse effects. They will sometimes internalize these difficulties where it is turned inward into self-destruction. In other cases, their suffering is manifested in hatred or violence towards others. Because nothing was ever done to prevent this deterioration and no serious action is being taken to resolve it now, many of our cities continue to be plagued with ghettos riddled with crime, violence, drug and alcohol abuse as well as other social ills.

Furthermore, the consequence of this neglect is not isolated to people of color. It has affected our whole nation and continues to corrode our communities. We can no longer afford to look in the mirror and keep rationalizing that our society's dysfunction is none of our business; that the drowning members of our country hit hard by racism wound up stuck in their own quagmire. We are all suffering from these social ills, even if only indirectly. King observed that *injustice anywhere is a threat to justice everywhere.*

If we are ever going to heal, we are going to have to follow the example of those who have successfully overcome such maladies. We will need to take a deep look at ourselves for the truth and then change collectively in addition to the changes we make individually. The section entitled *Principles in Action,* which focuses on the solutions for the root of our problem, describes exactly how we can do that.

However, many remain skeptical that change will help them personally. They are unable to understand why adjustments are still necessary or how it is their responsibility. They may disagree with this assessment of our history or the severity of our present problems. We wish to stay clear from debate, but if you are interested in opening up to new perspectives, the next chapter gives further details of these issues, how we all contribute to or collaborate with systemic discrimination. With this expanded knowledge, we will be better armed in our efforts to identify and then counter the effects of racism.

Chapter 8: Institutional Racism

Racism in the United States

Below is the definition of racism as adopted by "Teaching / Learning Anti-Racism"…

> Racism is an institutionalized system of power. It encompasses a web of economic, political, social and cultural structures, actions and beliefs that systemize and ensure an unequal distribution of privilege, resources and power in favor of the dominant racial group and at the expense of all other racial groups. A system of subordination is thus created and perpetuated (Hilliard, 1992). Further, the outcome of individual, cultural, and institutional policies and actions, rather than the intent behind them, determines the presence of racism. Lack of intentionality or knowledge, in a given situation does not change objective consequences for people of color. While most White people believe there is no racism if there is no intent to judge by race, "from the perspective of the recipients of racism, the expressed intention is relatively unimportant in comparison with the results" (Stroup & Fleming, 1995, pg. 31)
> "Teaching / Learning Anti-Racism"; pg. 9

Thus, racism exists when the actions and policies of the individuals or institutions of the dominant racial group harm or deprive other racial groups. The *outcome*, not the *intent* of those actions and policies are the determining factor as to whether or not racism exists. It does not have to be mean-spirited.

This misperception that we only bare responsibility of harms done when harms are intended, is often shared by people suffering from maladies that land them in other 12-step programs. Members often come in the doors baffled by the seemingly unprovoked resentments and expressions of hurt feelings from their friends and family concerning their behavior. After all, "they didn't mean to do any harm." Their disillusion results in thoughts such as "I'm a good person. Why are they over-reacting?"

Institutional Racism

After going through the process of self-examination however, they become aware of the damaging impact of their lifestyle. They come to the realization that although they wanted to perceive themselves as good friends, family and community members, not wanting to cause harm, in reality their actions were frequently neglectful and selfish. Many are often heard expressing the realization, "I wanted everyone to judge me by my good intentions, but instead, I am judged by my actions."

The same is true with Whites with respect to nonwhite groups. Most of us certainly don't want to be perceived as racist. We may have good intentions, but if either our behavior or our inaction results in harm to other races, it is still racism. The below definition is from the book *Dismantling Racism: The continued challenge to white America*. Like the previous definition, this author makes a link to power.

> "Racism is clearly more than just prejudice or bigotry. Everyone is prejudiced, but not everyone is racist. To be prejudiced means to have opinions without knowing the facts and to hold onto those opinions, even after contrary facts are known. To be *racially* prejudiced means to have distorted opinions about people of other races. Racism goes beyond prejudice. It is backed up by power. Racism is the power to enforce one's prejudices. More simply stated, racism is power plus prejudice.
>
> All of us, white people and people of color are racially prejudiced. We have been taught, or have developed by ourselves, distorted and unsubstantiated opinions about people from other racial and ethnic backgrounds. And we don't give up these prejudices easily. Often, we vigorously resist alternative points of view that conflict with our distorted racial biases. However, serious and damaging as it surely is, prejudice or bigotry is still not the same as racism."

> ***Racial prejudice is transformed into racism when one racial group becomes so powerful and dominant, that it is able to control another group and to enforce the controlling group's biases.****

---

* Joseph Barndt, *"Dismantling Racism: The continued challenge to white America"*, (Augsburg Fortress, 1991), p. 28

The above definitions differentiate racism from the destructive, yet less damaging problems of prejudice or bigotry. *Racial-prejudice* is a mild, sometimes subconscious, unfavorable feeling or opinion of another race that is formed without logic or reason. *Bigotry* is a much stronger conscious intolerance of differing races, creeds, beliefs or opinions and at the extreme, results in hate. *Racial supremacy* is the belief that one race is superior to another, but is not necessarily coupled with hate.

By these definitions, anyone can be prejudiced, bigoted or even a supremacist, but in the United States, Whites hold the vast majority of power in all major institutions, so nonwhites are much less likely to be in a position that would give them the power to exercise their bigotry in the form of racism that would deprive others from access to resources. Bigotry is of course still a major factor in racism as well as a destructive force even when not coupled with power. All such maladies are rooted in corrosive fearful disillusionment.

Both of the above mentioned texts distinguish between overt and covert racism. Overt racism includes actions and policies that openly and intentionally maintain an advantage for Whites. Despite the various laws that have been enacted to avert racial injustices, the FBI documents thousands of incidents of hate crimes[1], while the EEOC receives tens of thousands of race discrimination charges each year[2]. The watchdog group *Southern Poverty Law Center*, which monitors hate-groups across the country, reports annual increases in the numbers of hate-groups, with the count reaching over 1000 in 2011.[3]

These groups represent the most outspoken of those of us who hold bigoted sentiments in our country. The racist actions of such groups are calculated and openly orchestrated. Covert racism, on the other hand, is much more subtle and frequently unintentional. However, the outcome is essentially the same in that it consistently results in Whites maintaining an unfair advantage over other racial groups.

---

[1] http://www.fbi.gov/ucr/hc2008/index.html

[2] http://www.eeoc.gov/eeoc/statistics/enforcement/charges.cfm

[3] http://www.splcenter.org/get-informed/hate-map

Evolution of Systemic Racism in our Institutions

Institutional racism is almost always covert. Institutions included are governmental, political, financial, judicial, corporate and religious. They include education, the military, law enforcement, the arts and media. Others are more social or cultural in nature such as religious groups, clubs, associations and sports leagues. They can be found in the private and public sectors. Most of the significant institutions still active today were originally founded in the early stages of the birth of our country.

Our society was founded on overt racist laws and practices. The charters, codes, rules, regulations and laws that governed its institutions included explicit statements that denied nonwhites equal access to our country's resources. The very foundation of most of today's institutions were erected and legally operated as openly racist entities for hundreds of years. Their cultures were established and evolved in this environment. The psychological mindsets that were produced became etched in the foundation of these institutions. Even though laws were enacted to address the exposed overt discriminatory practices, the fundamental elements that result in the "Good ol' boy" network continue to be an ongoing problem.

Looking at the makeup of most of these major institutions shows that the foundation, on which they were formed, still provides disproportionate benefits to white males over women and people of color.

[1] 2010 Employment demographics: http://www.bls.gov/cps/demographics.htm#race
[2] 2010 Income statistics: http://www.census.gov/prod/2011pubs/p60-239.pdf
[3] 2009 PEW Study on net worth: http://www.pewsocialtrends.org/2011/07/26/wealth-gaps-rise-to-record-highs-between-whites-blacks-hispanics/
[4] 2012 Education study: http://nces.ed.gov/pubs2012/2012045.pdf
[5] 2010 General population census: http://www.census.gov/prod/cen2010/briefs/c2010br-02.pdf; State plus Federal prison population: http://www.bjs.gov/content/pub/pdf/p10.pdf; Combined prison plus jails population: http://www.bjs.gov/content/pub/pdf/cpus10.pdf
[6] 2010 Poverty statistics: http://www.census.gov/prod/2011pubs/p60-239.pdf
[7] 2010 Employment statistics: http://www.bls.gov/cps/demographics.htm

Why do Caucasians hold disproportionately higher ranking positions of employment?[1] Why are average incomes significantly higher from year to year for Whites than for minorities?[2] Why is the net worth of Whites more than 10 times that of Blacks?[3] Why do nonwhite children consistently get poorer statistics in school than Whites?[4] Why are far more black males incarcerated than white males even with white men outnumbering black men almost six to one?[5] Why is it that 1 out of 4 Blacks are in poverty, when only one out of ten Whites are poor?[6] Why are only 8.7% of Whites unemployed compared to 16% of African-Americans?[7]

If you are a white supremacist, you have likely justified these disparities in your own mind by subscribing to the rhetoric that Whites are superior intellectually and morally. But if you have rejected such divisive notions, you may naturally be confused. These deficiencies absolutely contradict these two notions that you may hold: *a) All people are equal (morally, ethically and intellectually);* and *b) The institutions of our country are built on principles that provide equal opportunity and justice and do not discriminate based on race, gender, religion or class.* We certainly have laws that are meant to deter such discrimination, but these deficiencies suggest that one of these statements is false. If they were both true, our institutions would reflect a more accurate representation of all racial and gender groups.

If you are experiencing the quandary of this contradiction, you are faced with a tough choice: *a) accept that you believe in the tenet of white-male supremacy;* or *b) concede that minorities must still contend with barriers as the result of racism and sexism in our institutions.* This is the dilemma we must all confront. We must either all take a stand to resolve this conflict in our logical reasoning and in our conscience, or we can try to somehow rationalize or ignore this discrepancy. One very effective and seemingly innocent way to explain the disparities is through the phenomenon of *blaming the victim*. This is discussed in a section later in this chapter.

For those of us who clearly see the fallacy of the rhetoric of the notion of supremacy and have studied *institutional racism, victim blaming* and *white privilege*, the answer for the statistical disparities is just as clear but belies the assertions of the supremacist. Persistent gaps in opportunities as the result of exclusionary racist constructs are the undeniable cause. First, the resources of these lands were accumulated by white males starting with the migration of the first European settlers; frequently through barbaric means. Racist foundations that excluded minorities were then established for the institutions that were built around this country's wealth and power. By means of inheritance and social exclusion, other communities have been left behind with no way to catch up.

The well-intentioned laws that have since been put in place attempting to end the resulting injustices and promote equal opportunity were obviously not meant to address the underlying causes of bigotry. Subsequently, they have had little effect on preventing racist practices. This failure is in part due to intentional resistance, but a more fundamental problem exists that is less nefarious. These institutions are machines whose parts were cast in racist steel and whose construction has gone fundamentally unscathed. Overt racism is no longer needed for the perpetuation of their unfair outcomes. The nature of the beast has been established and without an awareness or concern for the unavoidable inequity of this environment, the practices and mindsets that make up their cultures will continue to improve at an unreasonably slow pace. Accelerating the momentum of change will require a concerted effort to increase our social interactions to strengthen unity and root out our own prejudices.

Earnest attempts to modify these structures, however, will not likely take place as long as general perception of the dominant white population is that "racism doesn't exist" or "we don't care because it's not our problem." Except for the rare victories by women and people of color, the result of such attitudes will be the continued unfair treatment of minorities. Without an adjustment in perceptions, nothing will likely induce the necessary sacrifice to share more resources outside the current power-structure. We have no laws, incentives or initiatives with sufficient sway to provide a true level playing field. How can we claim equal opportunity when our institutions don't have comparable representation? And as long as nonwhites and females are denied an equitable partnership and not equally valued, how can we claim they are not oppressed?

Community Segregation and Social Oppression

One facet of institutional racism that has a significant direct effect on every child, woman and man in this country is community segregation. Like all of our country's institutions, urban planning and housing development were established with overt racist practices such as "restrictive covenants" that forbade land purchasers from reselling property to nonwhites and "redlining", which put barriers between minorities and resources such as banking and insurance. When strong social pressures failed to prevent integration from taking place, these types of practices threw up more barriers. Although such discrimination has been outlawed, nothing has been done to reverse the effects. Combined with unaffordable housing and the simple insidiousness of bigotry, the result has been the racial separation of our communities.

As some minorities managed to establish an economic footing in spite of the gauntlet of obstacles, some opted to move out of ghettos and into decent housing. As they moved into white neighborhoods, bigotry overcame many of those communities resulting in "white-flight" which perpetuated the race polarization. Along with the exodus of the white families went the bulk of the economic resources that kept those neighborhoods alive. The tax base used by the local government to fund the infrastructure and aesthetics of those communities no longer got replenished. As a result, the neighborhoods wither on the vine as those resources run dry.*

Because of this, if you are nonwhite, the chances are much greater that you live in a low-income section of town that seems to be neglected by the local government. They may find your part of town is the ideal location for city dumps, factories, junk yards and every other eye sore and health hazard of your city.**

---

* Sample study linking White Flight and Urban Decay http://www.iwu.edu/economics/PPE18/2Haines.pdf

**Sample studies of industrial pollution disproportionately found in minority communities: http://www.nbcnews.com/id/10452037/ns/us_news-environment/t/minorities-suffer-most-industrial-pollution/;

http://www.yale.edu/ynhti/curriculum/units/1996/2/96.02.01.x.html

Institutional Racism

If you are white, you are more likely to live in a neighborhood with pleasant aesthetics, decent schools and no polluting industries. If you are fortunate enough to have the means to live in a nice new home in a thriving community, you are likely to live a fair distance from neighborhoods that include a substantial percentage of nonwhites.

Is this segregation occurring because minorities don't want to integrate with Caucasians? Although many Whites proclaim this to be the roadblock, historically it has primarily been Whites who have prevented integration. Or maybe the reason is because the minorities who are stuck in poverty don't have motivation to improve their conditions? Of course this is not the case. People of color have the same instinctive drives as Whites. They want to be accepted into healthy communities with good homes where they can raise their families, but the economic effect of racism and the prohibitive social structures created by the underlying bigotry makes this nearly impossible for too many.

Blaming the Victim

Blaming the victim refers to evasive tactics for avoiding responsibility for racism. They evolved out of studies trying to get a handle on our failure to establish effective solutions to alleviate our country's racial problems. The book "Blaming the Victim" (William Ryan, 1976) describes the phenomenon as justifying racial inequality by finding defects in its victims. These defects are then used to redirect blame for the plight of the oppressed back onto themselves, subtly justifying the sentiment that they are causing their own suffering.

Although entitlement programs of the 60s and 70s provided some vital financial relief through job placement and financial assistance, they were often inadequately funded or cut short. Furthermore, like Civil Rights legislation that only addressed the symptoms of overt racism, these programs did little to resolve the root causes.

Exacerbating disillusionment over the merits of these programs was the relentless resistance from factions apathetic to racial disparities as well as those who deemed them as futile causes. Stigmatized as socialism, support for such programs became political liabilities and those who championed them were labeled as radicals.

Along with our failures in the War on Poverty, our government lost most of its initiative in financing the battle to modify the foundations of institutional racism.

Sociologists during this period, studying the causes of the plight of impoverished Blacks, did their research in this contentious environment. Probably the most important of these studies was the White House originated "Moynihan report". Although well-intentioned, this study focused mostly on social ills such as underage pregnancy, illiteracy and substance abuse that disproportionately affected the poor. It concluded that absent fathers and the breakdown of the family structure were the primary factors preventing Blacks from escaping poverty. Although the family breakdown was reported to be initially caused by exposure to centuries of oppression and bigotry, the report concluded the resolution to these problems should make a priority of focusing on fixing the broken family through efforts of educating the parents.

Ryan believed the authors of these studies were truly compassionate for the plight of the victims, but he raised concerns that such conclusions put the burden of the resolution on the shoulders of the victims who are powerless to resolve the root causes. He argues that a dilemma was created for some of the social scientists, who were caught between two extreme internal drives. On one hand, they experienced great discomfort witnessing the extreme inequities of prosperity for Blacks compared to Whites. This seemed to undermine our country's proclaimed ideals of equal opportunity and justice. On the other hand was the possibly subconscious concern that attributing these disparities to defects in our institutions might necessitate radical, burdensome changes that would upset the status quo.

Ryan believed that the sociologists, needing a way to resolve these conflicts within themselves, subconsciously found the answer through diverting the focus of responsibility back on to the oppressed. Their process followed a pattern of searching for defects in impoverished families, tying those defects to their inability to function in society then concluding these defects are the cause for their failure to free themselves from abysmal living conditions.

Such sentiments spawned criticism directed towards the so called "faltering Negro family." How could little black children do well in school when their families don't provide adequate stimulation such as newspapers or travel? How can a black boy become a man when his father is likely to not even be present? What chance does he have from being drawn into criminal activity in his crumbling neighborhoods? How can young girls succeed in life when they are having babies while they are no more than children themselves? With often absent fathers and working mothers, how can these children learn to articulate their thoughts and feelings if their family isn't there to speak with them?

Because oppression was cited as the initial cause leading to the family breakdown, this marked an improvement from the overt bigotry that disseminated genetic-inferiority as the reason for their problems. The more palatable assertion now was that behavioral and environmental factors rendered many Blacks scarred from childhood and hopelessly incapable of progressing. However, this seemingly positive shift still stigmatizes the victims, diverts attention away from the source of the problem and hampers the progress of social change.

Concerns were also raised that the seemingly benign labels that sprang up through this research such as "cultural deprivation," "socially deprived," "stuck in the cycle of poverty," and "inner-city child" sometimes caused further distortions in public perceptions. They seemed to become code-phrases that inferred hopeless psychological damage; broad-brush stereotypes that further stigmatized the oppressed.

Because they imply we are powerless to effect a change, guilt reduced absolution of responsibility now became possible. The destructive result produced by this perception is a reduction in efforts by the professionals who were empowered to make a difference. Why would schoolteachers work to address teaching issues if they are convinced the children aren't capable of learning? Why would members of congress waste resources on perceived futile causes?

These studies failed to raise questions for current problems born and now perpetuated through racism. How can children be expected to thrive in dilapidated and depressing buildings; outdated and worn out text books; over-crowded classrooms; sometimes frightened, bigoted and callous faculty; irrelevant curriculum and distorted history books? What can we really expect of families that are under the crushing pressure of bigotry, fear and disrespect from business owners, discrimination in housing and banking, exclusion from resources, opportunities and societal acceptance so freely exchanged within the confines of white communities?

With the distortion that racism's victims are causing their own suffering, the oppressed are chastised and made to feel guilty for problems caused by the transgressions of our country.

When African-Americans do verbally protest the system, pointing out racist practices, they are accused of "playing the race card" or "playing the victim." The term victim can dredge up a certain antipathy in some who believe that this status is abused, and that it is too often used to avoid personal responsibility. Most in our society who hold this sentiment will certainly agree that slaves were victims and that those exposed to Jim Crow laws too, were oppressed; but many have closed their minds to the possibility that those parts of our history have any bearing on the disparities of today. However, when you consider the effects of community segregation and social exclusion, connecting the dots to the imbalance of opportunity becomes clear.

A victim is a person who suffers from the destructive or injurious actions of another. As long as racism is prevalent in our society, those who are hurt by it are indeed victims. But as the result of this stigma, the casualties of these injustices are frequently denied compassionate support that can help them overcome the injury. They are shamed into stifling their protests and processing their pain. Michael Eric Dyson discusses this tendency in his book *Debating Race* (2007) along with contentious exchanges with others about several race-related issues. Here are some of his observations on obstacles that prevent Blacks from effectively processing their pain brought on by oppression. First are perception problems within the black community:

> "And let's not discount the black community's taboo on seeking therapy and strengthening our mental health." *p. 277*

> "For too many folks-and let's not lie, in the broader culture as well- therapy means that you are weak or that you're not sufficiently spiritual." *p. 277*

Institutional Racism

> "Black men are often left in tiny spaces to negotiate our psychic pain. That's why our suffering often opens up as wounds in the public for the world to see. We don't get much private therapy and relief from agony. We don't often turn to another brother to seek counsel and wisdom and direction. There are few spaces for everyday black men to do that." *p. 271*

Speaking directly about the shame placed on African-Americans for speaking out against racism:

> "You know, the reliance upon the language of victimization assumes that black people are not victims. So we stigmatize the notion of victimhood for those who are actually victims." *p. 305*

> "So those who have been literally victimized by the forces of oppression are now re-victimized because they're denied access to the very language that could express the horror and the tragedy of what has occurred to them." *p. 305*

> "…the advocates for the poor are barely as loud and abrasive as those who are willing to stigmatize them and those who defend the interests of the dominant society." *p. 303*

In his book, "Race Matters", Cornel West discusses various aspects of institutional racism, race relations, economics and politics. West touches upon concepts related to victim blaming and its effects on all communities. Below is an observation concerning an oppressive pecking-order.

> "In white America, cultural conservatism takes the form of a chronic racism, sexism, and homophobia. Hence, only certain kinds of black people deserve high positions, that is, those who accept the rules of the game played by white America. In black America, cultural conservatism takes the form of an inchoate xenophobia (fear or hatred of foreigners or strangers), systemic sexism, and homophobia. Like all conservatisms rooted in a quest for order, the pervasive disorder in white and, especially, black America fans and fuels the channeling of rage towards the most

> vulnerable and degraded members of the community. For white America, this means primarily scapegoating black people, women, gay men and lesbians. For black America, this means principally attacking black women and black gay men and lesbians."
>
> *"Race Matters"; p. 27*

We are all guilty of this scapegoating to some extent. Even some who are the victims of bigotry are ironically inclined to judge those they perceive to be lower in the pecking order. To resolve such problems, Cornell West presents guidelines that seem to speak directly to our organization:

> "Nihilism is not overcome by arguments or analyses; it is tamed by love and care. Any disease of the soul must be conquered by a turning of one's soul. This turning is done through one's own affirmation of one's worth; an affirmation fueled by concern of others. A love ethic must be at the center of a politics of conversion."
> *"Race Matters"; p. 19*

To recap, blaming the victim creates a diversion from addressing symptoms of racism by twisting the value of personal responsibility. Of course, both Whites and people of color must embrace this value. For practically every problem in our lives that involves others, we should always look at our own part. This value challenges *me* to look inside *myself* to determine my role and responsibility regardless of your part or who contributed the most to the problem. I should only focus on cleaning my side of the street instead of worrying about yours. It implies that me focusing on you is not only irresponsible, it blocks me from growing, since I am making my change contingent on your change, or simply ignoring my part altogether. Blaming the victim allows us to cunningly twist this ideal by criticizing others for not doing their part while we ignore our role. This distortion is the antithesis of this value while purporting to be in direct alignment with it.

We must all transform individually to resolve these problems. This will require us to change ourselves and to adopt the love-ethic that West mentions in order to address the root of the problem. Kennedy, Reagan and others advocated this level of responsibility. Reagan believed in grass roots organizations resolving social problems and removing reliance upon the government. Kennedy challenged us in his directive, "Ask not what your country can do for you; ask what you can do for your country." Imagine the possibilities we can achieve with a groundswell of individuals coming together willing to sacrifice in service for our fellow man. This is the true spirit of personal responsibility.

White Privilege: Racism by Proxy

The term "white privilege" names the phenomenon that gives Whites advantages over people of color, simply by virtue the color of their skin. They are the benefits all Whites receive as the result of racism. These may include special access to resources, exemptions from various burdens, or immunity from certain consequences. They are rights not made available to nonwhites.

If we are going to perceive ourselves as a just society with equal opportunity, we must operate evenhandedly and distribute benefits fairly. As a result, they no longer become advantages exclusive to Whites, but resources, protections, security and support in which everyone can prosper. In her book entitled *White privilege*, the author, Paula Rothenberg states:

> "*White privilege is the other side of racism*. Unless we name it, we are in danger of wallowing in guilt or moral outrage with no idea of how to move beyond them. It is often easier to deplore racism and its affects than to take responsibility for the privileges some of us receive as a result of it. By choosing to look at white privilege, we gain an understanding of who benefits from racism and how they do so. Once we understand how white privilege operates, we can take steps to dismantle it on both a personal and institutional level."
>
> Rothenberg , *White Privilege*, p. 1

Unity Initiative

Others of diverse backgrounds contributing to this book discuss their perception of the several ways in which Whites benefit. Most are very subtle, such as "being White means not having to think about it." Below are more of the listed examples.

1. If I should need to move, I can be pretty sure of renting or purchasing housing in an area which I can afford and in which I would want to live.
2. I can be pretty sure that my neighbors in such a location will be neutral or pleasant to me.
3. I can go shopping alone most of the time, pretty well assured that I will not be followed, harassed [or viewed with suspicion].
4. When I am told about our national heritage or about "civilization" I am shown that people of my color made it what it is.
5. I can be sure that my children will be given curricular materials that testify to the existence [and accomplishments] of their race.
6. Whether I use checks, credit cards or cash, I can count on my skin color not to work against the appearance of my financial reliability.
7. I can arrange to protect my children most of the time from people who might not like them.
8. I can speak in public to a powerful male group without putting my race on trial.
9. I can do well in a challenging situation without being called a credit to my race.
10. I can criticize our government and talk about how much I fear its policies and behavior without being seen as a cultural outsider.
11. I can be pretty sure that if I ask to speak to the "person in charge", I will be facing a person of my own race.
12. If a traffic cop pulls me over or if the IRS audits my tax return, I can be sure I haven't been singled out because of my race.
13. I can go home from most meetings of organizations I belong to feeling somewhat tied in, rather than isolated, out-of-place, outnumbered, unheard, held at a distance, or feared.
14. I can take a job with an affirmative action employer without having co-workers on the job suspect that I got it because of my race.
15. I can choose public accommodation without fearing that people of my race cannot get in or will be mistreated in the place I have chosen.
16. I can be sure that if I need legal or medical help my race will not work against me.

Rothenberg, *White Privilege,* p. 110, 111

Institutional Racism

Being the beneficiary of such privileges provides subconscious psychological nutrition needed to function and succeed while being deprived of such normalcy can create psychological barriers. They allow us to feel like we belong; that we are part of the system; part of this country and its institutions. Without this level of acceptance, we are less likely to feel respected or included.

Caucasians' ideas and feelings have historically been more quickly acknowledged and validated by our society's leaders. They are granted the psychological capital that provides the motivation, energy and confidence to carry on from day to day, to be productive and to succeed in life.

White privilege and institutional racism has the result of all Whites being racists by proxy. Eldridge Cleaver stated: "if you're not part of the solution, you are part of the problem." But even if strongly opposed to racism and bigotry, most Caucasians are unable to escape the stigma of being the beneficiary of unfair privileges. All Whites bare responsibility for its perpetuation as well as finding solutions for leveling the playing field.

White privilege sets up an environment as if all Caucasians are part of a family of organized crime, but don't necessarily participate directly in criminal activity. The wife and children may perceive themselves as being innocent, but they directly benefit from a corrupt system. They are the beneficiaries of ill-gained prosperity. The criminals may try to protect their loved one's innocence by shielding them from the knowledge of the origins of their income or the means for their comfortable lives, but the family most likely knows the dark secret.

The children are victims in that their innocence is taken away from them through their assimilation into the corrupt system. Fear, greed or simple complacency keeps them in line as willing accomplices. Protesting the immorality of the injustices or showing sympathy for the victims will inevitably get them ostracized.

Having not been educated on the unjust means for acquiring the wealth, descendants will naively inherit ill-gained assets. But regardless of the number of hands these riches pass through over the generations, there will always be a shadow over the integrity of the estate and the uncorrected injustice, in which the descendants of the victims must continue to suffer.

Although many signs make clear that racist institutions continue to operate in favor of Caucasians, the beneficiaries may still find ways to deceive themselves about their innocence by denying they have control. But some institutions and personal practices are not so easily dismissed. For example, whereas white privilege usually comes to Caucasians automatically without any action on their part, the community segregation described earlier is one area where the vast majority of white homeowners actively participate. Most Caucasians are directly responsible for some level of collaboration here. Whites are not forced to live or socialize in homogeneous communities. We may not consciously decide to live apart from people of other races, but we are not oblivious to it either.

This is a very visible facet of our society, yet we may give little thought to the effects it has had on distorting our perceptions and the role it has played in impeding equal opportunity. What measures have we taken to include exposure of other cultures into our lives in order to counter stereotypes? If we are to be honest, most would have to admit we can see these divisions, but have rarely "crossed the tracks" to reach out our hand or opened our homes to others of diverse groups. To ease our conscience and absolve ourselves of further responsibility, we may have contributed financial support to charities or organizations trying to address some of the symptoms of racism, but what have we done to resolve problems within ourselves?

Between community segregation and racial polarization, our society is largely devoid of dialogue between diverse groups. Because of high levels of fear and mistrust, we generally avoid addressing racial issues in most public forums. Although some corporations, institutions and organizations do foster gatherings of diverse cultures to provide these positive experiences, such assemblies are rare. Multiplying such activities will help us cross cultural boundaries to increase social unity.

An example of such an effort was the collaboration of two professors, one Black and one White, who teamed up for many years instructing a college-level anti-racism course. They worked to directly tackle these issues and educate others about racism and white privilege along with effective methods for overcoming these maladies. They shared their observations and experiences in the book *Teaching / Learning Anti-Racism*.

The expected tension that many may fear when considering taking part in public discussions on racism came to the surface in various forms in the behavior of their students. With each new semester, the instructors would observe anger in a few of the people of color while many of their White classmates were on the defense from the outset. Their defensive approach was to avert any responsibility by focusing solely on the negative social symptoms of racism's victims. They initially disregarded the impact of bigotry and would attempt to give advice for changing the behavior of minority groups. When their advice was rejected, they became hurt and confused, but time and education brought about clear understanding of the issues being faced. Once they examined the origins of the problems, they often became aware of their own contributions to institutional racism and desired to work to change those behaviors.

Part of the course requirement was to take *direct action* in some way to combat community racism. As all the students of every race continued down this path, they sometimes transformed into what the authors called "anti-racists"; those who continually take action to dismantle racism. At the conclusion of the class, many expressed a sadness to see it come to an end when they were just making a breakthrough of lifelong misperceptions. They wished for a united group to continue their efforts for social change and personal healing.

For those looking for this experience of personal involvement, we hope that after reading this book you find yourself inspired to take action. We invite you to walk with us on our journey by joining this fellowship, taking the steps to incorporate the suggested principles in your life, and getting involved in the initiative to unite our society. Together we can alleviate bigotry. Building this environment will allow each of us to experience the transformation made by the anti-racism students where each individual is able to focus on his or her own personal growth.

The first step in this journey will be examining ourselves for our own psychological barriers. This will then be followed up with the action required for overcoming these hurdles. Once we have worked through the steps and incorporated these values in our daily actions, we will be able to lead by example. This kind of humility will be a very difficult adjustment for many of us, but when transformed by these principles, we will find great peace and self-respect in the confidence that we are acting with the right motives.

After we all go through our house cleaning process and raise our awareness on racism, sexism and other manifestations of prejudice, we hope to build trust in each other through a better understanding of ourselves as well as a clearer perspective of our relationship with the world around us. Fellowships will be built that will foster frank and honest discussions. These dialogs will mostly be cordial, but some will necessarily be specifically structured to venture below the surface of our consciousness. Such discussions will certainly have an element of risk as we face highly impassioned and contradicting beliefs and perceptions. In the process, our innermost thoughts and feelings will be exposed. For most, this will mean giving up our innocence of our claim to being a non-bigot as our resentments, frustrations and criticisms surface.

Obviously, this means we may not always have the luxury of feeling safe. On the contrary, we will courageously be exposing ourselves to each other's pain. Our fears, resentments and disillusionments will be shared openly with fellow-members. But we will face these difficulties faithfully and with love, patience and tolerance. Honor will be extended to those who allow themselves to be put through the fire to expose their distortions then cleanse themselves of their shortcomings. We will not let fear keep us from accomplishing what we are set out to do, which is to clear our vision and to free our heart.

The payoff for this difficult journey starts with the peace, knowing we are doing our part in amending the past. Respect for ourselves and for our fellows will increase. Intimacy in relationships will grow stronger. We will be driving towards Dr. Martin Luther King, Jr.'s vision for uniting communities where trust and compassion are as natural with diverse others as they are with members of our own families. When this happens, the true benefits of integration will come to fruition. In these communities, social and economic opportunity should rise simply by virtue of proximity.

Our current segregation of communities prevents resources from crossing racial boundaries resulting in an economic embargo. This prevents possibilities of spurring new growth as envisioned by President Ronald Reagan's trickle-down economics theory. Reagan was also admired for his persistence in exposing, then challenging symbols of the dictatorship erected by the Soviet Union. To capitalize on his courageous quote, let's "tear down this wall!"

Then and now, walls of oppression are hurting our brothers and sisters. At that time they were physical barriers in Germany, but we have been ignoring the walls right here in our own back yard.

Excluded communities continue to decay, causing a drain on tax dollars. We can only speculate at the overall effects of addressing these social issues, but it will hopefully have the added benefit of leading to a stimulation of our economy. Providing sufficient opportunity along with community solidarity could possibly revitalize hemorrhaging neighborhoods, increasing productivity while restoring the tax base. We would be doing all this at no perceived expense to any other race. Ideally, instead of having to rely upon unpopular legislation like affirmative action to force a more equitable sharing of our resources, we will be doing it as a natural exchange across our communities.

We are a very long way from this level of healing, but we can imagine that a society with this structure could someday render quota-based programs obsolete. It is up to us.

Privilege of Class and Proximity

One of the most obvious and direct effects of Institutional Racism is the exclusion of employment opportunities and sales in everyday commerce exchange. Proximity is a major factor in the ability to take advantage of such opportunities. A large percentage of jobs and other economic resources are exchanged outside of public view. So often do individuals, store owners and their employees, corporate employees, home owners and others looking for help, naturally offer employment, home repair projects, service type jobs for businesses and individuals (everything from cleaning, to plumbing or painting, to remodeling, to book keeping or taxes), and other such work to their friends and family. Naturally, those looking to hire someone, whether for a fulltime job or a one day home repair project, will want to spend the least amount of time and energy to find someone to do the work.

Unity Initiative

Our method for seeking help will likely follow a pattern similar to this:

1. We will seek out a family member who is willing and able to do the job.
2. Next, the offer or request for referrals will be made available to friends.
3. Failing this, we will turn to local businesses in our community.
4. As a last resort, we will look in outside communities.

Companies often follow a similar process:

1. First they will look for a good fit for the position within their department.
2. They will then ask the employees of their department if they know of anyone who is qualified for the job.
3. Next, they may post the job on an internal bulletin board, only visible by company employees, to give them a chance to take advantage of the offer before they post it to the general public.
4. If no one can be found internally, they will seek help externally. At this point, qualified persons outside of the company can be offered the position.

Obviously, these are only generalities. Other hiring practices exist individually and institutionally, but this typical pattern for filling jobs illustrates the problems being faced by those who are denied access to these resources.

For both the case of the individual looking for help with a specific task and that of the business looking to fill a job or contract, a system of opportunity is created that can be visualized in the below diagram of concentric circles.

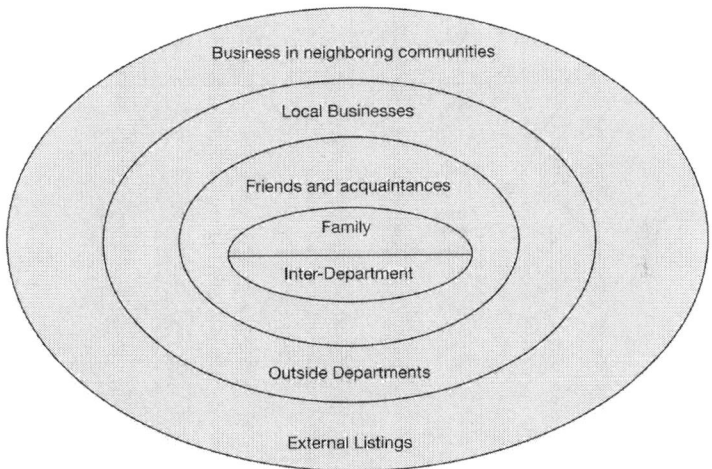

This cultural phenomenon is not race-centric but is the natural practice of all communities. The chance for receiving offers increases dramatically the closer we are to the inner circle. Those closer to the center have privileges not available to those in the outer circles, giving them a competing advantage. The old adage *"It's not what you know, but who you know"* rings true when you consider this phenomenon. Professional and social networking greatly improves proximity to the center, therefore increasing access to such offers.

Today however, most such networking takes place in homogeneous groups. Because of the division in our communities combined with these trading and job-filling practices, resources of the relatively affluent white communities are prevented from being equitably shared.

Another level of proximity exists when factoring in the previously discussed community segregation with class segregation. In the below diagram, the sets of concentric circles represent various

Unity Initiative

racial communities. The dominant white group is represented on the bottom right. Within each segregated community, the population is further segregated by class.

The darker circles towards the center represent the wealthy neighborhoods while the lighter outer circles are the poorer sub-communities. The wealthier neighborhoods will generally control the flow of commerce. The closer one is to the communities doling out these opportunities, the more likely they will come in contact with those seeking help with projects or filling jobs. Even when prejudice is not a factor, close proximity to those who control the resources greatly increases the chance of participating in available opportunities.

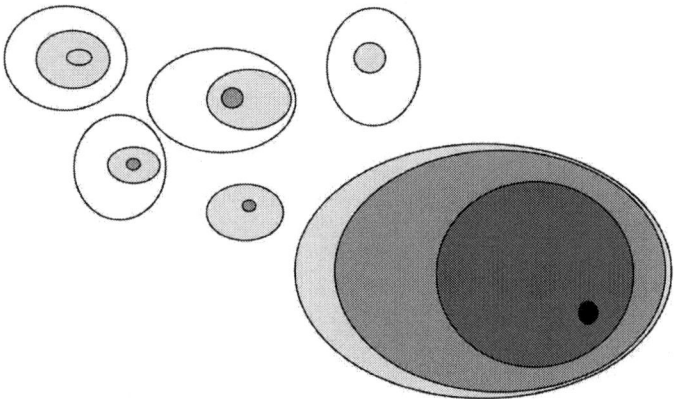

The combination of these two social constructs of racial and class segregation contributes to the perpetuation of institutional racism. With Whites controlling the vast majority of the economic power, this segregation ensures those resources continue to be recycled within these groups. The likelihood of participating, versus being excluded from commerce opportunities, is primarily a function of race and class-privilege plus proximity. Sex, age, ethnicity and religion all factor in as well, but are not directly addressed by this model. There is nothing illegal about these practices, and although prejudice obviously plays a role, it is not necessarily overtly racist. Much of this is because of our natural behavior combined with the historical racist development of our communities that are now largely self-perpetuating in their segregated form.

Regardless of the lack of intent to cause harm, the behavior patterns in these social structures consistently results in white privilege that is received to the detriment of all other races, reinforcing institutionalized exclusion. Through efforts to unite with diverse groups, we expand our horizons in our social networks. Over time, this will potentially lead to chipping away at institutional racism by increasing equitable access to opportunity for all.

Healthcare

Various studies have exposed disparities in healthcare between Whites and people of color.* To a large extent, many of these gaps are simply an extension of problems already discussed. Of course, better economic privileges will enable Caucasians access to healthcare resources by virtue of affordability. Because insurance is most frequently tied to employment** and because Whites are more likely to be employed in companies that provide such benefits, they have a greater chance of receiving health coverage.

In March of 2010, the *Patient Protection and Affordable Care Act* was signed into law in an attempt to ameliorate these disparities. Although every aspect of the bill has been hotly debated, stirring much controversy, proponents hope this legislation will shore up gaps in healthcare benefits by greatly expanding coverage amongst the poor. Regardless of the impact this bold act will have on our nation's healthcare problems, it demonstrates our widespread desire to make an effort to improve on our current insufficient policies.

Apart from the financial side of healthcare issues, race becomes an issue when distortions brought on by stereotypes produce prejudice and mistrust. When this is the case, people of color can be treated differently. The relationships between the service provider and patient are likely to be adversely affected. Studies have shown that these stereotypes have resulted in unequal treatment practices. They have caused barriers to access to physicians, healthcare facilities and other resources. Expanding awareness of such disparities in all our institutions is needed since we will not strive for improvement if we are not conscious of the problem.

* Disparities in health care: http://content.healthaffairs.org/content/24/2/398.full
**Health-coverage tied to employment: http://www.healthpaconline.net/health-care-statistics-in-the-unitedstates.htm; Disparities in health coverage: http://www.cdc.gov/Features/dsHealthInsurance/

Institutional Racism Conclusion

Our great country continues to move forward from the wounds of our racist pass, yet there is no denying that prejudice continues to inhibit the rate of our progress. It permeates every aspect of our lives. These problems are still prevalent in all of our major institutions. They continue to cause suffering to not only the immediate victims, but to those of us who recognize we all bear some level of responsibility for these inequities. Many share a sense of regret that we have allowed injustices to go on for so long without an official acknowledgement of harm done, let alone an effort to make amends.

As a civil society, we must surely continue to examine the symptoms of racism and explore solutions for making equal opportunity a reality. This will include continuing our efforts to expose then patch loopholes in our legal system that enables racist practices. We will need to continue setting policies in the institutions of government, law enforcement, military, healthcare, finance and education to ensure they don't continue to favor the dominant group at the detriment of others.

However, as important as these concerns are, they only address the symptoms of the problem. The true issues lie within us as individuals. *More important than anything else that we do in combating racism are the efforts we take to personally identify our own shortcomings at the root of our prejudices, take steps to have them removed, and take action to build relationships with people of diverse groups.* A true self-examination should carry on for a lifetime, but we can start with an intense directed self-survey as part of our step-work as described in the next section. Once we go through this exercise of self-analysis to discover our most glaring weaknesses, we can get started on cleaning up the shortcomings we expose.

While we are taking steps towards self-improvement, we will also take the initial steps for chipping away at our prejudices. The most effective way of doing this is to break down our social barriers and start participating in activities with diverse groups and individuals. These suggestions require rigorous action. Healing takes time, but if we put our best foot forward, positive results will follow. Our personal lives will become more joyful, our hearts will be freed from fear, and our unified fellowship will provide a healing center for others who desire to be liberated from their own biases.

SECTION III:
Principles in Action

Chapter 9: Getting Started

HOW

In the first section of this book, we looked at the principles that we wish to adopt for our organization and which we have suggested for the individual. We discussed the need for Direct Action, which is simply putting these principles to practical use. We also listed some of the humility-based personality attributes we can develop in our own lives to align with these precepts. By individually putting these ideals to practice, we will lay the foundation for a unified community. Only in the application of these principles in the actions of our daily activities will we begin to experience the true meaning of these values. The suggested disciplines develop the desired humility attributes, allowing us to move in the direction of the prescribed ideals. To start on this journey we must initially adopt the principles of *honesty, open-mindedness and willingness* (HOW).

We can first ask ourselves, "Can I be *honest* with myself and others in self-appraisal?" We can follow that up with the question, "Can I stay *open-minded* to the experiences and suggestions of those who apply these disciplines in their lives?" And finally, "Am I now ready to change? Am I *willing* to take action to incorporate these principles into my life, letting them become a part of who I am?" If you have answered 'yes' to these questions, then you are ready to move on to the program of action.

Sponsorship

The first suggested action on your journey is to get a sponsor. This is recommended before starting the steps or taking any other action. *A sponsor primarily acts as a mentor to guide you through the steps and help you incorporate the principles into your life.*

Getting Started

Sponsors can provide direction for working the steps, answer questions about problems they have successfully resolved, and support you in making tough decisions when facing personal difficulties. All this implies they should be someone with the following qualities:

- Successfully worked the step with which you are ready to take.
- Practices the principles in their own life.
- Currently involved in the fellowship.
- Humble, positive and constructive.
- Trustworthy and nonjudgmental.
- "Has what you want" (Peace of mind? Humility? Compassion?)
- Has the time to make the necessary commitment of sponsorship.

Those who partake in sponsorship receive no material compensation. They do it as part of the 12th step in the spirit of the principle of service.

Ideally we will be entirely ready to follow all recommendations from this mentor, but they will inevitably make suggestions that we will be reluctant to take. That is expected since we are letting them guide us on a new journey in unfamiliar territory. For this reason, we must find someone we *fully* trust and respect. As we go to meetings and get involved in the fellowship, we look for sponsors by observing fellow members and searching out those who exemplify the attributes we wish for ourselves. We then simply ask them if they will take us through the steps. The opportunity to work with others in a sponsorship role is a privilege, but we may ask a potential candidate who is incapable or unavailable. In these cases, we simply keep looking until we find someone who can act as our guide.

When you do settle on someone with whom you can place your confidence, listen to them. Take action. Commit to working the steps. This is one area where willingness is indispensable. You are fully responsible for your own growth, but to the extent you avoid taking action, the longer you delay your progress, and the more difficult it becomes for your sponsor to assist you. So make their job in helping you easier by being rigorous in your efforts. You will not regret it.

Each might approach the steps at a slightly different angle, and the action they suggest may vary, but here are some general suggestions to consider for working with your sponsor.

- ✓ Talk regularly and start building a relationship.
- ✓ Discuss your daily experiences during your talks (step 10).
- ✓ Share what efforts you have made to 1) Clean house; 2) grow spiritually; 3) serve others; 4) unite with diverse groups or others in our fellowship. *These four actions are the program in a nutshell.*
- ✓ Take their suggestions if in alignment with the UI principles.
- ✓ Emulate your sponsor. Don't put them on a pedestal to use that as an excuse for not following their example.
- ✓ Take full responsibility for your step-work. If it turns out your sponsor is not available to bring you through the steps in a timely manor, find someone else to work with you.
- ✓ Work together to help others. Combining your efforts will increase your effectiveness.

The tenth step will be discussed in more detail later, but you can use this and subsequent checklists as part of your daily, weekly or other periodic self-examination.

Chapter 10: Self-Assessment

Examining Our Egotism

In today's society filled with abundance and opportunity, the vast majority of families and individuals can earnestly report that they lead honest and productive lives, in which they find great satisfaction. They have incorporated into their daily practices, strong values passed down from previous generations. Through hard work, honest living and respect for others, they have found self-respect, peace and contentment.

On the other hand, most would also have to admit we are not perfect. Even though we may be happy, we all have flaws that prevent us from reaching our full potential. In some cases our shortcomings block us from living joyful lives filled with gratitude. For others, these shortcomings, often coupled with difficult struggles in life, have caused much emotional and psychological turmoil. At the extreme, some have suffered enormous amounts of pain by their defects and they have caused harm to others by their selfish behavior.

We all fall somewhere on this spectrum between pure perfection and being completely overrun by character-defects. To be effective in the efforts of our own growth we must be fully aware of the internal battle between our true selves and our ego and the extent egotism has crept into our lives.

At the core of every human is a being of purity; pure love, pure truth, pure compassion. This is our true self, free of egotism. This is the state of our minds and hearts at our birth. At this purest level of humanity we are all equal and invaluable. Although this part of our being always remains intact, our egotism can develop into what sometimes seems like an entirely separate personality, masking our altruistic self. While our pure self is strengthened by selfless ideals, inner peace and love, our ego is primarily driven by pleasure through external stimuli.

The drives of our ego and of our altruistic selves are often at odds with each other. It is often the case that for one to be satisfied, the other must be deprived. Our pure-self desires healthy relationships, strong family ties, stability and peace of mind, as well as happiness for others, while our ego craves excitement and pleasure, regardless of the consequences. While our ego will try to achieve this through material possessions, power and external stimulation, our pure self seeks truth, love and self-respect. With such incompatible drives, we are often ultimately faced with choosing between feeding our ego or our humility at the expense of the other. In order to nurture one side of our personality, the drives of the other must be sacrificed. This dilemma creates an internal civil war, which pulls us in the opposite directions of fulfilling selfless needs versus selfish desires.

If we have been taught the skill-set to strengthen our inner-self, our ego can be kept in check without becoming a big liability. But if we don't have or don't exercise these tools, our ego can grow into a destructive force that controls our lives. When we are subjugated by our ego, we are often driven to behaviors that can harm ourselves and others. We can possibly be brought down to the lowest depths of human existence. But no one is irredeemable. No matter what we have done in our past, a human being stripped of ego, lust, greed, envy and hate; free from all other negative attributes, is left with pure love and truth. These are fundamental concepts in which we can base our values that will guide our action and our relationships.

In the idealized state of consciousness of our perfect pure selves, we are virtually immune to emotional pain and suffering. There is no anger, jealousy, impatience, resentment, self-pity, hurt feelings or obsessive longing for external pleasures to relieve ourselves from a mundane or painful existence. At this level of purity we are absolutely free and at peace. We are content with life. We love others unconditionally as our equals and recognize their true value. We are selfless and want the happiness for all others that we have found for ourselves.

How can we put this ideal of perfection into practical use in our own lives? Although this perfect state may never be fully realized, the closer we get, the happier we become. To begin our journey towards that direction, we start off by stripping away as much of our accumulated debris of distortion and fear as we can, in order to expose our true pure selves. We then present this side of ourselves in all of our relationships. We become respectful and nurturing. We make an effort to accept the human shortcomings in others, looking for their positive attributes and loving them unconditionally.

Self-Assessment

To the extent that we can do this, we will receive an automatic benefit of freedom and joy by experiencing the purity of love and truth at our core being.

Just as these benefits are automatically received along the way of purifying our lives, there are inherent consequences when we pollute our being while living under the illusion that happiness is solely obtained through externally derived pleasures. With this misconception we live a life in constant search of external stimulation through over-indulgence of money, sex, food, drugs, alcohol, power, prestige and so on, in order to produce a feeling of euphoria so that we can simulate happiness. But because these indulgences do not provide long-term relief, our ego must soon seek out the next source of pleasure to sustain this euphoria. Its thirst is unquenchable. As the pleasure fades, the sense of longing returns and we feel like a hole is growing inside of us that we just cannot fill. We are never satisfied. As time goes on, we become more discontented with life and our dependencies grow for increased external stimuli for easing the pain and quieting the incessant clatter of our mind.

Without an understanding of what is happening to us and without healthy practices in our lives, our ego will get so out of control that chasing this euphoria becomes of utmost importance. We can become trapped in a vicious cycle of relieving our pain with behaviors that inevitably lead to more pain. Our ego separates further and further from our altruistic self. Our disappointments, fears, resentment and depression, continue to grow and our ego keeps convincing us that we will never be happy as long as we are deprived of external pleasures. In this state, we eventually lose touch with reality.

Early signs of these problems can appear as obsessive behavior in school, work, physical fitness or relationships. If we have a pleasurable experience, our ego can latch on to it and try to reproduce that feeling. We can be deceived by the notion: "If something makes us feel good, twice as much will make us feel twice as good." We might indulge in shopping therapy, incessantly spending money faster than we earn our income. We may become perfectionists or workaholics or become convinced that we'll never be happy until we find a relationship. How many of us look for the mythical "perfect mate" to fulfill our ego's unrealistic expectations?

Some of us will crave constant attention or try to become controlling and dominate in business, family and romance. We may start gambling on stocks or slot machines as we obsess over gaining enough wealth to quench our ego's nagging desires of greed. When these fail us, we might look for relief through chemistry; drinking more alcohol or taking pills to overcome anxieties or to sustain pleasure. As we pursue these stimuli, our ego becomes more obsessed. Simply fantasizing about them gives us a small taste of that exhilaration which causes our fixation to grow further still.

The more fixated we become, the more we surrender to our ego and the further we can drift from reality. The more insane we grow, the harder it becomes to control our behavior and to stick to our morals as we allow our ego to feed unabated. In this apathetic state, we may take emotional, physical or financial advantage of people who are vulnerable. Even in cases where another initiated the incident and we are able to rationalize that they are willing victims knowing what they were getting into, deep inside we know they are lost like us and we are contributing to another's destruction for our own selfish motives.

We are likely to hurt others if they get in the way of our ego's pursuits. We may indulge in behaviors that we had previously sworn we would never do. We are sickened by our own selfish acts and cannot believe what has become of us. We don't want to hurt others, but because we are disillusioned and equate pleasure with happiness, we insanely continue to act out in ways that keep us in this vicious cycle of destruction. If we continue down this path, we become utterly lost and the pure being at our core becomes so obscured that we no longer even believe that is who we are. We can become overwhelmed with depression and the persistent feeling of impending doom.

Obsessive behavior and addictions to drugs, alcohol, sex, gambling or other kinds of external stimuli, are all extreme manifestations of an ego out of control. The driving force behind the power of our ego is fear, without which our ego loses strength and is greatly reduced. As fear is removed, egotism relinquishes control over our lives.

Like other psychological disorders, our prejudices are based on disillusioned-driven fears. The emphasis on fear and delusion-driven egotism as the root cause of all our problems is a fundamental premise of 12-step programs. The various manifestations of behavioral transgressions themselves are only symptoms of the problem.

Self-Assessment

The 12 steps are designed to first address the insecurities that are at the root of these misbehaviors, which prevent us from forming healthy relationships. They then suggest disciplines that prevent a regression, while ensuring our continued growth.

But how did the disillusionment of our ego begin? 12-step programs make a connection to basic instincts such as love, sex and security. We get in a fearful state that our instinctual driven desires won't be fully satisfied. Our drive to meet these needs increases until they turn into obsessions.

Our modern culture seems to contribute to the problem by the amount of value we place on materialism, aesthetics and power. Although the messages are sometimes more subtle than others, the expectation to advance in these ego-feeding areas influences every facet of our lives. As children, we are often led to value these things as the true path to happiness. Seeking pleasure becomes a way of life.

Many of us are not given the tools needed to sustain happiness nor taught a set of guiding principles along with the specific action on how to put those values into daily practice. We do not learn how to express emotions when we are hurt. We aren't taught how to truly love unconditionally or how to freely give of ourselves by being of service without expectations of some external reward. We aren't given ongoing guidance on rejecting stereotypes while valuing and respecting individuals based on the merits of their character. We are sometimes discouraged from freely exploring our own understanding in spiritual matters. When it comes to the misbehaviors of others, we are often only taught minimal ideals of forgiveness. When someone becomes a detriment to society, we vengefully seek punishment and neglect rehabilitation. We callously lock them up so that we can forget about them in hopes that we'll feel safe.

Prison statistics are a staggering reflection of our intolerance as well as our ineffectiveness in turning lives around. Approximately one out of every one hundred three adults in our country is currently behind bars.[*]

[*] Based on 2010 U.S. population census and statistics of jail and prison incarceration; www.ojp.usdoj.gov

Incarceration is effective in putting an immediate stop to unacceptable behavior for a short period, but without arming the altruistic self with proper tools, the ego will continue to dominate. As a result, making positive behavioral modifications is unlikely. Our being's return to humility is the only viable solution. Without reorienting our culture with this basic understanding, we will not be motivated to find methods for rehabilitation. The result is that the recidivism rate will continue to escalate at the expense of our whole country. This change in perception will require more compassion and a desire to have each individual become free of their self-imposed prison.

Equipping our children with constructive coping skills will be to the benefit of our whole society. We can teach them the benefits of adopting healthy practices starting from early stages of their development. When we are only given cursory education to such ideals, they do not become part of our nature. We must have these principles and applicable actions engrained in our lives to give our core-being the tools needed to keep our ego in check. Without these implements, our ego can grow out of control until it rules our life.

Thankfully, most people never get to these stages of obsession or addiction. But if you have reached this state and you are addicted to drugs, alcohol, sex, gambling or other kinds of indulgences, your ego has taken over your life and your altruistic self is a prisoner suffering the consequences of your ego's impulses. However, this fellowship is not meant to be a substitute for recovery programs that address these issues. Because altering the way we think and feel with such behaviors inhibits our growth, removing overindulgences from our lives is essential. If you find you cannot control or abstain from such tendencies on your own willpower, we recommend you seek additional help.

A good way to measure egotism is by turning back to chapter five to the discussion of humility. Look at the table of personality attributes and for each attribute pair, determine if you lean more towards the ego side or the humility side. To go further, we can ask ourselves questions about perceptions we have and about the actions we take to strengthen each of the humility attributes. Am I able to be present in the moment, living in *the now*, or am I stuck in regrets of the past or fear of the future? To what extent do I still believe that I need a relationship, money, property or prestige to make me happy? Am I conscious and empathetic of other people's pain and suffering or do I only think of myself? Do I stuff my feelings or do I open up to others and reveal my problems to them? Am I free of resentment? Am I usually in a state of gratitude, or am I easily agitated through frustration, jealousy, fear or self-pity? Are my tendencies towards blame, or do I take full responsibility for these feelings? What tools do I exercise to process these emotions so they don't fester? What are my spiritual practices? Do I pray, meditate, read spiritual literature, listen to others about their beliefs or take similar action to allow myself to get spiritually centered? What do I do to help others? Do I have any commitments of service where I regularly give of myself? How much time do I spend judging or criticizing versus giving praise?

We can likewise ask questions that focus on the action of our daily disciplines. If we are honest in our self-appraisal, we will be able to gain clear insight into the extent of our egotism. Many of us will also realize we are lacking in our discipline for nurturing humility. When that is the case, we are more susceptible to our ego's influence. The disciplines practiced in the steps plus our involvement in the fellowship provide effective measures for ensuring healthy growth, as well as keeping our ego in check. Armed with this awareness, along with knowledge of how to apply these principles in our lives, we will be given a choice on which side of our psyche we will nourish. It will then simply be a matter of taking action.

Examining Our Prejudices

Our world has matured significantly over the last several decades and most people would like to be able to answer "no" to the question, "Are you a bigot?" Not only is overt bigotry explicitly condemned in the policies of government, employment and education, it has become socially unacceptable in most modern cultures. Overt bigotry is often associated with irresponsible scapegoat tactics and fearful narrow-mindedness. This is a stigma with which most people don't want to be associated; one that causes many of us to deny our prejudices. However, we are all products of a racist society. To live in today's modern world and not be negatively affected by the problems of the current racial climate resulting from an unhealed racist past is practically impossible. There are still many overt attempts to maintain the division between various races, while there has been no effective widespread attempt at overcoming negative images and perceptions within the individual.

Most of our communities, organizations and workplaces are still divided amongst racial and ethnic lines. Even when we are placed in the same rooms with people from various cultures, we tend to gravitate towards those who look most like ourselves. Of course, some of this is natural, as we feel more comfortable when we can identify with those around us; but it also prevents us from breaking down barriers that were erected during past generations of segregation that are still present today. Like all disciplines, we will need to move beyond these instinctual behaviors and step out of our comfort zone, if we are to face our fears of others.

Bigotry is a psychological disorder that is seeded by stereotypical misinformation. It then takes root when not exposed to objective personal experiences to counter such views. The distortion is fertilized by a fear-driven ego. When we avoid relationships with people from diverse cultures, we are prevented from broadening our perspective, which leads to our judging others' insides by the narrow glimpse we observe on the outside. As a result, we are rendered nearsighted and we are never given the opportunity to have our myopic vision corrected.

Communicating these distortions with others, who have no better insight, is how stereotypes metastasize. In this lifestyle shielded from exposure to diversity, we will unlikely escape our prejudices as much as we would like to. Misperceptions can then lead to unfair judgment of character traits, including morals and capabilities. These negative appraisals can produce unfounded fears of others that will lead to mistrust, resentment, and possibly hate. No race or culture is completely impervious to these problems. We must each individually look deep within ourselves to see how much of our thinking has been penetrated by learned stereotypes and by our own misperceptions.

Below is a list of questions for provoking such introspection and increasing awareness of our own bigotry. Some are based on controversial topics that are well suited for exposing deep-rooted perceptions. This is a self-survey, in which the responses are not meant to be judged, but to simply allow ourselves to examine our

Self-Assessment

own personal views at a level we might not normally contemplate. They should be used to search our innermost self to expose our true feelings. The only "right" answer is an honest answer. There is no incorrect response, if it is how you honestly feel.

1. What do you feel constitutes prejudice or bigotry in an individual?
2. What do you feel constitutes racism in a society?
3. Do you believe racism exists in our country? If so, name examples or signs you have observed. What percentage of our society would you guess carries some form of prejudice?
4. Have you ever been exposed to the prejudice or bigoted sentiments of friends, family or others in your environment?
5. Do you concede you may carry prejudices against others based on race, ethnicity, gender, religion, age or any other physical or cultural characteristic? If not, how are you able to make this determination?
6. Do thoughts of the various races and religions evoke feelings of love, compassion and respect, or of fear, anger, bitterness or disappointment?
7. Do you feel any discomfort when around people of other races, cultures or religions?
8. Do you often feel like you are disliked or judged by people of other diversities? If so, how does that make you feel about them?
9. Do you ever rationalize not uniting with people of other diversities by exclaiming either *"They're the ones who are prejudiced!"* or *"It's just natural to stick to your own kind"*?
10. Are there any religions or races you fear or regard with anxiety or contempt?
11. Do you believe it is acceptable to hate any person or group, including political or ideological? If so, where do you draw the line and consider hate to be a dehumanizing or destructive force?
12. Have you ever been the target of anyone else's bigoted actions or remarks? Have you ever been rejected, snubbed, insulted or threatened? Have you or a loved one ever been harmed? What impact did these experiences have on your view of the race of the offender?

13. Have you ever had thoughts that someone's thinking is distorted because of their genetic makeup?
14. Do you believe that some races are biologically superior and more capable in any way to other races? If so, what races are superior and in what way?
15. Have you ever attributed any undesirable traits to an entire racial or religious group?
16. Some believe that all races should be segregated. They base their reasoning on anything from "preserving racial identity" to unequivocal racist ideology. How do you feel about the idea of segregating the races?
17. Do you view any other racial or ethnic group as being lazy, unethical, greedy, irresponsible, less intelligent, naturally prone to crime or dishonest behavior, socially undesirable, naturally more inclined to abuse drugs or alcohol or immoral behavior?
18. Do you believe there are any natural differences in abilities between any racial groups?
19. Do you agree that slavery in the United States, followed by segregation, were morally wrong and an egregious injustice? If, so do you believe our country made amends for these wrongs and if so, when and how?
20. Do you believe all races are now treated equally in our society and that everyone has equal opportunity and that if they are trailing behind, it is their own fault? If you agree that slavery and segregation were wrong, but now believe all races are treated equal, at what point in history do you feel was the turning point of balance? What signs or statistics of the relative wellbeing of the health, education and economics do you see validating this perception? Also, if you believe all races are equal in capability *and* have equal opportunity, how do you reconcile the differences in the proportional statistics of poverty, unemployment, education, political representation, community segregation and prison population? If all races were treated equal and all races had equal capabilities, wouldn't there be smaller gaps in these statistics? If these big gaps are neither because of differences in capabilities or an imbalance of opportunity, what do you feel is the cause?

Self-Assessment

21. How do you feel about interracial relationships? Would you feel any discomfort if a friend or family member became involved with someone outside of your race? How do you feel when you see someone of your race coupled with a person of another race?
22. What are your opinions concerning Affirmative Action? If you have positive perceptions, can you state what they are? If you have negative feelings about it, can you state why? Do you know anyone who was hurt by it? Do you have any other knowledge of good or harm as the result of such policies? Whether or not you have personally observed perceived harms, if you agree that racism and discrimination still exist in our country, but believe Affirmative Action is wrong, what do you believe would be a better approach to overcome these problems in order to provide balanced opportunity?
23. Do you celebrate the Martin Luther King, Jr. holiday? What is your opinion about it and how do you think the country views this day? If your feelings are negative, are you confident bigotry is not a factor? Have you read books describing the Civil Rights Movement? Do you respect that part of our history, view it with contempt, or just simply give it no thought?
24. How has the media influenced your perspective on race?
25. When you hear or read news stories without seeing the participants, does the nature of the story or the role of the character affect the race of the person you visualize?
26. If you could somehow be transformed into another race, is there any other race you would prefer to be a part of or on the other hand, wish to avoid? What is the reasoning for your choice?
27. If you see someone of another race acting in an antisocial way, do you attribute their behavior to their race?
28. As an employer, would race affect your perception on candidates?
29. If interviewing for a job, would you have a preference on the interviewer's race?
30. If stopped by the police, would you feel more comfortable with an officer of one race over another? If the officer is of another race, would you suspect they were biased in his or her decision to stop you?

31. Would you consider moving to a neighborhood predominantly of another race? If someone stopped to ask you questions about the house for sale next door, would you be able to equally welcome prospective buyers of any race?
32. If you or a loved one is receiving medical treatment, would you have preference in the race of the physician?
33. Do you have close friends of other races that you spend time with as much as the friends of your own race?
34. Are the neighborhoods surrounding your home diverse and if so, do you feel comfortable around your neighbors?

While answering these questions, did you stay aware of your own level of comfort? Did any of the questions inflame any feelings of fear, anger or shame? If you are still not sure if your perceptions are distorted by bigotry, discussing these topics together with others of your own race as well as other diverse groups will give you a better chance of possibly exposing bigoted sentiments.

If you are now certain your heart is tainted with prejudice, you are not alone. Admitting this takes courage, but becoming willing to try to find a resolution will require further strength still. The next chapter will get you started on that journey. Regardless of whether or not you have concluded that you carry prejudice, working through the 12 steps places us in the best psychological and spiritual state to meet the challenges of unifying a diverse group. In this condition of strength, we can effectively begin our active participation of working towards unity. Together, these measures will guarantee the continued reduction of our own biases and provide an environment with a healthier future for generations to come.

Chapter 11: The Twelve Steps

Overview of the Steps

Unity Initiative is following the successes learned by many other organizations by incorporating the twelve steps of Alcoholics Anonymous into our program of action. Their descriptions are provided below, but more details of the original ideals behind the steps can be found in the two primary texts of Alcoholics Anonymous; chapters one through eleven in the book *Alcoholics Anonymous* (Also known as the "Big Book") and chapters one through twelve of *Twelve Steps and Twelve Traditions**.

Much of the foundation for the UI program of action was constructed from ideals outlined in this literature. They provide valuable information for living life on life's terms regardless of whether or not you have a problem with addiction.

The information in these books will raise your awareness and sharpen your skills for working through everyday problems. And like most organizations that utilize this program, UI has adapted the twelve steps by simply replacing references to alcoholism with the malady in which we are trying to overcome; prejudice. Except for this alteration, the steps have been adopted in their original form.

---

* *Upon asking permission for adapting the twelve steps and twelve traditions of Alcoholics Anonymous into the program of action for Unity Initiative, AA World Services reviewed the proposed adaptations and responded that they would not object, but asked that the original AA steps and traditions be re-printed in full, following the UI adaptation. In keeping with the fifth and sixth traditions, AAWS also requested we include a statement making it clear that our two organizations are unaffiliated. Below are the original twelve steps of Alcoholics Anonymous along with the statement of non-affiliation.*

The 12 Steps of Unity Initiative

1. We examined ourselves for prejudice, then admitted to any unfair biases we may carry.
2. Came to believe that a Power greater than ourselves could restore us to sanity.
3. Made a decision to turn our will and our lives over to the care of God as we understood Him.
4. Made a searching and fearless moral inventory of ourselves.
5. Admitted to God, to ourselves, and to another human being the exact nature of our wrongs.
6. Were entirely ready to have God remove all these defects of character.
7. Humbly asked Him to remove our shortcomings.
8. Made a list of all persons we had harmed, and became willing to make amends to them all.
9. Made direct amends to such people wherever possible, except when to do so would injure them or others.
10. Continued to take personal inventory and when we were wrong promptly admitted it.
11. Sought through prayer and meditation to improve our conscious contact with God as we understood Him, praying only for knowledge of His will for us and the power to carry that out.
12. Having had a spiritual awakening as the result of these steps, we tried to carry this message to others, and to practice these principles in all our affairs.

The Twelve Steps

The suggestions below a design for living, providing a framework in which we can *all* find meaningful contentedness. Many 12-step organizations present them as a program of recovery to free oneself from afflictions that usually manifest in specific destructive behavior such as gambling or drug use. A person suffering from these problems will certainly recover if they rigorously practice the steps, but these programs also found that they were having a much broader impact than just helping the suffering addict or alcoholic. Friends and family members without these specific afflictions followed the steps and were able to have the same transforming experience. They proved the steps could help anyone.

The Twelve Steps of Alcoholics Anonymous

1. We admitted we were powerless over alcohol—that our lives had become unmanageable.
2. Came to believe that a Power greater than ourselves could restore us to sanity.
3. Made a decision to turn our will and our lives over to the care of God as we understood Him.
4. Made a searching and fearless moral inventory of ourselves.
5. Admitted to God, to ourselves, and to another human being the exact nature of our wrongs.
6. Were entirely ready to have God remove all these defects of character.
7. Humbly asked Him to remove our shortcomings.
8. Made a list of all persons we had harmed, and became willing to make amends to them all.
9. Made direct amends to such people wherever possible, except when to do so would injure them or others.
10. Continued to take personal inventory and when we were wrong promptly admitted it.
11. Sought through prayer and meditation to improve our conscious contact with God, as we understood Him, praying only for knowledge of His will for us and the power to carry that out.
12. Having had a spiritual awakening as the result of these Steps, we tried to carry this message to alcoholics, and to practice these principles in all our affairs.

Copyright (c) A.A. World Services, Inc.

Statement of non-affiliation

The Twelve Steps and Twelve Traditions of Alcoholics Anonymous have been reprinted and adapted with the permission of Alcoholics Anonymous World Services, Inc. ("AAWS"). Permission to reprint and adapt the Twelve Steps and Twelve Traditions does not mean that Alcoholics Anonymous is affiliated with this program. A.A. is a program of recovery from alcoholism only - use of A.A.'s Steps and Traditions or an adapted version in connection with programs and activities which are patterned after A.A., but which address other problems, or use in any other non-A.A. context, does not imply otherwise.

Regardless of our psychological condition, background, social-class or beliefs, the steps outline a way of living from which <u>everyone</u> can benefit. The prescribed disciplines of love, honesty and spirituality are the necessary practices for living up to the *specifications of the human makeup in order to maintain mental, spiritual and psychological wellness. All human beings must exercise disciplines in these basic values if we are to nurture our altruistic self.*

For many, the 12-steps may seem complicated and intimidating. The truth is that they can indeed be very difficult. The action we take to apply these principles often takes us out of our comfort zone. The self-searching, the deflation of ego and the surrendering to a Power greater than ourselves will require us to face many fears. The apprehension of facing this discomfort will lead many into seeking out any rationalization for not taking the steps. But even if you believe you do not carry prejudice, the steps still allow you to review yourself for anything that may get in the way of our effectiveness in contributing to the efforts of uniting our communities. *For this reason, it is important that <u>everyone</u> in our organization do the best we can to work through all of the steps.*

Although this program is simple, it is not easy. The actions of the steps fall into one of three categor*ies: 1) cleaning house; 2) seeking spirituality; and 3) helping others.*

Cleaning house refers to the cleaning up of accumulated emotional and psychological baggage. This involves action, such as: self-assessment, self-cleansing through journaling and self-disclosure, and amends for past wrongs. It requires an immense amount of honesty, strength and courage.

The steps that include *seeking spirituality* involve coming to believe in a Power greater than ourselves, and trusting in that Power enough to be willing to rigorously clean house and work with others. Our practices may include prayer and meditation or they may involve strengthening ties with spiritual or religious affiliations.

The efforts for *helping others* can apply to any area of our lives where we are in a position to serve. This may include being of service to the UI fellowship by assisting in activities such as meetings, or by sponsoring someone and helping them through the steps. Service work also takes the form of helping anyone who is in need, as well as volunteering in our community.

The following chart breaks the 12 steps down into these three categories. Note that we are essentially trying to replace egotism with humility and that the actions of the three categories are specifically established for that purpose.

The Twelve Steps

12-Step Chart

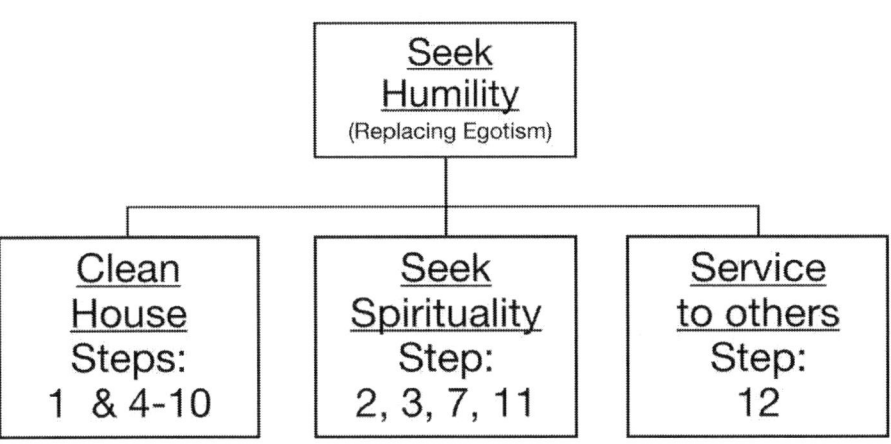

Cleaning house actions	Actions for spirituality	Actions of service
Getting honest. Self-Analysis. Self-Disclosure. Writing/journaling. Opening up to others by sharing our daily problems. Admitting when wrong. Correcting defects and mistakes. Paying off debts. Healing relationships. Facing responsibility. Staying accountable by soliciting feedback and advice.	Prayer and Meditation Positive Visualization Surrendering Participation in discussions of spiritual ideals with an open mind. Reading spiritual literature. Listening to spiritual teachers/mentors. Making yourself available for service to God. Looking for the Good in others.	Sponsorship Volunteering for your community. Carrying the message to outside institutions. Being kind and generous to everyone we meet. Listening to others unload their burdens. Empathizing to validate others feelings. Supporting the greater needs of a group and its service structure.

In cleaning house, we start with Step One, which requires honesty in admitting we have a problem. Steps four through nine involve cleaning up our past and Step Ten involves correcting any mistakes as we go along from here on out. In seeking spirituality, we have steps two and three for enlisting a power greater than ourselves. Steps six and seven are seeking God's help in removing our character defects that we discovered in the inventory taken in steps four and five, while Step Eleven suggests prayer and meditation. In helping others, we have Step Twelve where we provide services inside and outside of the rooms of our fellowship.

In general, the steps are meant to be worked in order. This is especially true for the first nine steps, which deal with cleaning up our past. We are not likely to do a thorough job in our inventory in steps four and five if we have not developed sufficient faith in our Higher Power. Likewise, we should not start making amends in steps eight and nine before we have made enough of a transformation in our lives in previous steps.

However, whereas steps one through nine primarily deal with our past, the last three steps address needs of the present. Because of this, we start working these steps from day-one. For example, part of Step Ten involves making amends for wrong-doings of today. If we make a mistake that harms someone else, we do not justify delaying an amends for new infractions simply because we have not completed steps one through nine. Similarly, Step Eleven includes prayer and meditation. If we desire to take these actions, we can get started at any time. Their practice does not require completion of previous steps. In step 12, although we do not want to try to give advice on something we have not yet personally experienced, even with a very short period of time in our organization, you are well positioned to reach out to the brand new member to make them feel welcome. Playing the Good Samaritan by showing kindness can also never be started too early.

Beyond incorporating the principles of the 12 steps into our daily routines, we will also be taking definitive steps towards unifying with people from diverse groups. These activities will be discussed in more detail in the next chapter.

The Twelve Steps

Step One
*We examined ourselves for prejudice, then
admitted to any unfair biases we may carry.
(Principles: Surrender / Truth / Humility / Self-Cleansing)*

For some of us, the admission of carrying any prejudice whatsoever will hastily be denied. We may truly believe we are completely free of any uneasiness or animosity towards any gender, race, religion, nationality, culture or belief system, but upon close examination, we may find some hidden feelings we were not even aware of. When we are honest with ourselves, most of us will have to admit that we carry stereotypical opinions that have resulted in unwarranted fear and unfair judgment of other diverse groups even though we wish to be free of such shortcomings.

Reading books about racism or going through questionnaires such as the one in the previous chapter will often expose deep-rooted feelings that reveal we are not free from these maladies. This may be the case even when our perceptions fly in the face of facts or logical reasoning. We may even discover that upon scrutiny, many of these beliefs actually contradict each other.

When truly asking ourselves these questions in the spirit of self-discovery, self-improvement and a desire to be free from such maladies, there is no shame in realizing and admitting that we are afflicted with prejudice, bigotry or racism. We are the product of our environment. Escaping these attitudes and misperceptions of our society is highly unlikely. Even when we are raised in surroundings that foster countering such biases, our human psyche will likely not completely filter out all of the negative clatter with which we are exposed.

After we are able to admit we carry these biases, we can examine ourselves closer for the feelings they produce. How do I feel when I am around various diverse groups? Do I experience stress, anger, jealousy, resentment or guilt? Do I have a general sense of discomfort? When I am the minority in a diverse group, do I feel disconnected or alienated like I don't belong? Am I self-conscious that I am different from the others or that someone may be judging me? When I am in the majority, am I uneasy about the presence of minorities in the group? Do I believe they are my equals and that they belong, or do I objectify them in some way and perceive they are outsiders that are simply passing through or possibly intruding?

How do I feel when I am in one-on-one dialogs with people of other diversities? Am I nervous? Do I feel like I need to stay on guard or that I am put on the defense? Am I more likely to mistrust them or question the validity of their views? Do I sense that I am being mistrusted or unfairly judged or criticized?

Most of us experience some form of anxiety when around others who are different from ourselves even if we don't feel animosity. These fear-based sensations inhibit our ability to communicate, keeping us in a state of apprehension. Even when our emotions are apparently non-bigoted we may be concerned with what others are thinking or feeling. We may feel like we are walking on eggshells in fear of exposing something about ourselves that will cause further stress. If this is true for us, we must become aware of the energy produced by these emotions and the potential they have for affecting our behavior. Although we cannot read each other's thoughts to reveal our discomfort, we cannot completely prevent the tension from affecting our interactions. Because most humans have some level of sensitivity to this emotional energy, those we expose to this anxiety may naturally reciprocate with uncertainty.

These are all consequences of a society born on the racist tenets that were allowed to endure from generation to generation. These issues are rarely addressed openly but we cannot deny the strained relationships of our society, formed as the byproduct of our maladjusted past. As a result, the tension has become the proverbial elephant in the room that everyone is keenly aware of, yet tries to pretend is not there. If we are ever to be free, we will need the courage to acknowledge the truth.

Like all other maladies that are being addressed by various 12-step programs, bigotry is only a symptom of the problem. We will need to get to the root causes then take action to relieve ourselves of fearful misperceptions and break down the psychological barriers that keep us divided. This first step of admission takes an immense amount of honesty and courage, but to the extent that we can overcome fear and denial to admit our faults will we be able to effectively use the rest of the steps to heal our lives.

The Twelve Steps

Step Two
*Came to believe that a Power greater
than ourselves could restore us to sanity.
(Principles: Hope / Humility / Spirituality)*

Sanity is soundness of mind and judgment. In Step One, we admitted to any biases we carried, which not only inhibited trusting relationships with people of diverse groups, but was corrosive to our own level of peace. Some of us have spent much of our life in disillusionment holding on to distorted perceptions of others that did little more than cause us anguish. We held on to misinformation even in light of evidence to the contrary. This thinking and behavior cannot be characterized as sound. The combined fear and twisted ideals amounted to a form of insanity that influenced our behaviors to our own detriment. If we had the awareness and power to escape this delusion on our unaided will, we would have. Most of us find that our distorted thinking will not fix itself. We must enlist a Power greater than ourselves to make this transition.

In this step, we embark upon finding this Power that will be our source of strength as we go through the rest of the steps to bring about a psychic change. We will need this strength if we are going to be thorough in our house cleaning steps and diligent in our service to others. Reaching the required level of honesty will take an enormous amount of courage, since we will be revealing then coming to terms with parts of our lives that we have so far successfully kept suppressed. We will need faith and courage to overcome the fear that we will certainly encounter, as we reach these depths of truth.

Whether religious devotee, spiritual student, confirmed atheist or agnostic, we can all find a Power greater than ourselves that will lift us to a higher level of consciousness, willingness and trust. This Power must be one that we can believe in and that won't fail us as we apply the magnifying glass to our lives in Step Four, bare our souls to another in Step Five, make restitution in Step Nine and start helping others in Step Twelve. As difficult as these steps are, we will find that if we have faith in a Higher Power that is strong, loving and forgiving, we will find the courage to take this action. If we don't have this faith, we are likely to let fear control us, stall in our step-work and stay locked up in our self-imposed prison of disillusionment.

For those who already have established spiritual or religious ideals, these will be the foundation for your source of strength. If you do not have such beliefs then reading spiritual books and talking to others can help in establishing the basis for your own concepts.

Many have started on this path by choosing the fellowship as their Higher Power, which provided immediate tangible benefits. We can physically touch, feel and see the effects that this Power has had in the lives of the individual. Even from our first contact with the fellowship, we experience the warmth of the love of others and our fears immediately begin to subside. As we start to attend meetings, we hear the wisdom of the collective group conscience that has evolved from the shared experiences of applying the principles in their daily lives. We are sometimes awestruck by the simple ideas and solutions we have found together that we could not find alone. Two heads truly are better than one.

The only thing that matters is that your concept makes sense to you and that you have faith that it has enough power to guide your thoughts and actions to restore you to a soundness of mind. Once we have settled on this Power greater than ourselves, we will next establish a set of ideals we feel this Guide wants for us by writing about our beliefs so that they are not simply nebulous thoughts without tangible meaning.

Don't worry about the accuracy of your description. If it is spiritual in nature, accuracy is impossible. The purpose of this exercise is for you to get to know yourself, develop your understanding of your Higher Power, and to use your own set of concepts as a guideline for your own personal life. This writing may also expose limitations we subconsciously hold, giving us the chance to expand our faith. You can update this writing in the future as your understanding evolves.

1. Describe the attributes of your Higher Power. What makes this power greater than you? What attributes do they have that you don't have? What frailties do you possess that are absent in your Higher Power?
2. Describe what you think your Higher Power wants from you in order to be happy or to live up to their expectations. List what principles you believe they want you to accept. What personality attributes are needed to fulfill the spirit of these values?

3. Write down the action needed to fulfill these ideals. To what extent do you currently exercise these disciplines? What grade would you give yourself for each discipline and personality trait? For those that need improvement, are you now ready to start incorporating these practices in your life?
4. Do you believe your Higher Power will provide you with the strength required to take the necessary action for changing your perceptions? If not, write down any reservations you still have and continue on your quest to find the sufficient faith to move on with the remaining steps.

The more detail we can put in this writing, the better acquainted we will become with our own subconscious perceptions on spiritual matters. Once completed, we have clearly expressed our beliefs in our Higher Power, our understanding of the nature of our relationship and exactly what disciplines we believe will allow us to live within the specification of our human makeup. We can then use these ideals as guidelines for our lives. We make a commitment to work towards these principles using the actions we take as the measuring stick for gauging the extent of our efforts.

As you go through the rest of the steps, determine if the prescribed actions will strengthen the personality attributes required to live in the realm of the principles you have listed.

Step Three
*Made a decision to turn our will and our lives
over to the care of God as we understood Him
(Principles: Humility / Spirituality / Surrender / Faith)*

At this stage in our step-work, we have admitted to some of our shortcomings that reduced our peace of mind and adversely affected our relationships. We realized we have not been able to resolve this problem alone, simply on our own willpower. But we then came to believe that a Power greater than ourselves could help us to make the necessary change. We only needed to seek understanding and practice those principles which we believed were intended for us to internalize.

If we are convinced of this, then we are ready to make a commitment to follow up on these beliefs with action. Making this commitment to translate ideals into action is what Step Three is all about. We are making a definitive and determined decision to align our will with God's or our Higher Power's will. *"Our will" is our conscious thoughts and "our lives" is our deliberate actions.*

In previous sections we took a preliminary look at ourselves by examining the extent of our egotism and bigotry. Some of us discovered that we are driven by fear, which often resulted in selfish behavior. We found our lives were sometimes running on self-will, causing problems for ourselves as well as those around us. When we got to Step Two, we started the groundwork of reducing selfishness by first solidifying our perception of our Higher Power. We listed the principles we believe this Power intended for us to adopt. Although that list may evolve as our ideals grow, they provided us an initial set of concrete guidelines, in which we can thrive. They became synonymous for *God's will* for us.

When we used those principles as the benchmark to compare against our current practices, most of us found we had plenty of room for growth. The remainder of the steps will help us to progress in that direction. They prescribe actions for cleaning house, continuing seeking our spiritual life and helping others. These efforts apply the principles of honesty, spirituality and service. When we take Step Three and decide to turn our will and our lives over to God's care, we are making a commitment to start practicing these disciplines.

The Twelve Steps

When we are ready, we voice our decision with a prayer similar to this:

"God, I am turning my thoughts and my actions unreservedly over to your care. Help me to replace fear and selfishness with love and humility. Please grant me strength and courage to align my will with yours, that I may better serve you and my fellow man."

Other prayers and meditations can be adopted for this same purpose. We choose whatever words we feel most comfortable with, in order to express our intentions.

We can enhance the experience by taking this step together with our sponsor or another loved one.

When we surrender, we become willing to change our thinking and behavior for a new way of living. We ready ourselves to live in accordance with how we believe our Higher Power would have us live. Although we may experience a certain amount of trepidation to the idea of assuming this new lifestyle, we will also feel a sense of hopeful-anticipation, knowing we are heading in the right direction. Paradoxically, by surrendering, we find that we are now giving ourselves an opportunity to succeed in the game of life. In this state of mind we are now able to move forward with courage while we continue on this journey through our work in the remaining steps.

Step Four
*Made a searching and fearless moral inventory of ourselves
(Principles: Humility / Honesty / Self- Cleansing /
Courage / Faith / Accountability)*

In steps one through three, we plotted the trajectory for the new direction of our lives. After admitting some of our frailties in Step One, we moved to Step Two where we made a list of principles we believed we were meant to live by, along with the action needed to fulfill those ideals. In Step Three we made a pledge to live by those values through our daily practices. Steps four through seven will be the first definitive steps in clearing the debris from our path, making our travels possible.

Now that we have mapped out where we are going, steps four and five will allow us to remove blocking obstacles by helping us first identify behaviors and mindsets we may have that contradict these standards. We then make an effort to remove counterproductive traits and avoid unhealthy habits in steps six and seven. In steps eight and nine we resolve conflicts in relationships that might hinder our progress and through steps ten through twelve we make daily course adjustments to keep us on track.

Step Four will be the first test of our faith in the Higher Power we have chosen, as we take an enormous leap into cleaning up any wreckage of the past. We have already taken our first small, but vital step at house cleaning when we evaluated ourselves for egotism and bigotry; then admitted our imperfections and the need for adjustments in our perceptions. But for some of us, these measures only touched the surface of the problems that lie within. They will not be sufficient to make the necessary change, which we are seeking. To become free of the bondage of self, our house cleaning will now need to go much deeper to examine ourselves for the root causes and conditions that have led to these problems.

To begin, Step Four will guide us through self-examination. Most of us carry painful feelings of our past that we have never fully processed. We try to block those memories in hopes they will not rise back to the surface. Some have had to face harsh realities in life such as living in conditions of intense poverty, suffering caused by disabilities or ailments, or a breakdown in family structure brought on by divorce, abandonment or death. In other cases we may have been the victim of crime, abuses, neglect or some other injustice. There are many such difficulties in life that an individual may have to face, which are usually beyond our control.

More common than these hardships though, are memories of events that caused suffering through intense exposure to feelings such as anger, embarrassment or humiliation. For example, our self-esteem may have been damaged or we may carry fears from childhood rejection by schoolmates or family members. We may have shame or humiliation from failure to make the grade in scholastics, sports or religion where we did not meet someone's expectations. We may carry resentment from situations where we were deeply hurt, betrayed, humiliated or made to feel like an outcast. Most people do not make it through life without experiencing this level of pain, at some point. We usually carry some of the baggage from such incidents into our adulthood, even if we had a good upbringing, live in a healthy environment and have a fairly normal way of life.

For those of us whose lifestyle was not so healthy, we became the occasional source of suffering in the lives of others, as we chased our own selfish pursuits. We sometimes manipulated friends and family to get what we wanted, regardless of their feelings or needs. If our behavior was controlling, we rationalized that we knew best; that it was "for their own good". We may have recklessly stooped to lying, cheating and stealing, seriously damaging valuable relationships. If our selfishness continued to grow without intervention, we have possibly gone much lower and reached depths in our lives where our ego completely dominated us to the extent that our behavior was controlled by fear and selfishness. In extreme cases, we went so low that we violated our most basic morals. We may have committed crimes or caused someone great harm; and we are horrified to think what might happen if others found us out. We feel bad about what we have done, but self-preservation kicks in and every instinct in our nature screams that no one must ever know. We plan on taking these secrets to our grave.

However, as long as we hold on to all these memories without finding an outlet to release them, we are doomed to continue suffering the torment of our past. By trying to deny the reality of the skeletons in our closet, we are also more likely to repeat destructive behavior.

We are destined to stay as sick as our secrets. Whether suffering from childhood memories or from experiences in our adult life, this step gives all of us the opportunity to get that baggage off our chest, freeing us from the refuse that blocks us from the sunlight of the spirit.

In this step, we will be writing these events and feelings down on paper. We write about fears, anger, guilt and shame. This writing will include harms others have done to us, as well as incidents where we were at fault. We are putting on paper all those memories that repeatedly haunt us and keep us from growing.

When possible, we also want to include any memories of incidents relating to both negative and positive feelings about other diverse groups. For positive experiences, what personal relationships did we have that favorably shaped our views? Were we part of any groups or associations that fostered diverse gatherings? Did we take part in activities meant to overcome prejudice, bigotry or racism? Whether we are at work, school, on a sports team or involved in other social activities, most of us have been fortunate enough to have had encounters with other races, religions or cultures that favorably shaped our views.

What about the negative experiences we've had, related to other diversities? Were we exposed to bigoted sentiments by any friends or family? Had we ever been harmed in any way by the words or actions of someone else's bigotry? Do we hold any suppressed anger, resentment, fears or pain, as the result of being exposed to bigotry fueled mistreatment or injustice? What stereotypes were we taught? Were we isolated from other cultures? Do we have any strong negative feelings about any ethnicities or religious groups?

All such experiences form our perceptions, so if we are going to free ourselves of our prejudices, we will need to face, then purge all negative emotions we may still carry.

We realize that for some, the thought of merely writing out our inventory will be a frightful prospect. If we have then looked ahead at Step Five and realize we are meant to share this inventory with another, our anxiety escalates. If experiencing these fears, we do our best to block Step Five out of our mind. This is necessary because of the importance of being able to be truthful with ourselves when simply writing these events down. We have found it helpful to divide our writing into the categories of feelings and incidents we are ready to disclose now, those which we may be able to disclose in the future, and memories that we may never be able to reveal.

When you go into your fifth step, you can bring with you everything you are ready to share; and if you wish, leave the rest at home. We are then less likely of being overwhelmed by the fear of putting these incidents down on paper. The more difficult events are for your eyes only, until you are ready to have them revealed.

Many useful guides are available that can help to get started on this writing. The outline below is one possible approach. For each incident in our lives, we write down the following:

1. **List the persons, places or institutions involved in the situation that evoke these painful memories from the past.** We include the nature of our relationship or association.
2. **Give details about the situation or the incidents that took place.** If exposed to harsh difficulties or traumatic events, we list those details. If we were wronged in some way, we write about how we were harmed and why we perceive they were responsible. If we caused harm to another, we include what actions and intentions we were responsible for that caused the damage. In most cases there is shared responsibility and we must try to look at what our part is in every situation, no matter how small, and state where we were at fault.
3. **Write down how <u>we</u> were emotionally, physically or materially affected by this incident or circumstance.** For material harm, was there a loss of property, physical injury or financial damage? Were relationships affected or reputations tarnished? Were there setbacks in employment, family or social standings? For the emotional effects, we write about what we experienced at the time of the event whether it was fear, sadness, jealousy, anger, humiliation, guilt, shame or disgust. Which of these feelings are still lingering? Simply writing about these is a very powerful tool for processing these memories. We sometimes find it necessary to do a very in depth journal about a difficult incident, as this will help us process those emotions by transferring them from our mind onto paper. When doing this, we use paper apart from what we present during our fifth step. We may use extensive "*stream of conscience*" writing to purge ourselves of all the poison,

continuing until we have nothing more to write.
4. ***If someone else was harmed, we write about how we believe they were affected emotionally, physically and materially.***
5. ***Determine if any character defects were inflamed or played a role in this situation.*** Turning back to the section on humility in chapter five, we write down each of the attributes in the column "Driven by Ego" that apply to our thoughts and actions for this incident. (This list of shortcomings will be used in steps six and seven).

On deciding what to write about first, there are various approaches we can take to get started for recording these events. They can be listed chronologically starting from our earliest childhood memories then working towards the present. The inventory can be divided into the consequential emotional states brought on by the incidents, such as resentment, fear, guilt and shame. In any case, it is sometimes best to start with the most prominent thoughts, feelings or memories that are on the forefront of our mind; those things that we frequently dwell on that keep us up at night. These will include people, places, institutions or events that evoke strong or persistent fear-based feelings. At the extreme, they will include memories of unhealthy sexual events or behavior, abuses, violence, debts and many other unresolved wrongs that we have caused others, or that others have incurred on us.

Our top priority in working through this step is to be completely open. We must be as honest as we can possibly be; providing enough details to thoroughly root out painful memories. We cannot afford to continue stuffing these feelings that are hurting our self-perception and affecting every area of our lives. We must get it all out on paper.

We can enlist our Higher Power's help by asking that we be granted the courage to be honest, thorough and selfless. However, this writing will still likely dredge up painful emotions. Before we become overwhelmed, we take a break to pray or talk to another person. Having these feelings come to the surface is healthy and necessary so that we can process them, but we don't want to get in such a fearful state that we are driven to impulsive behavior because we are unable to endure the pain. We should only expect ourselves to be able to take on a little at a time. There may be some incidents in our life that are so traumatic that we may want to seek professional help. We do whatever we can to free ourselves of our painful past.

This writing is usually very therapeutic since we transfer the thoughts spinning in our head onto paper. By asking for forgiveness or understanding as the case may be, we are allowing our Higher Power to become a part of the process. We are then able to come to terms with them and begin to let them go.

Although we have no set time frame for completing this writing, we should avoid procrastination. We don't want to rush our step-work, compromising honesty and thoroughness, but it is all too easy to find excuses to procrastinate and let it go undone. The sooner we can purge the toxicity from our lives, the sooner we will experience the freedom we are seeking that we can then pass on to others. When ready, we find a private room where we will not be disturbed, ask our Higher Power for strength, and start writing.

Step Five
Admitted to God, to ourselves, and to another human being the exact nature of our wrongs
(Principles: Humility / Honesty / Self-Cleansing / Courage / Faith / Integrity / Accountability)

If we have been thorough in the previous step, we have written down some of the most sensitive details of our lives. When we get to Step Five, we take the written pages from Step Four and reveal this personal information to another human being. To this extent, Step Five is similar to confession although there are notable differences. We often go much deeper in our self-examination and disclosure in order to free ourselves by ensuring we do not leave any refuse behind.

In the process of writing down our personal inventory in a format such as that outlined in Step Four, we likely uncovered our most objectionable behaviors and character flaws. As difficult as this exercise was, analyzing our lives in this way allowed us to see ourselves and the world around us with a whole new perspective.

Certainly, taking this exercise in honesty to the next level by bearing our souls to another person to this extent can be very daunting. Some will panic simply at the thought of disclosing such personal matters. Fear will consume many of us with every fiber of our being trying to resist. We find all sorts of reasons why divulging certain parts of our lives is not necessary for us. We can devise many excuses to postpone this disclosure, but it has been exhibited time after time that we will never find absolute freedom if we fail to take this vital step.

Know that no act or behavior has been committed that has not been revealed in some inventory somewhere. You are not unique and you are not alone. However, this information is certainly personal and likely very sensitive, so you will surely want to choose someone with whom you fully trust. This person will usually be your sponsor. After all, they have gone through this same process and have revealed their own life story to someone else. We have likely built a close relationship with them and they know exactly what we are going through. They know why we are taking this step and respect the absolute necessity for confidentiality. They understand how difficult exposing ourselves to others can be and for them to reveal parts of their own story to us is not uncommon. They are often insightful in feedback about what is revealed, but more important than anything is their ability to listen passively without judgment.

On the other hand, there may be some reason you don't feel comfortable sharing your entire fifth step with your current sponsor. You may have someone else in mind with whom you would rather share certain details. The choice is yours as to who will hear this personal disclosure. It may be someone else in the fellowship, a friend, a family member, your doctor or a spiritual mentor of a religious affiliation. The person we choose will be someone we trust enough to reveal all the skeletons in our closet, so that we have nothing left to hide.

Once you have chosen that person, immediately set up a date where you can meet to go over what you have written. To take a full day to complete this step is not uncommon, so make sure you have as much available time as needed in a place where you have complete privacy. When the time comes for you to get together, take a moment of silence to ask your Higher Power to give you the strength and courage to overcome your reservations so that you may be honest and thorough. Make yourself comfortable and read what you have written and allow yourself to start the process of healing from these toxic memories.

When we are done, what are we to do with our written pages? Many like to keep them as a valuable record of their former years so that they can review it later to see how much they have grown. Others find it cathartic to burn the pages in the symbolic gesture of letting go of this part of their past. If you fall into this latter group, make sure you save your inventory long enough to use as a reference when doing your eighth step.

After completing Step Five, we take some time alone to meditate and to review the step-work we have completed to this point. We examine each step and ensure that we have been thorough to the best of our ability. If we feel like we have omitted something important, we should discuss this with our sponsor and make the necessary effort to fill in any gaps. We can then thank our Higher Power for giving us the courage to complete this vital work.

Thoroughly following Step Five is a turning point in many people's lives. We often experience a great sense of peace as private burdens begin to be lifted off our shoulders. Much of the pain we have carried for years sometimes vanishes, instantly allowing us to breathe easier and sleep more peacefully. However, although we have gone a long way in cleaning up the wreckage of our past, the job is not fully complete and we are not entirely free. We have more house-cleaning to take care of in the following steps.

The Twelve Steps

Step Six
*Were entirely ready to have God
remove all these defects of character
(Principles: Humility / Spirituality / Self-Cleansing / Willingness)*

When we are confident that we have done the best we can to face our past with God and another human being, we are ready to continue with our journey of cleaning house. In the preceding steps we went through exercises of self-analysis and self-disclosure. We opened up, possibly taking a deeper look into ourselves than ever before in an effort to expose our defects of character. We were then able to tie these imperfections of our personal traits to problems in relationships and other areas of our lives.

In the section on humility in chapter five, many of these flaws are listed in the "Driven by ego" column of the personality attributes. While in Step Two we reviewed the "Guided by humility" column to select which traits we wanted to develop, setting the course of our direction, we now sharpen our awareness of behaviors and consequences to avoid which might cause a hindrance of our progress.

During the writing of our fourth step, we made note of the shortcomings we identified that were tied to the harms we caused others. Combining this exercise along with the fifth step, some of us discovered that we have suffered much in the areas of resentment, jealousy, fear and self-pity. In turn, our ego took over and we may have become materialistic, lustful, obsessive, controlling or overly critical of others. These shortcomings caused damage in our relationships and self-respect, thereby reducing our serenity.

In Step Six, we are simply acknowledging a readiness to have these character flaws removed. As long as we go on without addressing these defects, we will continue to suffer personally in addition to causing harm to those around us. To the extent we embrace humility and are willing to surrender the drives of our ego, our lives can be fruitful. If we are convinced of these facts, our readiness to have our Higher Power remove these maladies will come naturally.

Step Seven
Humbly asked Him to remove our shortcomings
(Principles: Humility / Spirituality / Faith /
Honesty / Self-Cleansing)

Once we have become ready to shed ourselves of our shortcomings, we request our Higher Power for help in having them removed. Complementing the work we did in Step Three when we made a commitment to follow the dictates of the list of principles we developed in Step Two, we now express our intent to avoid the liabilities we have uncovered in Steps Four through Six. We take this step through prayer and meditation, making an appeal to our Higher Power to give us the needed strength. When we are ready to make this request, we find it helpful to say a prayer similar to this:

"God, I am becoming aware of the problems that my fear-driven defects cause myself and others. I am convinced I will only be able to experience peace and joy to the extent I can become free of these shortcomings. I ask that You help me overcome these maladies and give me the strength and discipline to follow through with the action necessary to develop attributes of humility in my life."

Of course we are only human; none of us are perfect. The ideals behind the principles and the humility attributes are simply the direction we wish to travel. Progress towards these perfect ideals is all we can hope for. Asking our Higher Power for help in this way will get us started on that path. Willingness to take the necessary action will then be necessary to have these defects removed. We must continue on our journey of cleaning house, strengthening our spiritual pursuits and helping others.

The Twelve Steps

Step Eight
*Made a list of all persons we had harmed,
and became willing to make amends to them all
(Principles: Love / Honesty / Self-Cleansing /
Humility / Accountability)*

Making mistakes is part of being human. During the discovery years of our childhood, we innocently say or do things that hurt others. We make fun of our schoolmates not knowing the impact of our words. In anger, we may lash out and say hurtful things to our friends or family. As we age, our desire for external gratification increases and we become more skilled in our abilities of manipulation to get what we want. If we are not given the fundamental tools to live a healthy, happy life, we start getting pulled by temptations, at which point adhering to our morals loses its priority.

In the battle of our dualistic personality between egotism and humility, when an obsessive ego dominates our lives, we inevitably wrong others. We have quite possibly caused harm even if we were raised with a strong set of morals. We may not be over-burdened by guilt if the offenses were minor, but we may still have unresolved issues we would like to see cleaned up. In more severe cases, where our moral resolve was never developed in our youth or weakened by circumstance, we may repeatedly mistreat others, especially our closest loved ones. At these extremes, we cannot escape living a life filled with pain and remorse until we try to bring healing to those we have harmed.

Steps Eight and Nine are about the healing and rebuilding of these relationships. In Step Four when we did our written inventory, we included all the incidents in our lives that brought suffering upon ourselves or others. Extracting a list of the people, businesses or institutions we have identified in this writing will be the starting point for Step Eight, but we may think of others that need to be added as well.

As we go through this process, we may hesitate in adding some of the potential amends recipients to our list. Blame, justification and denial may stand in our way. Just as the fear of revealing indiscretions and defects in Step Five prevents many from doing an honest fourth step, the fear of facing the consequences for our behavior in Step Nine often prevents many from doing a thorough eighth step.

Self-preservation leads us to rationalize that an amends is not due by denying any "real harm" was done, or by unilaterally assuming we can write it off as "water under the bridge." Why should we reopen old wounds? We may alternatively decide that the other party was more at fault than ourselves and that they "got what they deserved", so why should we be the one to make the amends? But such diversion tactics will only keep us chained to our own defects of character. If we are going to be free, we must completely put aside the wrongs that others had done to us and focus only on cleaning our side of the street.

To help overcome our apprehension, we remind ourselves that in Step Eight we are merely making a list. To the best of our ability, we put the actual reparations out of our mind so that we do not become overwhelmed. Simply acknowledging the need for the amends by writing it down will provide a measure of healing, so we want to be as thorough as we can and not exclude anyone out of fear.

Just as we may have separated our fourth step into sections based on the sensitive nature of the events, it may be helpful to divide the list into categories based on the difficulty of correcting the infraction. Easy amends will be those for minor offenses that you have the courage to resolve now. Very difficult amends will be ones that you feel like you are not ready to address anytime soon, but think that you may be able to take care of in the future when you've gained more strength. Extremely difficult or impossible amends will be those that you are terrified to face because of the consequences or you may still hold deep resentments for their role, in which you are not yet willing to let go. Other circumstances such as deceased individuals or businesses no longer in operation may be included here. Keeping in mind the freedom we gain with each infraction that we are able to reconcile, limiting the number we categorize as being impossible is in our best interest.

To help decide on harms we may have caused that warrant an amends, we can ask ourselves questions about our personal relationships. "Is there anyone I have ever abused or betrayed? Have I ever caused physical, mental or emotional harm? Did I ever lie, cheat or steal? Have I borrowed any money I have not yet repaid? Did I ever evoke jealousy, fear or anger in others? Have I shirked on any responsibilities, putting an undue burden on friends, family or coworkers that I have not rectified? On the other hand, did I hold unrealistic expectations, then judge them for not meeting my unreasonable demands? Do I ever try to manipulate with either guilt or deception? Where have I been either controlling or overly dependent?"

But what should we do if we get to this point and still feel like we have not done any harm that still warrants an amend? We can make sure this is the case by soliciting the opinions of our closest loved ones. We can sit down with each friend or family member and ask if there is any infraction we had done in the past that they feel we have never fully rectified. This will give us the assurance that our slate is clean from their perspective, as well.

For each person or institution uncovered by this self-examination, we write down what we feel would be required to amend the infraction. Although it may not be feasible to fulfill the amends completely, we write down what we estimate would be ideal. What would make it right in our minds if the situation was reversed and someone owed us the amends? In some cases, we may decide the bare minimum is insufficient. For example, if we are paying back a debt or returning misappropriated property, we may consider paying extra to cover interest or penalties. We cannot afford to skimp here. It might be helpful to think in terms such as this: "If I had unlimited resources and was guaranteed I would suffer no consequences for making this amend, what would I do to restore what was damaged?"

We are not committing to fulfill this ideal, but this exercise will help us to overcome the fear driven by instincts of self-preservation, while laying the groundwork for the highest quality amends. In actual practice, we may have to settle for something a little less at the time of our atonement. At this point we are simply exercising honesty and accountability.

If we are thorough, we will find a measure of healing, simply by writing them out. We will overcome fears of the past while increasing our integrity and self-respect. We gain the courage to continue on this journey as we build confidence, knowing that we are on the right path and that we might help others to heal, as well as find freedom for ourselves.

Unity Initiative

For each person, business or institution we add to our list, we include the below items:

1. Name of person, business or institution harmed.
2. Brief statement of harm done.
3. Actions needed to completely rectify the damage.
4. Category of difficulty for making this amends.

When completed, we review our list with our sponsor or spiritual advisor. During this discussion, they may give us valuable feedback on the perceived harm, guidance on the action for amends we are unsure about and reassurance in the ones in which we have more confidence. We will also want to discuss the reason for our category of difficulty if we plan to postpone or never make reparations. Our sponsor may give us input on this as well. Sometimes they have good suggestions for approaching a difficult situation that we had not contemplated; but in the end, the final decision on how we categorize and carry out the amends is our own. Although we want to hold ourselves accountable, we must feel safe about our ability to openly discuss them without feeling coerced into something, for which we are not yet ready.

The Twelve Steps

Step Nine
Made direct amends to such people wherever possible, except when to do so would injure them or others (Principles: Honor / Honesty / Accountability / Self-Cleansing / Humility)

In Step Eight we made a list of all persons, businesses and institutions that we had harmed. It may be short with only minor offenses, but to the extent our lives were dominated by egotism, the list will be long and the infractions more severe.

Whether or not these misdeeds were known to others, our altruistic core will feel remorse for any harm we may have caused. In the cases where we were caught hurting those we cared about, we likely followed up with sincere apologies promising not to repeat such behavior. With a healthy life-foundation, we may have been able to keep our word, but if fear-based selfishness is driving us, we are likely to find ourselves returning to old habits and breaking our promises.

When this is carried on for extended periods, our close friends and family eventually lose faith that we will ever change. Exclamations that we are sorry will lose all meaning and verbal apologies begin to fall on deaf ears. In extreme cases, trust may have been so severely eroded that we feel we may never be able to repair the damage. Through this step, however, we discover the solution to mending the wounds caused by our infractions, often putting us on the road for rebuilding these relationships.

As a result of making our amends, we will find true forgiveness for self and for others; but we must first be sure we are on solid ground. This may be the most humbling of all our housecleaning efforts; and because seeking humility is our ultimate aim, we want to be as thorough and effective as possible.

By the time we get to this step, we should have already spent much time studying the basics of the humility principles and putting them to practical use. If we have been rigorous in our previous step-work, we will have undoubtedly made the necessary changes required for making a meaningful amends, but if we have skimped on our efforts, we will not likely be sufficiently armed for this undertaking.

If we are uncertain about the foundation we have built so far, it might be best to postpone this activity until we are confident we have done all that we can to ensure we will not repeat those behaviors. However, if we are confident that we are building upon firm bedrock, we will be ready to take this giant leap towards mending the relationships with those whom we have harmed or neglected.

All steps taken to this point have been building blocks in preparation for Step nine. Each one has returned a measure of sanity from our egotism, resulting in humility and spiritual growth. Along the way, we have mended our self-image, restored our self-respect and we have started strengthening our relationship with our Higher Power. We are now ready to start looking towards renewing our relationships with others.

To provide the best chance for the healing to take place, we must be ready to go to any length to correct our mistakes. More action will likely be required than simply expressing regret, which is important but probably not sufficient by itself. Further, although in some cases the change in behavior may be as simple as not repeating harmful behaviors, that too will likely not fit the bill. More often than not, rectifying the damage will require further action, which may necessitate some sacrifice on our part.

In any case, an effective amend will include a full acknowledgement of the infraction along with a commitment to right the wrong, followed up by taking the necessary action to make full restitution for the incurred damages.

To a large extent, this reparations process will have started long before we even reach this step through our work towards adopting humility attributes into our daily lives. We are becoming more thoughtful of the needs of others and we have started strengthening our practices of selflessness through patience, honesty, kindness and generosity. Such *living-amends* are vital to the success of healing all our relationships and for laying the groundwork of the other reparations we will soon be making.

The list that we created in Step Eight will be the roadmap, which we will use for navigating through Step Nine. Starting with the smaller infractions and working towards the more difficult ones, we approach each individual with a frank acknowledgement of our wrongdoings along with a proposal of what we will do to ameliorate the damage.

The Twelve Steps

Our initial amends are often made to close friends or family who have possibly already observed the positive changes in our personality, and will likely be very receptive when approached. From there, we may move on to coworkers and other acquaintances. With each resolved infraction, we will gain confidence in our efforts as we see years of friction begin to ease. We are then able to move on to the more difficult amends on our list, as they become less daunting.

For some of us, this will include facing atonement for misdeeds that we have so far successfully kept hidden. For those of us who have lived an extreme case of self-will, we may have committed crimes that, if revealed, might land us in jail. We may have embezzled funds from our company or taken property from a business or individual. What are we to do about such difficult situations? What about personal-offenses we have committed, including violence or other abuses? Just thinking about these being exposed causes us great distress. Must we put our own wellbeing at risk for these cases?

The reality though, is that the pain suffered while fighting to keep these crimes concealed will result in far more anguish than the repercussions from squarely facing them. We are trying to arrange to take our pain on the installment plan instead of one big payment, but the interest rate is much too high and we will never pay off the principle. We will suffer the rest of our lives under this plan. We must not let the fear of any personal repercussions we may face deter us from clearing our conscience.

If we are to ever be free, we cannot run from our responsibility. However, bringing unnecessary harm on ourselves will not make this process more effective, so as long as we are thorough in being honest and amending our infraction, we may try to work out the best negotiations that we can. But ultimately, even in cases where we must go to jail for our wrongs, we should be prepared to face those consequences in order to reach the level of freedom we are seeking.

Our lives are short and to go on to the bitter end without experiencing the complete freedom of a clear conscience would be a tragedy. Peace of mind and freedom of spirit while behind bars is infinitely better than physical freedom, when living in the bondage of self with the knowledge of the harm done to others.

Many have already gone before us that have shown the power of such courage by willingly taking responsibility and amending their wrongs in this extraordinary way. Those who have made such extreme reparations tell us they never regretted their decision and were in fact grateful for the peace, which they had been granted. Ironically, some found freedom for the first time while locked up behind bars.

The only reason we avoid approaching someone while working this step, is if we are risking bringing further harm to them or others. Broken romances or other damaged relationships, which resulted in a request that we no longer contact them and potentially bringing harm to an innocent party while unburdening ourselves of our own wrongdoings, are two examples of where we want to be careful about our amends. In any case, where we are not sure, we should talk to our sponsor or others who have faced similar situations. If requests were made for us not to try to contact them, part of our amends will be to honor that request. In cases where no such appeal was made, we use our intuition as to whether or not they should be approached. If we think someone is still very angry or hurt, we may be able to send a letter or get a message relayed through some other means. Having an advisor review our letter before sending it will help us to keep our motives honest and avoid saying something that might unintentionally inflame the situation.

Before making each amends, we want to prepare ourselves to adopt the best mindset that we can. We make an effort of freeing ourselves from debilitating fear that may deter us and high expectations that may set us up for improper motives. Making a request to our Higher Power similar to the one below will help put us in the ideal frame of mind for this undertaking.

"God, please help me to become willing to go to any length to make this amends. Grant me courage that I may overcome any fears that might otherwise prevent me from taking the action that would help others to heal. Allow me to find forgiveness for others, so that resentment will not deter me from cleaning my side of the street. Help me to forgive myself, that I may find freedom from the bondage of self."

During the amends, we can visualize our Higher Power being in the room with us, guiding our words while granting this willingness, courage and forgiveness. In this state, we present what we are doing and make no excuses to justify our behavior but instead take full responsibility for any harm we may have caused. If the situation presents itself, we talk freely about our spiritual beliefs and how they have affected our lives, but we do not want to prejudice anyone on our motives. Our discussion should include what we intend to do to make the amends and ask if they feel if this will be sufficient, or if there is something more they will require from us. If they have conditions that are acceptable, we gladly agree to them. If their requests need more thought though, we ask if we can consider their terms to discuss at a later date. We can then take time to pray about the proposal or consider their request in the presence of a spiritual advisor. This will allow us to make a level-headed decision and return to discuss the matter, after it has been well thought out.

As we continue to make our way through our list, we will find that some of our amends will go as we had envisioned, while in other cases, we may encounter reactions from the recipient that we did not anticipate. For this reason we should be prepared to expect the unexpected to avoid being derailed from our efforts, preventing us from reaching our final objective. We do not want to be deterred from thoroughly fulfilling our need to satisfy the amends, even if the surface response of the recipient is to deny its necessity. We will find that in some circumstances, individuals will either feel uncomfortable with our exhibition of humility, or they will be overcome by compassionate appreciation. They will try to protect our pride by dismissing our wrongdoings, thereby giving us a full pardon in an effort to minimize our discomfort. They may try to let us off the hook by refusing our money, or by denying they were seriously harmed.

Although taking them up on such generosity would be tempting, accepting this offer comes along with the risk that the uncompleted amend will not produce the necessary healing within ourselves or within them. We must not be confused into thinking our goal is simply to receive expressions of forgiveness. Although this may help the healing, it will not be sufficient. When met with these responses, we express our gratitude but explain what we are trying to accomplish and that completing the amends is something we must do if they will allow us. After we have made thorough reparations, we will be delighted at the results. We must not dodge our responsibility, depriving ourselves or the restitution recipient of the healing from this experience.

Some of the amends we face will be to those who have harmed us possibly more than the harm we caused them. Their wrongdoings may have been the excuse we used for rationalizing our own behavior. To provide the best chance for healing, we must be ready and willing to put their infractions aside and concern ourselves only with cleaning up our own side of the street.

In some of these cases, we will find that the other party acknowledges they were in the wrong as well, but at the other extreme they may not only stay silent about their part, but they may respond in a way that could potentially aggravate the situation. When this occurs, we never retaliate, criticize, or try to force an apology for their role. We are there only to focus on correcting our own misconduct. We humbly take the necessary action and thank them for being willing to help us complete the amends. Through this patience and unconditional accountability, we are well on the way towards our transformation. Such unselfish discipline in lifting ourselves above petty arguments about who is to blame will often leave a lasting impression that may help them grow in the future.

In other cases we will face individuals whom we have harmed more than any offense they may have caused us. They may be still suffering from our actions and express anger or other painful feelings when we bring up our infractions. When we are faced with such raw emotion, we do our best to avoid going on the defense. If they are not too elevated, we quietly and patiently allow them to get their thoughts off their chest without interruption. We can then validate their feelings by assuring them we are aware of the pain we caused and that we will do whatever we can in order to set the matter straight. If emotions become volatile or they refuse to hear our amends, we apologize for upsetting them, thank them for their time and let them know we are available if they would like to talk in the future.

If our motives are pure and we humbly approach each individual with a sincere desire to correct our mistakes, the recipients of our reparations will almost always receive us with open arms, allowing the healing to take place. But if our expectations are high that this will be their response, we are likely to set ourselves up for disappointment. If we are not prepared and their reaction does not meet our expectations, we may wind up on the defense and spoil the opportunity.

In some cases, our amends may be met with cool skepticism. Mistrust or bitterness may make them reluctant to accept the apology. Patience again will be the key. We cannot expect that every amends will be immediately well received. The tarnished trust occasionally takes time to restore, but if we are ready to accept their response and can avoid reacting negatively, we will inevitably see healing take place.

After making each amends, we can reflect upon them in self-examination with our Higher Power, reviewing our efforts to assess our perceived effectiveness. In most cases, we will have a deeply meaningful and positive experience; but if things didn't go well, we should review that with our sponsor and possibly write about it to decide on the next course of action. Above all else, we must keep the welfare of others at the forefront of our objective. We do not need to be the doormat for another person's scorn, but we must keep in mind the harms we have caused and ensure we do not add to the damage. If we have honestly put our best foot forward, we can walk with confidence in the knowledge that our intentions were honestly meant to right our wrongs and that we would do more to help them heal if it were possible. We can thank our Higher Power for giving us the courage to do the best we could do to heal these wounds.

In most cases, we will feel a real sense of joy from these experiences, even when we have to sacrifice in order to set the record straight. Long-standing resentments will be diminished. We not only mend our tarnished image, we reach new levels of respect with our community and greater depths of intimacy with loved ones. If we are thorough, fears of past events will no longer haunt us and we will develop an increased sense of self-esteem. When our amends result in a true healing of another's pain, our rewards are made tenfold and we experience a gratitude we have never felt. Although not all of these rewards will be fully realized immediately, they will continue to emerge as we persist in practicing these principles through our ongoing development of the humility attributes.

Step Ten
*Continued to take personal inventory and when
we were wrong promptly admitted it
(Principles: Honesty / Self-Cleansing / Perseverance)*

Through the rigorous efforts of the previous nine steps, we have done our best to clean up any wreckage of the past. We have cleared enough debris off our slate so that the sunlight has begun to shine through with a brightness many of us had not experienced in some time. With the weight having been lifted off our chest, we can now breathe freely. The energy produced by this experience is sometimes so strong that we are overwhelmed with joy. To hold onto this newfound freedom though, more action will be necessary. Although the most difficult step-work is behind us, we cannot stop here and end our efforts towards growth or we will surely backslide.

The remaining three steps, which combine the principles of all twelve steps, prescribe recommendations for cleaning house, spirituality and service that will pave the way for a lifetime of sustained growth and happiness. Whereas the previous nine steps focused mainly on healing wounds of the past, Steps Ten through Twelve address the here and the now. Through these practices, our relationship with the world around us will continually improve, but we must persist in shedding ourselves of old, ineffective ideas and continue to grow towards humility.

When we reflect upon our previous step-work, many of us will concede we approached the first nine steps with much skepticism. We believed we already had all the answers. The proposals either seemed irrelevant, unnecessary or beneath us. We had difficulty finding the willingness to surrender and take the suggested action. Finally going on blind faith, we went against our intuition and followed the advice of those who went before us. When we humbled ourselves and took the steps, we were able to discover the happiness we observed being enjoyed by others. Through these experiences, our apprehension faded, our perceptions changed and we gained confidence in the potential for these disciplines in helping resolve everyday problems.

In Step Ten our perceptions are challenged once again. The ideals presented will be hard for some to swallow at first, but with an open mind, tools will be forged that will allow us to stay free from the shackles of bondage that took so much pain and effort in removing through the previous nine steps.

Step Ten refines the principle of personal responsibility to its very essence. This is the value that each individual is responsible for his or her own wellbeing and accountable for their feelings, perceptions and behavior. The most difficult challenge we face when incorporating this principle is accepting the suggestion of fundamentally forfeiting reliance on the use of blame. Blame is a coping mechanism used for diverting responsibility to others. Since this is the antithesis of accountability, abandoning such practices is necessary to further develop tools for introspection and house cleaning. We may still acknowledge wrongs committed by others and hold them accountable for their actions, but we no longer hold them responsible for our continued wellbeing.

The most prevalent sign we are still holding on to blame as a diversion tactic is anger and its many manifestations. These include irritability, annoyance, resentment and rage.

While working the previous steps, we discover that we frequently held onto resentments that distorted our perceptions even in cases where we had truly been wronged. Disillusionment brought on by lack of factual information clouded our judgment causing us to overreact. Some of us spent years holding onto resentments not even aware we had a choice. We believed that until other people changed or righted some wrong, we would naturally stay angry. Yet with the help of our Higher Power and the example of others, we found that Steps Four through Nine could relieve us from our torment without any changes from those we were convinced were the source of our prolonged suffering.

As we matured through this process, the clarity of our new set of beliefs began unlocking our chains of bondage. But some may still hold onto the notion that others are at least occasionally responsible for our personal problems. To the extent this is true, our peace of mind and happiness are helplessly at the mercy of the conduct of everyone with whom we come in contact. As long as we continue to hold on to this perception, we are giving others control of our lives and we are susceptible to re-accumulating the debris that blocks us from joy.

To the degree that we can embrace personal responsibility will we free ourselves from this trap. The Alcoholics Anonymous book, *Twelve Steps and Twelve Traditions* clearly breaks this concept down, presenting simple attitudes and effective measures for adapting this attribute into our lives. Concerning taking responsibility for our feelings, this book makes the below assertion, which essentially gives no leeway for blame.

> It is a spiritual axiom that every time we are **disturbed**, no matter what the cause, there is something wrong with us. If somebody hurts us and we are sore, we are in the wrong also. But are there no exceptions to this rule? What about "justifiable" anger? If somebody cheats us, aren't we entitled to be mad? Can't we be properly angry with self-righteous folk? For us of A.A. these are dangerous exceptions. We have found that justified anger ought to be left to those better qualified to handle it.
>
> Few people have been more victimized by resentments than have we alcoholics. It mattered little whether our resentments were justified or not. A burst of temper could spoil a day, and a well-nursed grudge could make us miserably ineffective. Nor were we ever skillful in separating justified from unjustified anger. As we saw it, our wrath was always justified. Anger, that occasional luxury of more balanced people, could keep us on an emotional jag indefinitely.
>
> Other kinds of disturbances–jealousy, envy, self-pity, or hurt pride–did the same thing. *

* Twelve Steps and Twelve Traditions; pg.90. Go to Appendix-D for the statement of non-affiliation from Alcoholics Anonymous.

This interpretation of personal responsibility raises the bar on this principle to its highest level. A *spiritual axiom* is a fundamental truth of spirituality which needs no further proof. When we become convinced that *every time* we are hurt, angry, fearful, jealous or experiencing any other negative emotion, that these disturbances are actually exposing a problem within ourselves regardless of the cause, then it becomes clear that blaming these feelings on the wrongs of others only prolongs our pain.

However, this concept is not easily digested and in spite of the attempt to head off anticipated skepticism, many still respond dubiously, "but if someone really harms us, isn't it only human to become disturbed?" Of course, in many cases this is only natural. For example, being attacked or observing acts of violence will surely result in a strong emotional reaction. But we must be careful not to use such exceptions as wholesale justification for the continued use of unwarranted condemnation for every perceived offense. We reduce our peace of mind and inhibit our growth when we set limits on our ability to let go of *any* negative experience.

Our capacity to move past negative feelings will come quicker if we can separate the acknowledgement of the wrongdoings of others from our responsibility of our own emotional state. With this capability, we will avoid diverting our attention in the wrong direction, needlessly prolonging our suffering.

This excerpt also mentions that many are not skilled in separating justified from unjustified anger. From our ego's perspective, "our wrath was *always* justified." But how often are we really exposed to extreme offenses, such as personal attacks, compared to the frequency in which we encounter anger or self-pity? And who among us is not guilty of occasionally overreacting in day-to-day experiences and letting the disturbance linger far beyond the initial emotional reaction? Many of us have at some time resorted to letting friends, family or coworkers stew in our seething silent scorn to punish them for their deeds. We have used guilt to keep people in line or to hold someone responsible for our own self-pity. Such behavior usually resulted in strained or damaged relationships that eventually brought us more pain than the original perceived offense.

One of the many contributors to the personal stories in the book *Alcoholics Anonymous* provides the below personal discovery. Their insight gives clarity to the assertion of the spiritual axiom that something is wrong with *us* whenever we are disturbed with any negative emotion.

And acceptance is the answer to *all* my problems today. When I am ***disturbed***, it is because I find some person, place, thing or situation, some fact of my life, unacceptable to me, and I can find no serenity until I accept that person, place, thing or situation as being exactly the way it is supposed to be at this moment. Nothing, absolutely nothing happens in God's world by mistake.

>...unless I accept life completely on life's terms, I cannot be happy. I need to concentrate, not so much on what needs to be changed in the world, as on what needs to be changed in me and my attitudes.
>
> *Alcoholics Anonymous: fourth edition*; pg.417

Perhaps the best thing of all for me is to remember that my serenity is inversely proportional to my expectations. The higher my expectations of other people are, the lower is my serenity. Acceptance is the key to my relationship with God today. I never just sit and do nothing while waiting for Him to tell me what to do. Rather, I do whatever is in front of me to be done, and I leave the results up to Him; however it turns out, that's God's will for me. I must keep my magic magnifying mind on my acceptance and off my expectations, for my serenity is directly proportional to my level of acceptance. When I remember this, I can see I've never had it so good. *

Expectations are said to be the seeds of resentment. With this awareness, we can stay on guard for these insidious ego-bated traps that lead to blame and leads to a grudge. Acceptance is the key to returning us back to serenity. When we do become disturbed, responsibility for unreasonable expectations need always fall back on our shoulders if we wish to end unnecessary suffering since waiting for resolution of our agitation to come from those who "let us down" is tantamount to blame.

* *Alcoholics Anonymous: fourth edition*; pg.420; *Go to Appendix-D for the statement of non-affiliation from Alcoholics Anonymous.*

There will certainly be times where we encounter others stepping on our toes in the quest of self-serving pursuits. People will come into our lives who are weakened emotionally and suffering from insecurities or a dominant ego. We may occasionally face insults, betrayals unwarranted criticism, or humiliation. We may encounter situations where someone casts an unflattering light on us in an effort to protect their own image. Or we may find that someone has been gossiping about us, spreading untrue rumors.

This step has us examine ourselves for how we react to all such situations. "Do I become hurt or fearful and go on the defense?" "Do I become angry and retaliate?" Although we do not want to simply put our heads in the sand after such infringements, we must rise above fearful condemnation in order to avoid being poisoned with cynicism. We do a self-examination looking for selfish expectations and adjust our own perceptions, regardless of the circumstance.

In their "unsparing self-survey" of their malady, the members of Alcoholics Anonymous make the following discovery:

> Selfishness, self-centeredness! That, we think, is the root of our troubles. Driven by a hundred forms of fear, self-delusion, self-seeking, and self-pity, we step on the toes of our fellows and they retaliate. Sometimes they hurt us, seemingly without provocation, but we invariably find that at some time in the past we have made decisions based on self, which later placed us in a position to be hurt.
>
> So our troubles, we think, are basically of our own making. They arise out of ourselves, and the alcoholic is an extreme example of self-will run riot, though he usually doesn't think so. Above everything, we alcoholics must be rid of this selfishness. We must or it kills us! God makes that possible. And there often seems no way of entirely getting rid of self without His aid. Many of us had moral and philosophical convictions galore, but we could not live up to them even though we would have liked to. Neither could we reduce our self-centeredness much by wishing or trying on our own power. We had to have God's help.*

* Alcoholics Anonymous; pg.62. Go to Appendix-D for the statement of non-affiliation from Alcoholics Anonymous.

Being open-minded to accept such a self-appraisal is much easier when you've been beaten down by a disease such as alcoholism. However, many who will join Unity Initiative will likely be fortunate enough to have never had to cope with such addictions. These members may therefore have not experienced the extreme levels of fear-driven selfishness described above, yet all humans are potentially susceptible to such frailties. Each individual must evaluate how well the shoe fits. If we cannot completely exclude ourselves from these appraisals, then we must keep this self-knowledge in the forefront of our mind as we practice our daily inventory.

We come to realize that although our instincts continue to tempt us to blame others for our disturbances, fear-driven selfishness is usually a bigger factor. We have indeed come a long way in our spiritual growth when we are able to come to this conclusion. We find that we need only change our perception to prevent negative feelings and avoid giving others control of our emotions. Responsibility is consistently put back on the individual since that is the only path to freedom.

To continue growth in our thinking and behavior, the members of U.I. will need to adopt similar uncompromising self-examination. A new set of tools will need to be developed to help us avoid the traps that lead to resentment and self-pity. Once we have digested the concepts presented above, we will find that the actual actions are not at all difficult. To develop our skills in taking personal responsibility, we will simply apply the disciplines we started in Steps Four through Nine in our day-to-day lives. Instead of allowing debris to accumulate, we deal with it as soon as we are capable. To do this we must take inventory daily and when we realize we have subjected another to selfish behavior, we promptly make our amends.

Like a business, we may periodically take a formal, all-inclusive inventory that is rigorous and self-searching such as the house cleaning we did in the fourth and fifth steps.

However, a business cannot afford to wait extended periods before uncovering a potential disaster. To avoid this situation, they might incorporate a perpetual inventory, keeping a watchful eye on all items in stock from day to day so that they can then respond proactively before problems grow out of control. Defective items can then be discarded while deficiencies in higher quality assets can be developed. We can do the same thing with our temperament throughout the day as suggested below.

> A spot-check inventory taken in the midst of disturbances can be of very great help in quieting stormy emotions. Today's spot check finds it chief application to situations, which arise in each day's march. The consideration of long-standing difficulties had better be postponed, when possible, to times deliberately set aside for that purpose.
>
> In all these situations we need self-restraint, honest analysis of what is involved, a willingness to admit when the fault is ours, and an equal willingness to forgive when the fault is elsewhere. We need not

The Twelve Steps

be discouraged when we fall into the error of our old ways, for these disciplines are not easy. We shall look for progress, not perfection.

Our first objective will be the development of self-restraint. This carries a top priority rating. When we speak or act hastily or rashly, the ability to be fair-minded and tolerant evaporates on the spot. One unkind tirade or one willful snap judgment can ruin our relation with another person for a whole day, or maybe a whole year. Nothing pays off like restraint of tongue and pen.

We must avoid quick-tempered criticism and furious, power-driven argument. The same goes for sulking and silent scorn. These are emotional booby traps baited with pride and vengefulness. Our first job is to sidestep the traps. When we are tempted by the bait, we should train ourselves to step back and think. For we can neither think nor act to good purpose until the habit of self-restraint has become automatic. [1]

As we go through the day we pause, when agitated or doubtful, and ask for the right thought or action. We constantly remind ourselves we are no longer running the show, humbly saying to ourselves many times each day "Thy will be done." We are then in much less danger of excitement, fear, anger, worry, self-pity, or foolish decisions. We become much more efficient. We do not tire so easily, for we are not burning up energy foolishly as we did when we were trying to arrange life to suit ourselves. [2]

It works - it really does.

[1] *Twelve Steps and Twelve Traditions;* pg.90-91
[2] *Alcoholics Anonymous;* pg.87-88

To get started on the right footing each day, we can arm ourselves by enlisting our Higher Power with a morning prayer such as the following example.

"God, please allow my thinking to be divorced from fear, dishonesty, selfishness, and self-pity. Help me to replace egotism with humility. Let my heart and my thoughts be filled with love, strength, wisdom and joy that I may be of better service to you while maximizing my effectiveness in helping others. How can I best serve you today?"

Having aligned our will with God's will with these thoughts, we are ready to face the day. When we fall down and get caught up in emotional turmoil, we promptly renew our thoughts with this prayer and bring God back into the picture.

Of course, developing these skills takes practice. When we start off, our self-examination will occasionally come in the aftermath of damage already done. In the evening before we go to bed each night, we may review the day with our sponsor, another friend or with our Higher Power in prayer and meditation. We can scrutinize any difficulties we encountered, as well as acknowledge our progress. We examine our emotions throughout the day for disturbances and take a look at contention in our interactions with others.

Asking ourselves reflective questions at the end of the day will help in this review. "Was I able to diffuse conflict and avoid confrontation? Did I bring harmony and peace into communications, or was I irritable, divisive or defensive? Was I flexible and open-minded towards the ideas of other's or was I obstinate? Did I treat people around me with respect and kindness, or was I impatient, terse or abrasive? What action did I take to clean house, seek God, or give of myself? Did I journal or share my difficulties with another? Did I pray or meditate? Who did I make time for; to listen to and support? What action did I take in the realm of unity? Did I go to meetings or talk to others of diverse groups? How can I improve in these areas?"

In some cases during our daily activities, pausing when agitated is not always possible such as when feeling backed into a corner during a disagreement. If we carried on dialogs while in this state, words will possibly have come out sideways adding to the tension. If that is the case, we must examine these situations to honestly appraise our role. If we are still upset about something from the day's events, we will find that writing about it can make a big difference in quieting our mind and putting us at ease. With pen in hand, we dump the chaos in our head onto paper. As recommended in the fourth step "stream of conscience" journaling, we write until all negative feelings are purged. This tool can clear the murky thoughts of our mind and bring us soothing tranquility. If we find we owe an amends, we may want to discuss it with our sponsor then take care of it as soon as the opportunity arises.

As our skill in taking a spot-check inventory grows, we will find that we are eventually able to automatically catch ourselves at the very first sign of agitation, averting painful situations by immediately adjusting our perception. We learn to listen without becoming defensive. Patience becomes natural. We begin to see that others are simply children of God just like ourselves; neither better nor worse. When we cross paths with those who allow fear to control their behavior because they do not have these tools, we lift ourselves above any turmoil, love them unconditionally and avail ourselves to them so that they can break free of their own bondage. These thoughts and attitudes must be practiced every day, in every area of our lives. Whether at home with our family or at work in a stressful situation; whether in line at the grocery store, or stuck in traffic, we try to take on each challenge with kindness and patience.

In addition to keeping our side of the street clean when relationships are in conflict, practicing our house cleaning in Step Ten will also help us in strengthening bonds through open and honest communications. As our trust grows, we become more inclined to openly communicate feelings with an ever-expanding circle of loved ones. Regardless if our head is in a good space or not, regularly opening ourselves up to others prevents emotions from bottling up and turning into anxiety.

For some, talking about our innermost joys and sorrows is a skill that can seem very awkward, at first. Finding a vocabulary beyond, "I feel fine", takes practice. A good place to start is within a step-study group that includes other friends who are making use of these tools. These groups give us a chance to delve below the surface to communicate the health of our wellbeing. Such dialogs will create long-term bonds of trust and help keep our minds free of clutter. A good way to start such group dialogs is to go around the room, in turn sharing our state of mind. Using an agreed upon scale, similar to the below example, will allow us to clearly communicate and understand each other's overall level of peace.

1. Devoid of hope. Consumed with thoughts of destruction, due to unbearable fear or rage.
2. Mostly suffering with thoughts of hopeless destruction, but not resulting in absolute despair.
3. Persistent depression or self-pity fueled resentment, but with fleeting moments of relief.
4. Much depression and occasional hopelessness, but with short periods of hope.
5. Moderate depression, confusion, self-pity and anger, mixed with occasional periods of peace and connection with others.
6. Periodic bouts of mild depression or anger balanced with a

good amount of hope, happiness and fulfilling relationships.
7. Occasional discontent or irritability, but mostly happy and grateful.
8. Very happy, but with a small sense of anxiety.
9. Filled with much love, gratitude and joy. Mostly yearning and worry-free.
10. Absolutely free: free from fear, worry, regrets, obsessive yearnings and any other feeling that causes internal disturbance. Completely contented in relationships. Secure in all areas of life and filled with delight. Happiness will never be greater than it is at this moment.

In addition to discussing our level of well-being, we can include the actions we have taken to clean house, seek spirituality, help others and become active in diverse groups. We are then able to make a direct link between the action we take and the impact those measures have had on our life. Opening ourselves to others with this level of honesty in exposing our feelings and accountability for our actions forces us out of our comfort zone, but with practice, becomes natural. The benefits we gain from this open communication will soon overcome any reluctance we may have.

As we continue, we are able to reach new levels of depth into our conscience that we could not do alone in our solitary spot-check reviews. We more effectively avoid accumulation of unwanted debris, such as anxiety, anger and envy, thereby making way for happiness. Fears of people, places and things begin to vanish, becoming replaced with faith and compassion. We find understanding and intimacy in our relationships with those around us. Our whole life becomes more stable because our emotions have less control over our behavior. We are able to stay calm and at peace, even during moments of strife or chaos. The regular use of these practical tools keeps our head clear and our heart free. When rigorous house cleaning is turned into a daily practice, we safeguard ourselves against re-accumulating debris that could inhibit our growth.

The Twelve Steps

Step Eleven
Sought through prayer and meditation to improve our conscious contact with God as we understood Him, praying only for knowledge of His will for us and the power to carry that out
(Principles: Humility / Spirituality)

Continuous practice of spiritual disciplines is the theme of Step Eleven. In Step Two we took definitive action towards searching ourselves for our ideals about our spiritual beliefs. We first wrote down the attributes that we believe our Higher Power possesses that makes them greater than ourselves. We then wrote down what principles we believe they want us to live by and the necessary behaviors and character traits we must adopt to live by those principles. After establishing this foothold on our spiritual beliefs, we carried those ideals forward and relied upon our Higher Power to guide our action and deliver us through each step. From the beginning, we have adopted the discipline of prayer to maximize our conscious contact with God. In Step Eleven, we continue to refine the use of prayer and begin to practice meditation to strengthen our spiritual unity. With these tools, we find truth in the statement *"Repetition strengthens and confirms habit and then faith becomes natural."*

The forms of our prayers may differ greatly. Prayers can be performed in solitude where we incorporate self-survey while seeking guidance. They can be shared with friends or family to set the foundation of relationships, or we may join large groups in this practice to strengthen our unity. We may follow religious customs handed down from past generations, or we may adopt the disciplines we observe by spiritual advisors. In each case, we develop routines that are customized to fit our own beliefs.

The reasons for prayer may also vary. We may pray to unload our burdens or to ask for guidance and direction. We may pray to give thanks, to make a plea or to pledge our devotion and service to God and to our fellow man. So how should we pray and what should we pray for? Of course, there is no set answer to this question and it will vary depending on our own concepts of spirituality. However, here are some practices that many have found effective in their daily use of prayer.

When praying alone, finding a quiet spot where we will not be disturbed will keep us from being distracted. Praying in the morning gives us a chance to align our thoughts with God's will for us by asking for direction and how we can best be of service. We are then put in a frame of mind that allows us to focus on living within the principles we established in Step Two, while leaving the results in the hands of our Higher Power. Throughout the day, short prayers can be used to maintain spiritual-mindedness and help us through trying times. In evening prayers, we can review our day and give thanks.

When attending meetings within our fellowship or at our places of worship, we are given the opportunity to participate in group prayers. A common favorite adopted by many groups is the *Serenity Prayer* given below. This succinct petition eloquently expresses our desire to live in harmony with God and the world around us.

"God, grant me the serenity to accept the things I cannot change; Courage to change the things I can; And wisdom to know the difference."

With these words we convey our desire to be at peace and let go of people, places and things that are not in our control. We entrust these to the domain of our Higher Power, releasing them to God's care. In doing so, we avoid frustration, self-pity and resentment. We increase our effectiveness by minimizing wasted energy on perceived problems of the universe in which we have no control.

We next state our willingness to change that which we can. We ask for courage so that fear does not inhibit our growth. We always first look inward for this change, since we have minimal direct influence over the behavior and attitudes of those around us. We are most effective at shaping our universe by embracing guiding principles, then practicing them in our lives.

Finally, we ask God to make us aware of where the line is drawn between those things we can change versus those which are out of our control. With this knowledge, we can let go of situations when holding on will only exacerbate a problem, and we can engage in a solution when our efforts can contribute to a positive outcome.

However we choose to pray, we find this act of humility to be a very stabilizing tool in our lives. In prayer we face God directly and review our most personal thoughts and difficulties. If we are overwhelmed in fear, prayer will often lead us the way out of our suffering, but like all other disciplines, we must be rigorous and persistent. If need be, we must be ready to stay in prayer for as long as necessary until we find peace. Along with our personal connection with our Higher Power, the daily practice of prayer will increase serenity, patience, forgiveness, and improve our intuition and our relationships.

Like prayer, there seems to be unlimited forms for practicing meditation. This discipline involves spending varying periods of time in thought, reflection or contemplation in order to reach a deep state of relaxation and heightened awareness. Also like prayer, many prefer to practice this discipline in a quiet place, such as a candle-lit room. Others experience the same benefits of meditation through nature-walks, exposure to the arts, or contemplation of spiritual principles.

Meditation too, need not be practiced alone. Exercising this discipline in a group setting can be very enjoyable and beneficial. We strengthen our relationships with others, while we are increasing our spiritual wellbeing. But unlike prayer, which usually involves voicing what is on our mind and in our heart to our Higher Power, in meditation we are usually quiet and try to clear our thoughts.

To start, we can make ourselves as comfortable as possible by sitting or lying down in a quiet room, then closing our eyes to further limit sensory input. We can then continue in this relaxed state while in silence for periods ranging anywhere from a couple of minutes to over an hour. During this time we may focus on our breathing, a specific word or visualized images in order to block out all other thoughts. When our mind starts to wander, we simply let those thoughts pass by so we can return to the relaxed state. Other techniques involve contemplation of the meaning of an inspirational passage, phrase, prayer or poem. Meditation can make use of visualization where we see ourselves in a peaceful setting, such as a rainforest or a sunlit meadow.

You may find that sitting quietly for even a few minutes can be very difficult when you are just starting out. If so, playing recorded sounds or music or using guided meditation can help. Guided meditation is a form of visualization, in which a guide takes us on a mental voyage by describing imaginary scenery. Alternatively, the guide may repeat certain words or phrases to help us reach a state of tranquility. The guide may be an individual in a group, but recordings are also available. Accompanying our meditation with soothing sounds, such as ocean waves, or tones from an instrument, or calming music can also help us get in the desired state of mind.

Many books are available to guide us in various techniques, but the goal of meditation is almost always to enter a deep, peaceful state by quieting our thinking. While turning our attention to a single thought, we block the random noise-producing activity of our mind. When we are in fear or suffering in any way, our thoughts are racing in our subconscious, preventing a tranquil state and prolonging our anxiety. By freeing our mind of such clatter, we are able to calm ourselves down and return to peace.

Some believe that while we pray to relay our thoughts to God, we meditate to open ourselves up to receive God's message. A heightened mental awareness can enable a closer connection with our Higher Power. Regular practice of meditation will result in increased health and happiness by reducing stress. Increased joy is also achieved due to its effectiveness in bringing us into the moment. The clatter of our thoughts frequently traps us in the past or the future, which is a symptom of a fear-controlled mind. We may dwell on regret, shame or guilt of past events or fear of looming future difficulties, or we may be fixated on upcoming events that we fantasize will deliver us from unhappiness. In this state, we are letting our life slip by without enjoying the present. When we meditate, all points in time are returned to their proper place. We find contentedness in the moment; we are able to *live in the now*.

The Twelve Steps

Step Twelve
Having had a spiritual awakening as the result of these steps, we tried to carry this message to others, and to practice these principles in all our affairs
(Principles: Humility / Love / Service / Self-Sacrifice)

With the growth we've gained through our rigorous efforts in the past eleven steps, we find a level of hope and joy we had never known. We acquire a renewed sense of faith in God and in our fellow man and we sometimes feel as though a miracle has occurred in our lives. We have been granted a gift. Now filled with gratitude, we continue to practice the principles of house cleaning and spirituality while we seek to give away what was so freely given to us. With these disciplines in place we are guaranteed to flourish with happy, abundant lives.

We have likely started the practice of giving, long before we reached this step and probably before becoming involved in our fellowship. Anytime we are selflessly kind and helpful, we are living within the spirit of Step Twelve. Now armed with valuable principles that consistently bring us joy, we are in a position to increase our effectiveness in service. Our transformation through our step-work gives us the necessary training that uniquely qualifies us to carry this message to those seeking to adopt these values. Introducing others to these principles and bringing them through the steps adds richness to our lives.

Watching fears evaporate, happiness grow, and relationships strengthened are wonders you must see for yourself. In some cases individuals are suffering from various trials and tribulations of life and find relief in the steps that they were unable to find elsewhere. Broken hearts become mended, lost dreams restored, families are put back together. Witnessing these miracles never becomes mundane. They consistently fill us with humbling delight. These encounters are vital to our own continued growth, so exercising these principles must become a regular practice. We ask each day in prayer and meditation how we can best serve God and our fellow man.

Many ingredients of our personality can be developed to increase our effectiveness in giving to others. Starting with the attribute of *spirituality,* the first part of this step assumes we have had a *spiritual awakening* as the result of working the previous steps. The forms of these awakenings vary from member to member. In most cases, they come in the form of a psychic change; a transformation of our perceptions and beliefs that slowly redirects our life. For some though, the experience is much more dramatic. In some cases, they are so acute that they include physical sensations that facilitate in an immediate transformation.

One well-known episode of such phenomena was reported by AA-cofounder, Bill Wilson, in his story written for the Alcoholics Anonymous text. He describes having a vision of a bright light along with an immense emotional upheaval, after taking the recommended action to overcome alcoholism.

He was so overwhelmed that he reported the incident to his doctor. Although neither Bill nor his physician could conclude what brought on the experience, he was so deeply moved it became a key factor to his forming that society. However, such immediate "burning bush" encounters are rare. Awakenings are usually gradual, coming slowly as the result of our accumulated knowledge from the education and experiences we receive when taking the steps. This process can potentially take several months. Those close to us sometimes notice the growth in us before we acknowledge it ourselves. In any case, we find that we have had a transformation in our lives that enables us to completely change our perceptions and behavior in a way that did not previously seem attainable.

Only through thoroughly cleaning house is this transformation made possible. We will reduce the benefits if we do not have a sufficiently clean slate. To be effective in teaching others the principles of the steps, we must experience them for ourselves. We cannot give away something we do not have.

The next set of ingredients we will need for this step is *love, compassion and kindness*. In this service we will be helping people of all walks of life; rich and poor, young and old, healthy and sick, those with and without jobs or family. We want to avail ourselves to people of all races and ethnicities as well as everyone on the spiritual spectrum regardless of belief. Some of those we assist will have lived through unimaginable trauma. Some will have legal difficulties and some may even have mental or psychological problems. We may not have the answers to all the complications our members may face, but we give our love to all and we approach them with understanding compassion. We provide them emotional support and walk beside them as they face their difficulties. When we earnestly seek to be of maximum service in this way, we find that God will provide us with abundant love, courage and strength to share with all.

The quality of our service will be determined by the ingredient of *humility*. This could be the most important attribute when serving others. Since this is a key element that we are seeking through working the steps, our own level of humility will be the example for those we are guiding. We live in a glass house and make no attempt to hide our frailties. We are honest when we are afraid and we admit our mistakes. The rewards from our life of humility will be our testimonial for this model of living. We must also set aside self-righteous evangelism. We do not want to come off like we are talking down to anyone. We only try to be helpful. We are not offended when someone declines to walk this path.

When serving others, we must keep in mind that we benefit just as much as those seeking our guidance. Their problems in life, their desire to change, and their willingness to work through the steps are our opportunity to give to another so that we may stay free from the bondage of self for another day. By serving them, we give ourselves the vital nutrition needed for our daily strength. They are a blessing and we let them know this up front. But we also let them know that their own growth will be contingent on how well they pass it on to those who follow them. Some hold that helping others is our effort to compensate for the support we received while going through the steps. This work is certainly a privilege. With this perspective, we stay in gratitude and consistently experience joy through this discipline.

This leads to the next ingredient we must take on which is *willingness to sacrifice* along with the ingredient of *selflessness,* which is an integral part of this attribute. We give of ourselves unconditionally and without expectations on those who we serve. To reap the rewards of service work, we must be ready to give of our time and our care. Requests for help frequently seem to come when most inconvenient, but we selflessly sacrifice when called upon, making their needs a priority.

The next attributes we will need are *patience* and *tolerance,* which will be most needed when we walk others through the steps.

Ideally, everyone we work with will be completely ready to surrender with the willingness to take the suggested action. In such cases these attributes are obviously not necessary. However, this is not the usual circumstance most of us find ourselves in when starting on this path. In the beginning, the proposals suggested in the steps seem foreign or unnecessary. Our egotism resists the humility of self-examination, spirituality and service. Some will have difficulty mustering up the courage or willingness to meet these challenges. In some cases following these suggestions will be entirely rejected. If our motives are in the right place, responding to such outright refusal will require very little patience as well. Since we can only assist those who desire to take the required action, we simply respect their decision and let it go at that.

Where patience will most be required in sponsorship is when we, as sponsees, are caught on the fence between the hope of the growth we see in others and the intimidation of dredging up our past during our step-work. Most going through the steps will naturally have some level of trepidation here. We find all forms of rationalization and excuses for dodging these efforts. When we face this reluctance, a firm but gentle nudge can sometimes help us stay accountable and keep us on track. Of course, no one wants to be forcefully pushed into doing something they are afraid to do. We should not try to control others, nor manipulate them into action they are simply not ready to take. Discipline-tempered patience will be required to allow ourselves to step back before we cross a personal boundary, while working against a high level of resistance.

The ingredient of *perceptive intuition* enables us to understand where the line is drawn between a gentle nudge and forceful control; a boundary that is different for each individual. Some of us appreciate a very firm approach from those we trust and respect. We welcome their confident clear-cut direction and unwavering insight as positive authoritative guidance. Others will perceive such an approach with great skepticism and view it as an intrusion into their personal space. Those of us in this category respond much better to a gentle guide that simply lays out the program of action and respects the autonomy of the individual to follow up with the necessary work.

Patience is also tied to our *ability to listen*. This simple ingredient goes a long way, but is not so easily exercised. To be able to sit passively and focus our attention on what is being said without interrupting with interjections of your own thoughts takes practice. In most cases, when someone comes to us with a problem and they are ready to take responsibility but simply need to vent, listening requires no feedback. We simply need to acknowledge their feelings and give them a chance to state what's on their mind. This builds trust, since we are not placing judgment.

There will naturally be some circumstances where we will want to give responses during such house cleaning discussions. One example is when our advice is requested, and another is when we are in a sponsorship role, guiding someone through the steps before they step in a common pitfall.

The *ability to give constructive feedback* is probably the most difficult of all service skills and will come with experience, but there are general guidelines that can help. First, is to remove judgment from your heart and mind. We want to be as loving and gentle as possible. Negative criticism or forceful control will not be helpful. We do our best to empathize with their situation and acknowledge the difficulty of their struggle. Since many of the problems brought to us will involve emotions of agitation brought on by conflict, we will next want to guide those we serve to likewise lift themselves above judgment and take ownership for their state of mind. We gently help them see what their role or responsibility is in each circumstance.

Beyond validating their feelings, we usually want to focus on their own personal role in the conflict. Taking sides is a mistake. We have no power to change the other person who is not there to defend themself. To demonize them will cause distortions that will create a diversion from finding a healing solution. So we guide those we are helping into seeing the perspective of the other person, present a human face and grant them the benefit of a doubt they are doing the best they can in the situation with the tools they have. To the extent they can empathize with the person who they are in conflict with, will they be able to free themselves of their distress.

Finally, we try to avoid giving advice on any situation, which is beyond our own personal experience. We especially do not want to try to guide someone through any step we have not yet completed ourselves. If a problem is presented that we have not personally had to work through, but we know someone who has, we direct them to that individual.

However, there may be some cases where we are asked for advice on situations that we are neither familiar with, nor know of anyone else with such experience. In these situations, we can sometimes offer a recommendation based on the principles, but we make it clear that this is just our opinion.

Regardless of whether we are confident in our advice or we are just giving an educated guess upon request, we offer this feedback as a suggestion and do not become offended if our advice is not taken. We can be content that our ideals have been conveyed and keep in mind that they helped us by letting us play a part in helping them.

All of these attributes for being of service, as well as the "Guided by Humility" traits listed in chapter five take time to develop. Although some of us appear to be more naturally gifted with our ability in reaching others, we will all increase our effectiveness as we continue to grow through the practice of these skills. Because there is no "one size fits all" approach that best suits everyone, we are all uniquely valuable in this service. We each have our own set of gifts that we have developed from a lifetime of individual experiences. We inevitably find that we are each able to touch some people that others may not have been able to reach. Because of this, we are all needed for this work.

So, in what ways can we be of service and how do we get started? Below is a breakdown of the *twelve steps of Step Twelve* which summarizes the advancement of involvement in helping others. The progression starts from the beginnings of a newcomer and advances to the matured member who has rigorously worked the steps and exemplifies the principles in all their affairs, as suggested in Step Twelve. This is a recommended path that will guarantee our success. The progression of these practices can start as soon as we are ready. And although we do not want to rush into the next sub-step before we gain a solid footing, we also want to make sure we don't unnecessarily delay our progress. On the other hand, we want to keep a humble attitude and maintain our willingness to participate in any service that is needed from us, no matter how trivial.

The Twelve Steps

- 12.1 – Go to meetings and listen with an open mind. From the beginning, start thinking about the principles and the personal attributes required for service work. Start observing those who exemplify these ideals and begin incorporating them into your own life.
- 12.2 – Get a sponsor who exemplifies service-oriented attributes. Talk to them regularly and start working through the steps. Be thorough in your house cleaning so that you will be able to unblock yourself from debilitating debris that could hinder your effectiveness in helping others. To the extent we clean house can we confidently relay the benefits of these practices.
- 12.3 – Contribute to your group. Come to meetings early to help set up and greet members. Stay late to help clean up and meet up with others after meetings. We will benefit by a sense of usefulness and humility by these basic services regardless of our longevity.
- 12.4 – Share/contribute in meetings. Relay the experiences you have had as the result of taking action to adopt the principles.
- 12.5 – Talk to at least one person, one-on-one, at each gathering of our fellowship. Share with them and your sponsor any difficulties you are facing. The simple exercise of getting our burdens off our chest will help alleviate these emotions. This is the act of cleaning house.
- 12.6 – Invest yourself in the fellowship. Get in the center. Develop close relationships with several other men and women committed to putting these ideals into practice. Hold yourself accountable with these friends in the same way you do with your sponsor. Share your most intimate thoughts and feelings.
- 12.7 – Reach out to newcomers and welcome them. Help them to get involved by answering their questions and introducing them to members of the group.
- 12.8 – Take part in the responsibility of your group's welfare and volunteer for a service commitment, such as: meeting chair, group coordinator, treasurer or secretary.
- 12.9 – Participate in 12-step calls and service commitments to outside institutions. Observe how experienced members exercise the principles in their own lives and apply the humility attributes in their service work.

- 12.10 – As soon as you have a solid foundation in step-work, start reaching out to those going through difficulties. Listen to them, share your experience, strength and hope and make yourself available for sponsorship.
- 12.11 – Bring others through the steps, giving freely of yourself. Spend time with newcomers and those you sponsor, studying literature that can help reinforce your ideals and increase your understanding of the principles. Guide them in the specific actions for cleaning house, seeking God and being of service. Walk with them as they take action in their step-work. Involve them in your service commitments. Be an example to them of truth, love and unity.
- 12.12 – Get involved in carrying this message to the outside world. Present informational panels and when appropriate, offer meetings to any institution interested in our service. Examples will include colleges or places of worship, but we will also be needed in places of confinement such as jails, prisons, halfway houses and shelters. Taking this message directly to those who are confined can potentially be a lifesaving measure.

When deciding to adopt these practices we can put our thoughts in the mode of service with a prayer such as this:

"God, I offer myself to you to be a channel of your loving grace. If it is your will, help me to serve you by allowing me to help those in need. Let me bring comfort, peace and clarity, where there is suffering, turmoil and confusion. Help me to listen without judgment or criticism, but with understanding compassion. Allow me to continue my own personal growth, that I may maximize my effectiveness when helping others."

When we see people who are facing difficult challenges, this step takes us beyond simply asking God to help them through their troubles. We express our willingness to serve God by being a channel of love, sharing the experience and strength that was so freely given to us. We contact those in need and let them know we are there for them. We talk to them and help them work through their difficulties. In extreme cases we may go as far as providing assistance with resources such as food, clothing or finances. If the conditions are right, we may even offer shelter. We should open up our home as long as their presence does not create an undue burden and the rest of the household is supportive of our generosity.

Such compassionate giving is an absolutely altruistic expression of love. However, although we wish to maximize our service to God and to our fellow man and not exclude such assistance out of cynicism, we must also be practical and learn how to set boundaries. Doing what we can to set up a healthy environment of accountability and open communication is in the best interest of all parties. This may include setting guidelines and clearly communicating conditions and limitations.

Before we decide to offer such help, we make sure our own life is on solid ground. This level of aid is not advisable if you are new on this path. Waiting until we have enough practice with sponsorship and other forms of giving will allow us time to develop the necessary balance of service ingredients discussed above. When we start to consider providing such resources, we should talk to others who have embarked on this kind of giving to seek their advice. This use of prudence will safeguard against unexpected problems and increase the likelihood of a mutually beneficial experience.

The twelfth step also suggests that we *practice these principles in all our affairs*. We do not limit our goodwill to the confines of the fellowship. We bring our helpful attitude everywhere we go, looking for opportunities where we can contribute in our daily lives within our schools, our families and our workplaces. Anywhere we have contact with another person is a chance for us to practice these principles and strengthen our humility attributes. Volunteering in our community is another wonderful way to be of service. Whether at a public library, a shelter or volunteering your time and energy to your favorite cause, getting involved to make your town a better place to live is a great way to feel good about yourself.

Certainly, adopting rigorous service work into our lives can be very demanding, requiring enormous sacrifices. Exercising this discipline has similarities to exercising our body. When we first start off, we tend to get drained easily, becoming burnt out in a short period. We may then back away to regain our strength to give our batteries time to recharge. This is a necessary part of finding balance. But when most of us get to this stage, we often back off for extended periods or even permanently. We may rest on our laurels, patting ourselves on the back for a job well done; concluding we did our part and that someone else should pick up the reigns from here. Unfortunately, just as the effects of exercising our bodies will wear off with time, we cannot expect that since we were disciplined for many months resulting in good health and energy, that we can now completely end this regimen and continue enjoying the same level of health. We must continue exercising the discipline as long as we wish to continue reaping the benefits.

If we end our service work, we often find our egotism creeping back causing a diminishing of our happiness. Many who do backslide to this point are baffled as to how it happened. They become disillusioned, concluding the luster has simply worn off and that this way of life had lost its effectiveness. And although such situations are atypical, at the other extreme some who become burnt out may continue forward at full speed without giving themselves a chance to recuperate. Not surprisingly, our experience has shown that we are more inclined to error in the former category, retiring prematurely, than in the latter crowd, continuing on, even when feeling drained. To stay effective in service work, we must find balance. We rigorously give, emptying our cup to avoid complacent stagnation and we surround ourselves with nurturing friends, refilling our cup to avoid burnout.

As we mature in service work, we grow stronger and become less susceptible to depleting our energy. Just like doing physical exercise, over time we are able to do more with less effort, allowing us to gain more benefits. Eventually we reach a stage where we are charging our batteries while we are doing service work. We are giving and receiving at the same time. In order to reach this maximum level of efficiency, we do our service work while also maintaining our house cleaning in Step Ten and our spiritual pursuits in Step Eleven.

If we wish to practice discipline in all areas of our life - physically, mentally, spiritually - the key for endurance is finding balance so that we do not exhaust our energy at one extreme or stagnate at the other. To do this, a progression that has worked for many of us is to rigorously push ourselves, until we start to tire out. We then take a breather to enjoy some downtime with family and friends. We then pick up where we left off, pushing ourselves a little further. To avoid stagnation and lethargy, we should not prolong the next round of service for too long. We want a good rest, but we do not want to risk having our efforts permanently derailed.

Finding balance takes practice, but when we are persistent, we eventually hit a stride that provides a sense of complete wellbeing. We will find that we are more easily able to relate to *all* people with love and understanding. We are able to work through life's challenges with ease and our growing faith protects us from fear-based disturbances. Our life becomes filled with abundant joy and gratitude. Our self-esteem grows with our sense of usefulness. We are given renewed energy with the sense we are living up to our purpose in life. Our experience has proven time and time again that rigorous action will not only bring about these rewards, but that they will grow throughout our lifetime, as long as we make an effort to continue on this path.

Chapter 12: Taking Direct Action to Unite

Uniting of Diverse Groups

We have finally reached the crux of the primary purpose for this organization; to unite with others of diverse groups. The efforts we have been making for integrating the principles in our lives through step-work will have already removed most of the underlying causes of our prejudices. Along the way, we have also already started taking action of involving ourselves in diversity activities. We are now ready to focus our efforts specifically on continued improvement in freeing our hearts of our prejudices, as well as negative personal effects developed from observing racism in our society.

The root causes of the problems of prejudice, bigotry and racism lies within our own tainted hearts and disillusioned perceptions. The inoculation or neutralizing of these maladies within ourselves will only take place through persistent social interactions with those with whom we hold our prejudices.

The below list provides specific Direct Actions that can be used as a guide for working towards personally integrating with others of diverse groups and further shedding ourselves of our own prejudice.

1. Get started on your education of the history of racism. Read books, take diversity and "anti-racism" courses, and talk to others about their experiences.
2. Examine yourself for bigotry or bias in your own attitudes and perceptions.
3. Become attuned to the level of prejudice in today's society.
4. Take the 12 steps for personal growth to root out the causes that lead to our own prejudices. Continue to examine yourself for hidden bias and continue using the 12 steps for ongoing progress.
5. Educate yourself on the pioneers of integration who exemplified the principles that became the foundation for this organization.
6. Attend meetings and social events with diverse races and cultures.

7. Become an active member in a racially and culturally diverse group. Show up with the humble desire to find common ground, learn and participate.
8. Engage in regular one-on-one dialogs with persons of other diversities.
9. Make a commitment to spend time to build relationships with diverse individuals. Nurture those relationships with regular communications and personal meetings.
10. Help others in the fellowship seeking to follow this path. Focus on helping those of your own race to overcome prejudices and take steps towards integration. Helping your own race is the key to passing on these values while strengthening your own convictions. Become a unifier/anti-racist through these actions.
11. Learn to unconditionally love those you meet in your daily life who are still unknowledgeable in these principles and still holding onto fear-driven misperceptions. If the opportunity arises, present these ideals and help them to see a new perspective.
12. Educate yourself on the ideologies of hate groups. Learn to understand that they are driven by fears, which are the source of their hatred. Use this knowledge for strengthening your own confidence in your beliefs. Learn to unconditionally love even those who hate.

By following these suggestions, we become educated on the dynamics of racism, remove clutter from our own lives and tackle the obstacles that block us from uniting with others. Through this direct action, we guarantee a life enriched with love and peace.

Our Fellowship

The fellowship of UI plays a vital role in the process of our unity. If we are fortunate, our groups will attract individuals from a broad range of racial, cultural and religious diversities. We will benefit by the contributions of women, men and children of every age and background. Most of us will go through a period of feeling anxiety stepping out of our comfort zone, but as we grow closer, our joy will increase as uncertainty begins to dissipate.

Meetings will give us a venue for refining our ideals as we discuss our common principles. We will learn how to listen without judgment and share without fear as we open ourselves up while working through life's challenges. In our gatherings, we will share meals, laugh together and learn about each other's cultures. We will open our homes to our new friends and they will become a part of our family.

Through our combined experiences, we will increase our effectiveness in helping others. As each group matures, they will provide a new safe haven for our expanding society. Newcomers coming into our fellowship will face the same level of trepidation we encountered ourselves, but like those who went before us, we will welcome them into the group with open arms, inviting them to join us on our voyage.

Children growing up in our fellowship will potentially have an enormous influence in the future of our country. They will ideally have the opportunity to be raised in an environment filled with mutual love and respect and challenged with the same disciplines adopted by their parents. They will have a much better chance of avoiding the strained relationships and distorted perceptions in which many of us were raised.

These future teachers, parents, and community leaders will be able to shape our world with a whole new outlook on life. Unencumbered by fear and resentment, motivated by compassion and unconditional love, our children may someday guide us into a new era of social prosperity that we can only dream about.

—

On August 28, 1963 from the steps of the Lincoln Memorial, during the "March on Washington for Jobs and Freedom", Martin Luther King expressed his vision for this dream for the transformation of our society. Referencing the struggles being faced primarily in the south, King conveyed these conciliatory statements, sharing his hope for reconciliation.

Taking Direct Action to Unite

"I Have a Dream"

"And so even though we face the difficulties of today and tomorrow, I still have a dream. It is a dream deeply rooted in the American dream.

I have a dream that one day this nation will rise up and live out the true meaning of its creed: "We hold these truths to be self-evident, that all men are created equal."

I have a dream that one day on the red hills of Georgia, the sons of former slaves and the sons of former slave owners will be able to sit down together at the table of brotherhood.

I have a dream that one day even the state of Mississippi, a state sweltering with the heat of injustice, sweltering with the heat of oppression, will be transformed into an oasis of freedom and justice.

I have a dream that my four little children will one day live in a nation where they will not be judged by the color of their skin but by the content of their character.

I have a dream today!

I have a dream that one day, down in Alabama, with its vicious racists, with its governor having his lips dripping with the words of "interposition" and "nullification" -- one day right there in Alabama little black boys and black girls will be able to join hands with little white boys and white girls as sisters and brothers.

I have a dream today!

I have a dream that one day every valley shall be exalted, and every hill and mountain shall be made low, the rough places will be made plain, and the crooked places will be made straight; "and the glory of the Lord shall be revealed and all flesh shall see it together."

This is our hope, and this is the faith that I go back to the South with.

With this faith, we will be able to hew out of the mountain of despair a stone of hope. With this faith, we will be able to transform the jangling discords of our nation into a beautiful symphony of brotherhood. With this faith, we will be able to work together, to pray together, to struggle together, to go to jail together, to stand up for freedom together, knowing that we will be free one day.

And this will be the day. ... this will be the day when all of God's children will be able to sing with new meaning:
My country 'tis of thee, sweet land of liberty, of thee I sing.
Land where my fathers died, land of the Pilgrim's pride,
From every mountainside, let freedom ring!

And if America is to be a great nation, this must become true.
And so let freedom ring from the prodigious hilltops of New Hampshire.
Let freedom ring from the mighty mountains of New York.
Let freedom ring from the heightening Alleghenies of Pennsylvania.
Let freedom ring from the snow-capped Rockies of Colorado.
Let freedom ring from the curvaceous slopes of California.
But not only that:
Let freedom ring from Stone Mountain of Georgia.
Let freedom ring from Lookout Mountain of Tennessee.
Let freedom ring from every hill and molehill of Mississippi.
From every mountainside, let freedom ring.

And when this happens, when we allow freedom to ring, when we let it ring from every village and every hamlet, from every state and every city, we will be able to speed up that day when all of God's children, black men and white men, Jews and Gentiles, Protestants and Catholics, will be able to join hands and sing in the words of the old Negro spiritual: Free at last! Free at last! Thank God Almighty, we are free at last!" *

Our fellowship can make this vision possible. It can become a reality for everyone of all diversities. As we walk hand in hand as brothers and sisters in our mutual quest of freeing our hearts, our beloved community will pave the way for a better life for ourselves and for our children.

> * *Reprinted by arrangement with The Heirs to the Estate of Martin Luther King Jr., c/o Writers House as agent for the proprietor New York, NY. Copyright 1963 Dr. Martin Luther King Jr.; copyright renewed 1991 Coretta Scott King*

Community Outreach

Once a fellowship has been fully established with a solid foundation of members who have worked through the steps to incorporate the principles in their lives, we will be ready to take a more active role in presenting these ideals of unity to our communities. Beyond seeking support from friends and family, we can look for interested individuals or groups from outside institutions.

Armed with pamphlets to pass along these concepts of unity, information panels can be offered to schools of all levels, ranging from elementary schools through universities. Studies have revealed that even the youngest of school children, susceptible to messages from their environment can carry racial-prejudice; they pick up and assimilate subtle cues from others in their surroundings. When they are not made aware of ideals of equality nor exposed to positive images to counter divisive views, they are more prone to show bias. They are much more likely to perceive others in a positive light when they are presented with concepts for valuing all individuals. In this environment, the impact of prejudice is reduced.

We can engage teenagers and young adults from middle school through high school in dialogs to understand their perspectives and use that input for guiding the direction of our organization. College students with fresh perspectives on world issues will further influence our course. Whether for the purpose of advancing peace, awareness of our ecological environment or taking a stand for social justice, universities have played an important role in setting the direction for our country.

Campuses will hopefully be interested in going beyond hosting panel discussions. They may provide ongoing anti-racism training courses or diversity fairs. Our organization should be prepared to support and participate in all such activities as long as they are within the boundaries of our traditions.

The informational panels will be tailored for the specific audience, but here are some suggestions that can assist in the general structure. The panel will ideally include a diverse range of members. A facilitator will be appointed who can start with an overview of our organization and its primary purpose followed by introductions of the panel members. Each participant may then briefly share their personal experiences with prejudice before their involvement, what it was like working through the steps and the impact the principles and fellowship have since made on their lives. The panel can then open up to the audience to ask questions or participate in the seminar.

At the end of the discussion period, the facilitator can emphasize the importance of community involvement, raising the awareness of the audience in their power of helping reshape our future. Each new member will strengthen the initiative, taking our nation one step closer to unity. Pamphlets, meeting schedules and contact information can then be provided along with an appeal for individual participation.

In such cases where we are invited to give a presentation, we must always try to stay within the bounds of the traditions. Such symposiums are to be provided as a free service of our organization on a volunteer basis. If there is a chance that reporters or other members of the media are present, we ask that the tradition of anonymity be respected. Neither identifiable images nor full names of members should be included in stories broadcasted from mass-media sources. If questions of politics, religion or other controversial issues are initiated by the audience, we explain our primary purpose of unity; that our organization must stay clear of outside issues in order to preserve that objective. By continuing to seek expanded participation while safeguarding our traditions, the positive impact on our communities will continue to grow.

Integration: The Final Frontier

Our combined efforts to remove prejudices and form a united fellowship will take us far in our pursuits of personal freedom from bigotry, yet the communities around us will likely stay divided for many generations to come. Even within our fellowship, some of our members will likely need to drive from one homogenous racial or cultural community to another relatively homogenous community of another race. These social structures have developed over several centuries and the barriers that divide our communities will not come down overnight.

This text was written for the purpose of sending out a call to action to free ourselves of the shackles of our subconscious biases, breaking down our own psychological barriers that prevent us from opening our lives to those who are not like ourselves. The end goal is to heal our country from a history of divisiveness that has been passed from generation to generation to the contentious society of the present. To do this, we will need to carry our activity to the final end of truly integrating our communities. Integration will require a certain amount of risk and sacrifice for those who take the initiative to move away from their safe haven into uncertain territory.

If the call to action to unite is well received and increasing numbers take up the challenge to embrace the suggested principles, our fellowship will flourish and the comfort zone of individual members will expand. Our compassion and personal confidence will increase as our fears dissipate. Our meeting places and the homes of our fellow members will provide the social safe harbors that will allow us to increase our comfort away from our homogeneous neighborhoods. When we become at ease regardless of our environment, we will be more likely to consider moving to a diverse location, but lingering anxieties will still keep most of us from naturally choosing this option.

To make strides towards integration, we will need sufficient numbers of our communities to overcome these apprehensions and become willing to move to a diverse neighborhood. With our confidence raised and our resolve strengthened, our members can earnestly consider this final challenge. The initial trailblazers will then ideally inspire increasing numbers to follow their lead. If the trend continues, we will someday be able to visualize a cross-cultural migration that will bring us closer to fully integrating our communities. Whether this takes another century or another millennium, every measure will take us a step in the right direction.

Appendices

Appendix A

Unity Initiative Preamble

Unity Initiative is a fellowship of families and individuals who take action in freeing themselves of personal prejudice through their involvement in a diverse, yet unified community. By sharing the solutions we have found in our personal experiences, we set up an environment where others can benefit from what we have learned. By changing ourselves, we hope to make a positive impact on our communities and our society as a whole.

If you are new to this organization and you are feeling a little uneasy about being out of your comfort zone, we understand; we've been there. Please don't let that deter you from joining our fellowship.

We assume that you are here to take part in solutions for overcoming problems of bigotry in your community. We are all products of a racist society and most of us must admit that we too carry some form of prejudice. Regardless if you recognize the need for your own transformation or you are solely here to support changes in our society, Unity Initiative needs you! Community involvement is vital to our success, so everyone interested in participating in this endeavor is encouraged to join. You will make a difference. All who enter our doors are welcome and are greatly appreciated; every one of every race, belief system, social status and background. We value each individual of *every* diversity.

The only requirement for membership is a desire to support a culture of harmony where mutual respect is nurtured. However, where there is diversity, there will surely be differences in cultural, political and religious ideology. We must therefore stay sensitive and respectful of each individual's right to their own opinions. When sentiments or perceptions are expressed that we disagree with, we redirect our focus back to our primary purpose of finding common ground. We generally steer clear from the pitfalls of impassioned debate which can divide us. We instead allow the highest ideals of the group conscience to shape individual views.

Appendices

Over and over again, we will need to rise to these values. Taking the high road in this manner will give the fellowship a chance to help each of us grow past our own misconceptions and overcome personal prejudice.

To ensure the continuity of our organization, our society is following the example of other successful 12-step groups by adopting customs that will allow us to keep our focus on our primary objective of unity. UI must sustain a policy of non-affiliation with other organizations and institutions. We are not aligned with any political group, sect or denomination. We wish to stay free of all controversial issues and we neither advocate nor oppose the efforts of any other causes.

To avoid problems of money, property and prestige, we charge no dues or fees for membership, take in no funds from outside sources, and our members maintain a profile of personal anonymity. Unity Initiative expenses are covered solely through our own contributions. With these standards in place, we establish a foundation in which our united community can thrive.

Appendix B

The Twelve Steps of Unity Initiative

1. We examined ourselves for prejudice, then admitted to any unfair biases we may carry.
2. Came to believe that a Power greater than ourselves could restore us to sanity.
3. Made a decision to turn our will and our lives over to the care of God as we understood Him.
4. Made a searching and fearless moral inventory of ourselves.
5. Admitted to God, to ourselves, and to another human being the exact nature of our wrongs.
6. Were entirely ready to have God remove all these defects of character.
7. Humbly asked Him to remove our shortcomings.
8. Made a list of all persons we had harmed, and became willing to make amends to them all.
9. Made direct amends to such people wherever possible, except when to do so would injure them or others.
10. Continued to take personal inventory and when we were wrong promptly admitted it.
11. Sought through prayer and meditation to improve our conscious contact with God as we understood Him, praying only for knowledge of His will for us and the power to carry that out.
12. Having had a spiritual awakening as the result of these steps, we tried to carry this message to others, and to practice these principles in all our affairs.

Appendix C

The Twelve Traditions of Unity Initiative

1. Our common welfare should come first; personal healing and growth depends upon UI unity.
2. For our group purpose there is but one ultimate authority—a loving God as expressed in our group conscience. Our leaders are but trusted servants; they do not govern.
3. The only requirement for membership is a desire to live in harmony with people of all diversities.
4. Each group should be autonomous, except in matters affecting other groups or UI as a whole.
5. Each group has but one primary purpose - to foster an environment of unity and to carry its message to all who wish to be free from prejudice.
6. A UI group ought never endorse, finance or lend the UI name to any related facility or outside enterprise, lest problems of money, property and prestige divert us from our primary purpose.
7. Every UI group ought to be fully self-supporting, declining outside contributions.
8. Unity Initiative should remain forever non-professional, but our service centers may employ special workers.
9. UI, as such, ought never be organized; but we may create service boards or committees directly responsible to those they serve.
10. Unity Initiative has no opinion on outside issues; hence the UI name ought never be drawn into public controversy.
11. Our public relations policy is based on attraction rather than promotion; we need always maintain personal anonymity at the level of press, radio, TV, films or any medium broadcasting to the public at large.
12. Anonymity is the spiritual foundation of all our Traditions, ever reminding us to place principles before personalities.

Appendix D

Alcoholics Anonymous Statement of Non-Affiliation

Upon asking permission for adapting the twelve steps and twelve traditions of Alcoholics Anonymous into the program of action for Unity Initiative and including excerpts borrowed from AA literature, AA World Services reviewed the proposed adaptations and responded that they would not object, but asked that the original AA steps and traditions be reprinted in full, along with the Unity Initiative adaptation. In keeping with the fifth and sixth traditions, AAWS also requested we include their statement of non-affiliation, making it clear that our two organizations are not affiliated in any way. Below is the statement of non-affiliation. The twelve steps and traditions of Alcoholics Anonymous are listed in the following appendices.

Statement of non-affiliation from Alcoholics Anonymous

The Twelve Steps and Twelve Traditions of Alcoholics Anonymous have been reprinted and adapted with the permission of Alcoholics Anonymous World Services, Inc. ("AAWS"). Permission to reprint and adapt the Twelve Steps and Twelve Traditions does not mean that Alcoholics Anonymous is affiliated with this program. A.A. is a program of recovery from alcoholism only - use of A.A.'s Steps and Traditions or an adapted version in connection with programs and activities which are patterned after A.A., but which address other problems, or use in any other non-A.A. context, does not imply otherwise.

Appendices

The Twelve Steps of Alcoholics Anonymous

The Twelve Steps of Alcoholics Anonymous

1. We admitted we were powerless over alcohol—that our lives had become unmanageable.
2. Came to believe that a Power greater than ourselves could restore us to sanity.
3. Made a decision to turn our will and our lives over to the care of God as we understood Him.
4. Made a searching and fearless moral inventory of ourselves.
5. Admitted to God, to ourselves, and to another human being the exact nature of our wrongs.
6. Were entirely ready to have God remove all these defects of character.
7. Humbly asked Him to remove our shortcomings.
8. Made a list of all persons we had harmed, and became willing to make amends to them all.
9. Made direct amends to such people wherever possible, except when to do so would injure them or others.
10. Continued to take personal inventory and when we were wrong promptly admitted it.
11. Sought through prayer and meditation to improve our conscious contact with God, as we understood Him, praying only for knowledge of His will for us and the power to carry that out.
12. Having had a spiritual awakening as the result of these Steps, we tried to carry this message to alcoholics, and to practice these principles in all our affairs.

Copyright (c) A.A. World Services, Inc.

Statement of non-affiliation from Alcoholics Anonymous

The Twelve Steps and Twelve Traditions of Alcoholics Anonymous have been reprinted and adapted with the permission of Alcoholics Anonymous World Services, Inc. ("AAWS"). Permission to reprint and adapt the Twelve Steps and Twelve Traditions does not mean that Alcoholics Anonymous is affiliated with this program. A.A. is a program of recovery from alcoholism only - use of A.A.'s Steps and Traditions or an adapted version in connection with programs and activities which are patterned after A.A., but which address other problems, or use in any other non-A.A. context, does not imply otherwise.

Unity Initiative

The Twelve Traditions of Alcoholics Anonymous

The Twelve Traditions of Alcoholics Anonymous

1. Our common welfare should come first; personal recovery depends upon A.A. unity.
2. For our group purpose there is but one ultimate authority—a loving God as He may express Himself in our group conscience. Our leaders are but trusted servants; they do not govern.
3. The only requirement for A.A. membership is a desire to stop drinking.
4. Each group should be autonomous except in matters affecting other groups or A.A. as a whole.
5. Each group has but one primary purpose—to carry its message to the alcoholic who still suffers.
6. An A.A. group ought never endorse, finance, or lend the A.A. name to any related facility or outside enterprise, lest problems of money, property, and prestige divert us from our primary purpose.
7. Every A.A. group ought to be fully self-supporting, declining outside contributions.
8. Alcoholics Anonymous should remain forever nonprofessional, but our service centers may employ special workers.
9. A.A., as such, ought never be organized; but we may create service boards or committees directly responsible to those they serve.
10. Alcoholics Anonymous has no opinion on outside issues; hence the A.A. name ought never be drawn into public controversy.
11. Our public relations policy is based on attraction rather than promotion; we need always maintain personal anonymity at the level of press, radio, and films.
12. Anonymity is the spiritual foundation of all our Traditions, ever reminding us to place principles before personalities.

Copyright (c) A.A. World Services, Inc.

Statement of non-affiliation from Alcoholics Anonymous

The Twelve Steps and Twelve Traditions of Alcoholics Anonymous have been reprinted and adapted with the permission of Alcoholics Anonymous World Services, Inc. ("AAWS"). Permission to reprint and adapt the Twelve Steps and Twelve Traditions does not mean that Alcoholics Anonymous is affiliated with this program. A.A. is a program of recovery from alcoholism only - use of A.A.'s Steps and Traditions or an adapted version in connection with programs and activities which are patterned after A.A., but which address other problems, or use in any other non-A.A. context, does not imply otherwise.

Appendix E

Starting a New Unity Initiative Group

Those who rigorously work through the steps, taking the action to incorporate the suggested principles and making the effort to unite with people of diverse backgrounds will undoubtedly find a life filled with abundant delight. We have found paradise on earth through the process of changing our lives. This gift enriches all that we do. Our next objective will be to expand our fellowship, making it available to anyone interested in joining us in this undertaking. The larger we grow while maintaining the quality of our message, the better equipped we will be at providing these benefits to anyone else wanting to free themselves of prejudice by taking part in this endeavor.

There may be others reading this book that desire to have this experience, but are not within proximity of established groups. Whether you are looking to expand the reach of our fellowship in a community which already has meetings available, or you live in a city that does not already host meetings, you will be doing your community a valuable service by establishing a new group in your area. Our organization is new, so no process has yet been formalized to guarantee success, but here are some suggestions for getting started on opening a group in unchartered territories:

- Find close friends expressing interest in unifying diverse groups.
- Hold group studies of our literature to become familiar with the principles.
- Open up group discussions.
- When you get to the section "Principles in Action", find a sponsor and start working through the steps. If no sponsor is available in your town, contact a group office in the most convenient city, ask for help finding a sponsor and then work with them remotely.
- Seek out a variety of "open" meetings of local 12-step programs to get a feel of the different formats they provide. Find large diverse meetings to observe the community spirit.

- **Become intimate with the 12 traditions. For starting a new group, this is more important than knowledge of the steps or principles. Ensure that all activities are within these boundaries.** *The 12 traditions are vital to the continuity of our organization.*
- Once you have a good handle on the steps and traditions, contact local leasing businesses or places of worship to search for meeting-space available to rent. (Per tradition seven, we do not accept any outside donations, including rent-free accommodations).
- When you are confident in your direction for getting started, contact another group (or intergroup* office if available) to order literature, pamphlets, suggested meeting outlines and anything else that will help in getting started. Pamphlets should be given out free of charge at meetings, while literature prices should not exceed their cost to the group.
- To get the word out about meetings at your new location, flyers can be made to pass out at other groups. Places of worship, schools, or other institutions can be contacted to see if they would like to get involved in the efforts of unifying diverse faiths, races and cultures. Anonymous public service announcements can be made through media sources, but whatever methods we employ, we must make sure we stay within the bounds of the traditions (*See tradition eleven*).
- To meet the group's ongoing expenses for rent, literature, beverages, etc., baskets or collection plates can be passed around, but the group should only maintain a prudent reserve to cover expenses for an established period (such as three months). No dues or fees should ever be requested. This is in accordance with the third and sixth traditions. No funds should go directly to members for purposes of profit, but expenses can be paid to individuals in or out of the fellowship for required services such as electrical work, plumbing or carpentry.
- Hold a business (or group conscience) meeting to first elect a secretary, coordinator, treasurer and any other needed position. These monthly democratic meetings will also be the time to discuss and vote on group business matters. Allow for periodic (e.g. bi-annually or annually) elections to rotate service

Appendices

positions. Appoint or request volunteers for meeting chairs, coffee makers, literature coordinators, greeters, etc. and rotate these periodically, as well.

- Before each general meeting begins, the chairperson will find volunteers to read selected material, such as the steps and traditions. At the opening of the meeting, after standard greetings and introductions are given, an invitation is extended to join in on a moment of silence followed by the serenity prayer. Next, the preamble is read, after which each volunteer is queued to go through their selected readings. Time may then be allocated for acknowledging newcomers and out-of-towners, recognizing membership anniversaries, making announcements, and asking for volunteers to stay after the meeting to help clean up.
- Exercises of unity may then be initiated, such as going around the room introducing ourselves or having each person greet the people around them.
- The chairperson can next convey the type of meeting (speaker, open discussion, step study), introduce speakers or present topics. Instructions are then given for breaking into groups, meeting duration and so on.
- Discussion groups usually try to give each person a chance to participate.
- Most meetings end by circling up, hand in hand, and concluding with a prayer.
- After the meeting, make sure established members stay long enough to reach out to newer members.

As time goes on and the fellowship size becomes large enough, consider adding more meetings to the schedule or opening another group in your community. Once multiple groups are established, an intergroup* office can be opened to service a specific geographic area.

See the preface concerning the establishment of this organization. As of 2013, no Unity Initiative groups have been formed and plans have not yet begun for establishing intergroup offices.

Unity Initiative

Although each group is autonomous (tradition four), they will inevitably have common needs that can best be met by the efficiency of a coordinated effort. This is the role of an intergroup; to take care of area administrative needs so the fellowship can concentrate on their primary purpose. The intergroup becomes the de facto information center. They are responsible for answering calls, and purchasing literature to then resell to groups or individual members at cost.

Like the fellowship groups, the charter of the intergroup is not for profit per tradition six, but because the demands of these offices usually require a fulltime worker, a paid position of office-manager is usually made available and paid from the incoming voluntary contributions of the groups it serves. If enough resources are not available, such coordination must wait until the surrounding groups can provide funds through their meeting collections. Financing must not come from outside sources per tradition seven.

For any questions or controversy over finances, public relations, media, etc, leaving these concerns to the decision of the group-conscience guided by the traditions will usually provide the best answer in handling these matters. Much helpful literature has been published by other 12-step organizations that lay out the entire service structure of their organization. Some of these entities have been around for several decades and have successfully found a framework that has allowed them to function efficiently, while avoiding the potential pitfalls of money, property and prestige that can cause a movement to lose its focus. All rely upon the traditions to provide the solid foundation that gives their structure stability. By following the successful practices of those who went before us, we will increase our likelihood for longevity and effectiveness in our service.

Appendix F

FAQ: Frequently Asked Questions

Question: What is UI?
Answer: UI is a fledgling newly starting organization that will combine the principles of 12-step organizations with those of civil rights movements to create a united fellowship of diverse races, religions, cultures, etc. The below Q&A is based on the planned structure and charter of this organization.

Question: Is UI a charity?
Answer: UI is not a charity. It is a society with the intent of uniting diverse groups. UI includes a suggested 12-step program that places us all in the best position to effectively help in this endeavor.

Question: Is UI a political or religious organization?
Answer: No. UI is neither a religious or political organization, nor does UI have any political leaning. It is against the UI traditions to take a political stand. The goals of unity are a universal concept. Making strides towards unity will require involvement from all political and religious sectors.

Question: Why is UI needed?
Answer: Historical social, economic and political maladies such as racism, classism, chauvinism and bigotry continue to plague the whole world. Those taking part in this endeavor recognize this and wish to take part in addressing the root causes of this global epidemic. Most of us carry some form of prejudice. Joining a diverse fellowship that is active in taking steps to overcome such maladies is an effective measure for healing ourselves and influencing our society.

Question: Who is UI intended for? Is it only intended for people with prejudices, bigotry or problems with racism?
Answer: This fellowship is for everyone; *not* just for people who carry prejudice. If you acknowledge that prejudice, bigotry and racism are prevalent problems in our society and you would like to participate in solutions by joining our fellowship, UI is for you.

Question: Why would I or anyone else join UI?
Answer: There are two main reasons why someone may want join

Unity Initiative: First, you recognize prejudice, bigotry and racism are still maladies that permeate our society to the detriment of present and future generations and you see hope in Unity Initiative's approach for helping resolve these problems and would like to be a part of the solution. Second, like most of us, you may be able to admit you too carry some form of prejudice and would like to overcome your own distortions through the steps, education and fellowship UI offers.

Question: Does UI charge for membership?
Answer: No. UI is a non-profit organization and charges no dues or fees for membership or its services. We do this for enjoyment and for the benefit of our communities. Expenses are paid through the voluntary contributions of its members through collections at meetings.

Question: How do I get Involved?
Answer: To get involved, you can attend any of our meetings (starting sometime in 2013) and let us know you wish to partake in this endeavor.

Question: What measures does UI recommend for overcoming prejudice?
Answer: First, we recommend participating socially in our fellowship. This simple act of exposing yourself to other diverse groups is a very good starting point for overcoming stereotypical misperceptions. UI then recommends following the twelve steps for self-examination, spirituality and service. The steps and the principles behind them are outlined in the Unity Initiative text.

Question: Why does Unity Initiative recommend using the 12-steps for overcoming prejudice? Aren't they designed for addiction?
Answer: The root of prejudice is fear and insecurities and the purpose of the 12-steps is not to overcome addiction, but to overcome the fears and insecurities, which are also the root of such problems. The 12-steps are a proven and well-established solution, as well as a respected program of recovery from fear-based maladies.

Question: The first step states "We examined ourselves for prejudice, then admitted to any unfair biases we may carry", but I don't have prejudices. Why do I need UI or why would I need to work the steps?
Answer: Some of us carry subconscious prejudices, in which we are

not aware. The steps include measures for self-examination that can uncover these prejudices. If that happens, you will be very pleased at the results of your courage in taking action. However, even if you don't have prejudices, that is just one small aspect of step-work. The true aim of the steps is to replace insecurities, fear and egotism with humility. They are designed to help everyone grow, regardless of your state in life. The risk of not taking the steps, is that you will not be as effective in breaking down social barriers or in addressing the root causes of prejudice. If you concede you are not perfect, you stand to gain enormous benefits from these humbling acts of growth. The steps are intimidating for some, but don't let apprehension stand in your way! You won't regret it!

Question: How does one go about working the UI steps?
Answer: Working through the steps should be done with the help of a sponsor who has already successfully worked through the steps. Once you choose a sponsor, they should guide you through the steps with the help of the UI literature.

Question: What is a sponsor, where do I get one, and how much do they charge?
Answer: A sponsor acts as a mentor to get us oriented into the fellowship and answer questions. But most of all, their purpose is to guide us while working through the 12 steps. Sponsors do this at no charge as part of the twelfth step. You choose a sponsor by listening to people at meetings. When you find someone you trust and admire, that has a good working knowledge of the program, ask them to be your sponsor to assist you in your step-work.

Question: Since UI is a 12-step program, can it be used to address maladies such as drug-addiction or alcoholism?
Answer: No. Because identification is so important for recovery, help for such maladies should be sought through programs that address these problems. However, we encourage anyone struggling with these issues to also attend UI meetings. Also, adopting these principles early in life and being part of a healthy supportive fellowship will likely help young people from facing these other maladies.

Question: Who personally profits from UI finances? Who receives salaries?
Answer: Unless being compensated for a specific job or task, no individual benefits from UI finances per our traditions. UI may employ special workers to fulfill needs, such as running offices that answer phones; or we may hire contractors for services, such as: cleaning, plumbing and electrical; but no one receives funds or salaries outside of such services.

Question: Who runs UI?
Answer: UI has no governing leaders and we are not organized per our 2nd and 9th traditions. Running UI is a collective effort. Elections for service positions are held to fill service positions, which are to be rotated. Each member has an equal opportunity to participate in the affairs of UI.

Question: How is UI funded?
Answer: UI groups are self-supporting through individual membership contribution, but UI service offices may also be funded through sales of UI literature along with group contributions.

Question: Where do funds from book sales or meeting collections go?
Answer: Meeting collections first go to paying the expenses of the group, including rent and utilities. Groups may then contribute to inter-groups that service a geographic area in answering phones and distributing literature. Groups may also contribute to the UI foundation office. Literature sales will go to support the foundation office, including salaries for special workers. Some funds will be retained at various levels of service as a prudent reserve. If the amount of prudent reserve is exceeded at the foundation level, UI literature will be discounted to shrink the reserve.

Question: Can I donate money or property to UI?
Answer: Generally speaking, no. As part of the 7th tradition, UI does not accept donations, but groups will collect funds by "passing a basket" to raise the necessary monies to run their group, inter-group or UI foundation.

Question: Won't this movement stir controversy?
Answer: UI has an honest desire to avoid controversy. This organization is meant to serve our communities through unity. We take no stand

in politics or religion. We hope community citizens appreciate the possibilities of our endeavor and get involved regardless of ideology.

Question: What religious beliefs does UI subscribe to?
Answer: UI includes references to God in our steps, yet we advocate no particular spiritual belief. People from all faiths are needed and encouraged to join our organization.

Question: What happens if the courts want to mandate a "hate-crime" offender to UI?
Answer: UI hopes people suffering from bigotry will find their way to our doors. If they want to find peace in freedom from this malady, we can help. All that is required is a willingness to support a culture of harmonious diversity. This is the only requirement for membership.

Question: Does UI offer any professional help?
Answer: No. We offer no counseling, nor do we proclaim to be experts or professionals in any area of sociology, psychology, history or the like. All we offer is our personal experience of participation in a diverse fellowship along with the growth we found through our step-work. However, most will find that these are very effective tools in overcoming almost any problem.

Question: Is UI affiliated with any other organization?
Answer: No. Per the 5th and 6th traditions, UI is not affiliated with any other enterprise. Although individual members may personally support the efforts and get involved with other endeavors, the UI traditions deter us from forming affiliations at the organizational level.

Question: How big is the organization and what are the demographics of UI?
Answer: Such information is not available as UI is a fledgling organization whose membership will only begin after the printing of this text in 2013.

Question: Where and when will meetings be held?
Answer: Meeting information will be posted on the unityinitiative.org website.

Appendix G

Why we are here

Upon first hearing about Unity Initiative, many respond back with various questions about its purpose. Why is UI needed? Why would someone join UI? Many of these questions are answered in the "Frequently Asked Questions" of this text. In these paragraphs, we will list various reasons why we participate in this organization.

> *We are here to join with other diverse groups in helping our communities unite. We are here to personally learn from the experiences of others; to heal from our own prejudices; to follow; to contribute and to serve. We are here to help other individuals when that help is requested of us.*

> *We are not here to give unsolicited advice, force our opinions or to criticize. We are not here to form political opinions or seek political or religious agendas. We are not here to take up other causes regardless of their merit. We are not here for profit or for any other self-serving interest.*

Striving to limit our scope to these ideals will help us stay within the bounds of the traditions and keep us on track in pursuing our primary purpose of uniting our communities.

Made in the USA
Columbia, SC
09 June 2020